Blind
Mazes

Blind Mazes

A Study of Love

George W. Kelling

nh Nelson-Hall/Chicago

LIBRARY OF CONGRESS CATALOGING IN PUBLICATION DATA

Kelling, George W
  Blind mazes.

  Bibliography: p.
  Includes index.
  1. Interpersonal relations. 2. Love. I. Title
HM132.K45   158'.2   78–24254
ISBN 0–88229–242–0

Copyright © 1979 by George W. Kelling

Manufactured in the United States of America

10 9 8 7 6 5 4 3 2 1

1/17/86 Dalbert typh 20.95

Contents

Preface

The most important discoveries of social psychology will be made by those who, while playing a part, filling a role and so on, can be their own audience.[1]

THIS BOOK IS about love and its problems. It is written by a social-personality psychologist. While it is critical of the work of other psychologists and contains a brief account of an experiment, it is not technical. It is a theoretical, logical, and speculative book, based on my thought and observation; I do not think or observe in the technical language of psychology. Thus it is not nontechnical because I oversimplify or talk down; but neither is it nonpsychological or "merely" a report about psychology because it is not technical. As the epigraph indicates, I am subjective but still respectable and scientific. This book, while completely accessible to the general reading public, should be considered an example of a new kind of approach to psychology, currently recommended by an increasingly large number of psychologists.

Thomas S. Szasz has suggested that ". . . human relationships are inherently fraught with difficulties." In addition, he believes that "Man's awareness of himself . . . seems to be a steadily expanding one, bringing in its wake an ever larger *burden of understanding.*"[2] Szasz has attempted to demolish the myth of mental illness; I believe he has substituted another myth, that of inherent disharmony. This book shows that disharmony, unquestionably present, is not inherent, and does not result from increased understanding.

A note on terminology. Social scientists often use the letters *P* and *O* to represent two people in interaction. I do too. More often I use *Joe* and *Mary*, who are not representatives of their sexes, but empty symbols. They do appear, however, in stereotypic situations—situations in which males and females are often found, in real life or fiction. Such situations are not necessarily representative either, but they provide good examples—everyone knows the plot.

When not writing about two sexes or a particular sex, I usually employ the pronoun "he" rather than one of the clumsy locutions in current use. Because this book does not treat males and females as different sorts of people, the generic "he" is used more often than one might expect in a book about relationships between the sexes. In *this* case, it is not a symptom of sexism; quite the contrary.

I use writers, philosophers, and Jean Piaget as if I knew something about them.[3] I've read them. They are in the public domain. Some scholars may object that I haven't read the requisite scholarship on these people. I have at least read them carefully, and make no further apologies.

This book is not intended to be, or to stem directly from, a complete review of the literature. It is based on literature *and* real life. In most cases, I have not mentioned research because it has not been relevant to the specific task at hand. However, my rather strident pessimism concerning the willingness of psychology to deal with intimate relationships is less appropriate now than it was in 1975, when the manuscript was completed. Since then, several promising lines of investigation have opened.

I have certain acknowledgments to make. The first is to my teachers, especially Peter G. Ossorio. He directed my dissertation, portions of which are discussed in the final chapter of this book, and has been a major influence on my thinking. Others who have influenced the kind of thinking exhibited in this book are Stuart W. Cook, Desmond S. Cartwright, Keith E. Davis, and William A. Scott. None are responsible for any errors contained herein.

I thank Connie and Curt Colby for reading and criticizing the manuscript; they were of considerable help. The people at Nelson-Hall involved in the editing process were also of great help.

I would also like to thank all the people, including myself, who have, usually unwittingly, provided data for this book. However, any resemblance between an example or anecdote in this book and real life is only because this book is about real life. I have not borrowed anything directly from anybody.

1
Blind Mazes

Our closest human relationships do not bring out the best in us. People fall in love. Love is the highest, the best, the most noble and human emotion. It is all downhill from there, down past the warm and joking affection of friends; past the mannered courtesy and respect of social and business relationships; past even the cold politeness or ill-concealed disdain of transactions in stores, into a pit of hatred, contempt, violence, despair, and chronic misery.

It is not always this way, but it is this way often enough; and even in the best of love relationships there are descents into the pit. This book is an attempt to explain why. Why do love relationships that proceed, as most American ones do, from romantic love into a more formal stage, have the problems they do? The answers are many and varied, but some major themes can be set forth here.

What does it mean to say an individual is a person—or that a person is an individual? If we behave as others do in our groups, classes, and roles, it means nothing at all. Personality and individuality are terms for what is left over, protrudes, or interferes.

How much personality does a person have? Some people have more than others. The answer to the question depends to a great extent upon who answers it. The more an observer knows a person, the more that person appears to be an individual. Busy people, for example, don't have time to observe individuals.

If a person has a unique individuality and nobody observes it, does it exist? Does the tree falling in the empty forest make noise?

Such questions are philosophical; this book is psychological. Unrewarded, however, unnoticed individuality is likely to vanish.

Personality as a mass phenomenon is, I argue, a relatively recent development. If it is just emerging, we, who are just emerging as personalities to observe it, can expect to have difficulties dealing with it. The developmental psychology of Piaget will be used to explain why.[1] Many of the difficulties relationships encounter can be explained in terms of the general difficulties novel objects (infants) have when trying to deal with other novel objects (everything they encounter). Infants learn to deal with simple things first. As adults, we can deal adeptly with hydrogen atoms, Chevrolets, baseballs, and hearts. Personalities are more complex, and we deal with them as well as we dealt with hydrogen atoms 100 years ago.

Romantic love has been around throughout recorded history, but in western civilization, particularly in the United States, it has become epidemic. This book does not attempt to explain why. Perhaps we are less busy simply surviving. Perhaps we are therefore more complex than our roles and groups, and more able to deal with such complexity; hence, romantic love, an unchoreographed dance of courtship. For whatever reason, romantic love is now the normal beginning to adult love relationships. Historically, this is a dramatic change.

Romantic love will also be described as an emotion; it is translated into behavior. A person in love wants to do something to or with his loved one. The behavior a couple settles upon comprises their love. The better the translation of emotion into behavior, the less residual emotion will remain. Paradoxically, then, people who love each other do not feel love for each other.

This is not a particularly esoteric formula. It is a cliché that the husband feels love for his wife most strongly when he is threatened with her loss, through divorce or death. He then realizes "what he had." But it is not merely his wife he will lose. He also loses his behaviors, his translations of the powerful emotion of romantic love.

Relationships, I will argue, have a life of their own. The notion that relationships are translations of emotions helps make this clear. As we come to know someone, our behaviors become tailored to their peculiarities. We no longer have a general way of doing things. It really won't "be the same" with anyone else. These specifically tailored ways of doing things with our loved ones are *ours*. We are not happy to lose them; nor is the artist happy to lose a painting. Many personalities do not need love; hence we have had artists, madmen, prophets, and poets throughout history. We cannot all be artists, and most of us seek our outlet in the medium of interaction with other people. People are not a second-rate medium; they are rather more difficult to work with than clay. Neither are relationships second-rate products; they have a life of their own in much the same sense that a painting does. Both are produced by people; both attain independent existence.

If personality is relatively recent, it is not fully detached from the groups from which it grows. The members of the groups have no reason to love personality, for it destroys solidarity. It is hard on the person who possesses a personality. He is observed and objected to. Naturally, he feels alienated. Naturally, he seeks company. Hence romantic love, the search for another individual as separate as oneself. But hence it is not surprising that there is a tendency for personality to be attacked, from without and within. In chapter five I discuss three trends, all of which involve a progressive tendency to squash the individual.

If it is true that love relationships tend to go bad, it is equally true that this does not necessarily mean they will end. In fact, chapter four is devoted to explanations of why bad relationships are not terminated.

All in all, then, this book is pessimistic. It is, in addition, without redeeming salutary exhortations or incantations. I do not believe that the usual patent medicines (patience, hard work, awareness, sex, or therapy) are valuable; in fact, I believe they are often counterproductive. It would not be timely to attempt to rescind the tenor of the book now. There is every reason to face the facts—squarely, directly, head on. After that, perhaps a beer.

I do not, however, take a position about the basic nature of man. Recent writers like Ardrey, Lorenz, and Morris take the position that man is by nature aggressive or unpleasant. Others such as Gaylin and Brain believe that man is basically good. To take either position is to prejudice the results of one's deliberations and observations. It is also a little simpleminded.

Since this book is about relationships, it would be well to define them. Most of the time, a relationship can be defined as the interaction between two people, verbal and nonverbal. This makes the process of acquisition of relationships nonproblematic. All you need do is say hello. It also frees us from attempting to decide at what point a couple qualifies as having a relationship of the kind this book is concerned with. A relationship qualifies if the couple has said hello and consists of people eligible in a very broad sense for such a relationship. It also allows us to discuss the decay of relationships without specifying at what point they end. Old relationships don't die; they do fade away. When all overt and covert interaction is gone, so is the relationship—by definition. But it has not died, there is no corpse, and there is the possibility of resurrection.

Most of the time I use the term *relationship* in its ordinary language sense, which is quite vague. The preceding definition is given merely as a base of operation. It is not a radical proposition about the nature of relationships, but a definition that clears up some problems by showing that they are illusory.

There are other problems to surmount before we can proceed with the task at hand. It will be necessary to criticize some previous thought and research that has stalled progress in understanding relationships. Theorists have had difficulty accepting the simple fact that relationships exist; they have therefore come forth with some strange descriptions of what goes on between two human beings. Social psychologists, in particular, have become stuck in attempting to explain the beginning of relationships. I have argued that this is a nonproblem, and have presented a simple and useful concept of how relationships begin.

Most people believe that people and relationships are different kinds of things. I shall argue that this is not really the case, but will then attempt to indicate the distinction between the two concepts. Similarity between members of a relationship has widely been considered important. I argue that it is not, and attack other beliefs that have been supported by research. Perhaps all of us have sometimes sought advice or rules for handling relationships, and several writers have made much money peddling advice and rules. I argue that this approach is harmful. Even more harmful is the "advice" to argue, and I argue against that also. Finally, most of us have a tendency to blame such scapegoats as sex, money, the past, in-laws, and again I argue that this is a fruitless venture.

This section of the book is to some extent throat-clearing. But it is necessary that we abandon and in some cases demolish old buildings so that we may move to better ones. I do not believe that civilization is a scholar. Writers are often said to influence the habitual modes of thought of a given era; it is more probable that the causality goes the other way. The old buildings I attempt to demolish do not belong to psychologists, sociologists, philosophers, and historians. They belong to all of us, and their presence blights all of our landscapes. Let us remove them.

SOME STRANGE CONCEPTIONS OF RELATIONSHIPS

This book is about relationships between people. The topic seems well-defined; but an examination of some conceptions of relationships reveals interesting ambiguities.

The existence of individual persons is phenomenologically obvious. Individual persons come together and interact and then, sometimes, have a relationship. The individuals existed prior to the relationship and it was the individuals who entered the relationship.

This assumption or base of operations, which has not been empirically validated, has been uncritically if only implicitly adopted by experimental social psychologists. Naturally, therefore, much research and theorizing has been devoted to the determinants of interpersonal attraction. Description of existing relationships has not been entirely ignored. Most of the terms are borrowed from the physical sciences: *cohesion, bonding, valence, attraction.* These terms are not descriptions of relationships. They merely mirror the fact that people—conceived of as separate and individual objects—are often, in a vague and unspecified manner, "stuck together."

While experimental social psychology has largely ignored the middles and ends of relationships, two important conceptions of relationships are further removed from phenomenological reality.

Psychoanalysis focuses on the individual and tends to isolate him. The individual's behavior is determined by the structure and dynamics of his psyche. The immediate environment is accidental and random in its effects. A real life event may precipitate a disturbance, but only if it has symbolic significance to the individual. For example, Mary is not unhappy because Joe left. Mary is unhappy because Joe's leaving reminds her of a fantasy about her father. Not, however, her father as he is today—her father as he was during her childhood, or perhaps her father as she fantasized him to be during her childhood. Should Mary consult a psychoanalyst and develop strong feelings about him, she would be experiencing a transference neurosis. Mary would be said to be treating her analyst as she treated her father or wished she had treated her father—or her fantasy of her father.

From the point of view of psychoanalysis, the world consists of isolated individuals acting out fantasies with people who exist only as characters symbolic of other people, who may themselves be symbolic. Relationships between people are not at all what they seem to be. They consist of two isolated psyches, each weaving the other into his private fantasies. What we would call the relationship is a success if each person facilitates the other's fantasy. Note that to do so, it is not necessary to do anything in particular, although it may help. The two people are not in contact with each other. In Piagetian terms, they assimilate each other without accommodation. That is, Joe treats Mary as if she were the kind of woman he wants, regardless of whether she is or not.

Sociology's view of what actually exists is different, but equally removed from what seems to be the case. Berger's *Invitation to Sociology* presents a strong statement of a sociological position, of which the following is an oversimplified version.

A person's behavior is determined by the groups to which he belongs, the roles he plays, and other causal entities larger and more powerful than the individual. In a phrase, the individual is caused by society. This is so much the case that there is little point in treating individuals as if they were causal entities. We are not prisoners of society; a prisoner wants out and is held in. We are allowed to rattle around the prison yard at will. This accounts for our illusion of freedom. Because we have always known the walls and nothing but the walls, we do not consider them walls; we do not even perceive them.

From this point of view, relationships are like plays. In the East, where marriages are still arranged, a woman may marry a man she has never met. She will have an ideal of a husband (D. Mace and V. Mace, *Marriage East and West*, pp. 133, 166). Furthermore, she is expected to treat her husband as if he fit this role perfectly, regardless of his actual behavior. Usually, her husband will have been sufficiently well programmed by society so that she will succeed in finding him in correspondence with the ideal. All *she* must do to be regarded as the perfect wife is treat her husband as a god (D. Mace and V. Mace, *Marriage*, p. 232).

In the West, we believe we have freedom of choice in marriage; but study after study, year after year, shows this belief to be an illusion. With monotonous regularity people marry people from the same social class, ethnic background, education, and geographic region. They raise children. The husband works. The wife cleans the house. The husband calls his wife "dear."

What else is there to know? The strong sociological position says that aside from differences attributable solely to group affiliation, there is not much.

The psychoanalytic and the sociological theories of the nature of social reality seem absurd when their extremity is revealed by the removal of stylistic hedges. They nevertheless have their uses. There are people who employ other people solely as characters in neurotic fantasies. There are people who are "not really there" in the sociological sense— people who seem to be nothing more than the groups to which they belong.

Most of us, however, are not like that; not usually. Nevertheless, it is important to keep these two positions in mind as limits and boundaries. The psychoanalytic position describes pseudorelationships in which the participants are self-contained. They initiate contact with the outside world when their internal equilibrium is disturbed (it is not disturbed by the immediate environment). When they do, they do not encounter the other "as an individual" or "as he really is," but as whatever they want him to be. The encounter is pure assimilation. Reality is forced into a desired shape, often occasioning misperception of reality—or, simply, failure to perceive. The sociological position describes pseudorelationships in which the participants have no real selves to contain. It is not that they are subservient to the groups to which they belong; they are the concrete embodiments of these groups. Their behavior is pure accommodation. The person (rather than reality) is forced into the shape society desires. The man *becomes* a husband (and nothing more or less). While successful adaptation is a balance between assimilation and accommodation, the psychoanalytic and sociological positions describe cases of extreme imbalance.

The phenomenological position adopted by social psychology seems sane and harmless by comparison. That experimental social psychology has yet to deal directly with relationships seems due to a wise decision to begin with beginnings rather than middles and ends. It at least recognizes that individuals exist and interact. Furthermore, it may be unnecessary to talk as if relationships existed. Possibly, all relational behavior can be described as a function of the individuals in a relationship.

Let us try it: Joe loves Mary. Therefore, Joe does nice things for Mary. How do we know that Joe loves Mary? Because he says so? No, there must be some behavior directed at Mary. This behavior is Joe's.

Why does Joe love Mary? She is warm and beautiful and nice and intelligent; but so are millions of other females. One thing special about Mary is that her warmth is directed at Joe. Why? Joe is warm and handsome and nice and intelligent; but so are millions of other males. One thing special about Joe is that his warmth is directed at Mary.

Joe's behavior is understandable, it would appear, if and only if Mary loves him. If Joe directs loving behavior toward Mary and Mary does not love Joe, Joe does not love Mary in the normal sense of the term—he is playing neurotic games. In addition, Joe cannot direct loving behavior toward Mary unless she lets him. Love is not the sort of thing one can force on people.

It seems parsimonious to admit that Joe and Mary have a love relationship. All typical loving behavior follows directly from that. If we try to start with Joe and explain his behavior as a function of the kind of person he is, we will have to accept, as part of the natural environment, that Mary loves Joe. That is, Mary directs loving behavior toward Joe, and that serves as the reinforcement which causes Joe to direct loving behavior toward Mary. If Mary does not direct her good qualities at Joe, there is no good reason for Joe to *single out* Mary.

But Mary had to start somewhere. The relationship had to have a birth. Let us say Mary begins directing loving behavior at Joe when she sees him smile at a party. This smile warms her heart. But who does Joe smile at? Joe smiles that smile at Susan and Mary sees it from the other side of the room. Mary crosses the room. If Joe smiles that same smile at Mary it is not his love smile, but his social smile, and Mary is being taken in by another pretty face. A social smile is not a smile to fall in love with. (People do fall in love with such smiles, but it is not considered normal love—it is, for example, considered being "taken in.")

If it *is* Joe's love smile, then Joe loves Susan, and Mary will not receive *that* smile when she comes across the room.

But perhaps she doesn't care. Perhaps she sees Joe's love smile and decides she wants it directed at her, and so she approaches Joe and gives him *her* love smile. *But she cannot.* Unless she and Joe are already in love, she can not give him her love smile, but only her hustling smile. Therefore, Mary's smile will not be the kind of smile Joe will fall in love with. People do fall in love with hustling smiles, but then it is not normal love, as argued previously. In addition, the hustler is not in love, at least not while in the act of hustling, and cannot be counted on to continue presenting loving behaviors. If Mary is hustling Joe but finds he is lacking something essential, she will stop directing loving behavior at him. If she loves him, she won't let a little lack stop her.

So if Joe falls in love with Mary because of Mary's hustling smile, we have discovered why Joe fell in love with Mary; but we have had to abandon Mary's love for Joe, which is what we were most recently trying to explain.

Thus, while we can describe the birth of (abnormal) love, we cannot describe the birth of a relationship. If Joe falls in love with Mary and Mary is not already in love with Joe, then either Mary has been hustling Joe—which precludes her loving him—or Mary is indifferent to Joe. In either case, we cannot count on Mary to continue the loving behaviors that we need in order to describe the growth of Joe's love (and note that even to describe the birth of love we have had to assume full-grown love at first sight). In addition, such nonreciprocal love is not normal love. Similarly, we can describe Mary falling into nonreciprocal love with Joe. But as soon as she begins directing loving behaviors at Joe, unless Joe already loves her, she is hustling rather than loving. If Mary really falls in love with Joe, we expect her to stammer, blush, pretend to be indifferent, or blurt out her love—none of which are particularly lovable behaviors, *unless Joe already loves her.*

How *do* relationships get started? Earlier I said they start when the couple says hello; but that seems a rather empty formula now that we are dealing with the beginnings of love. It looks as if it will be very difficult to describe these beginnings, but surely we must try.

Consider, however, the famous paradox. If you want to get from A to B you first must go halfway. You must still, however, go half of the remaining half. Then you must go half of the remaining fourth. You can never get to B because you always have to go half of the remaining distance before you can go the other half. And yet people get from A to B even more often than they fall in love.

So let us assume that the attempt to describe the birth of a relationship is like the attempt to get from A to B by halves—that is, let us assume that relationships exist and that their birth cannot be described in terms of individual human beings. The next section will make sense of and legitimate these assumptions.

THE ONTOGENETIC PRIMACY OF RELATIONSHIPS

The existence of individuals seems obvious; however, ontogenetically, relationships precede individuals. Individuals differentiate themselves from relationships with difficulty.

The child's attempt to differentiate himself from his environment is a major theme in Piaget's description of cognitive development. If the child sees a hand attached to his arm whenever he looks, he has every reason to think that the hand is part of the arm. If the child's mother does all he desires before he knows he desires it, he has no grounds for concluding she is not part of himself. Later, he comes to know that hands *are* parts of arms but that mothers aren't parts of self. Incomplete differentiation, however, is common in adults: some people claim they don't feel "whole" or "complete" without various persons or objects near them; such people are not considered crazy. Great hitters are said to use their bats as if they were extensions or parts of themselves. In fact, great hitters use their bats as if they were as in tune with them as we are with our hands (and often as if they were more so). Our clothes are very much a part of us. To insist that there are human beings on the one hand and clothes on the other is to take an overly literal and concrete view of reality. Most of us feel a good deal less ourselves with our clothes off than we do with them on, even when we are alone (the shirt hides the paunch).

The examples could be continued, but the point is clear: the self-other distinction is often either arbitrary or unclear. It may appear obvious that human beings are separate; we can't see relationships. But visual reality does not coincide with reality. Much of our thinking about people is hindered by an obeisance to physical reality. Younger children tend to judge a person's guilt to be proportionate to the amount of harm the person has done. (J. Piaget, *The Moral Judgment of the Child.*) The amount of harm is more assessable, visible, and quantifiable than the intent to harm. It is understandable that children focus on it first. Adults can take intent to harm into account, although they never abandon amount of harm. People are more visible and quantifiable than relationships; but adults do not deny intent, and should not deny the reality of relationships.

Norman O. Brown, in *Life Against Death,* has argued that western civilization is a disease—a disease largely reflective of the infant's, and later the adult's, unwillingness and inability to accept the "fact" that he is an individual separate from his mother or, more generally, his environment. There is, however, no need to adopt such an extreme position. The child grows in his mother's womb, and during that period it is a moot point whether the child is an individual. When the child is born he is visibly separate from his mother, but it does not seem likely that he comprehends this in any adult manner. As both Freud and Piaget have emphasized, with no objection from hard-headed empirical scientists, it does not make sense to attribute to the child the concepts of self and other.

As indicated, relationships are not as concrete as people, and it may be that our thinking about relationships is primitive in much the same way a child's thinking about guilt is. As Piaget has demonstrated, children pass through an Aristotelian phase in their thinking about physical reality, as did the human race when Aristotle was alive. Perhaps we are in something of an Aristotelian phase in our thinking about ourselves—after all, we are less visible to ourselves than physical objects and we are more than merely physical objects.

The primal relationship is considerably different from adult relationships. Adults have differentiated themselves to some extent from their environment and then enter into relationships with other adults. The primal relationship is not a relationship between individuals; it is an undifferentiated unity. Most adult relationships, however, involve a somewhat blurred self-other distinction. For example, if a wife always does what her husband tells her to do, neither will have any way of knowing that she does not belong to him as much as his hands do.

If the preceding discussion has demonstrated the reality of relationships, it has also demonstrated the difficulty of defining them. The definition given in the preface does not specify that the relationship is separate from the individuals comprising it. If one could isolate the component parts of an interaction (as one isolates the constituent elements of a chemical substance), then one could isolate the participants of a relationship. But just as a chemical combination of two elements may yield a substance quite unlike the elements when isolated, relationships change the nature of people. The notion of self-other confusions has blurred the sharp outline of our basic unit, the individual. If a couple in love claims to be "one," or if Joe feels Mary is part of him, how can we isolate Joe from the relationship? In fact, how can we isolate Joe from Mary?

In the next section, I make the distinction between behavior expressive of relationships and behavior expressive of people. I will not attempt to further define relationships. I will, however, attempt to develop the psychological reality of the concept of relationships. It is as if relationships are as difficult to see as intentions. If children have difficulty attributing blame to bad intentions, we should have difficulty attributing fault to bad relationships. We should instead focus on the most visible feature of relationships—people. And we do. One of the most painful aspects of divorce is the necessity everyone feels for giving and accepting blame. It is little consolation to blame both or to say it is nobody's fault. It would be helpful if we could blame the relationship—that which was peculiar to the interaction between two people but not predictable on the basis of knowledge of the people as they are "in isolation."

RELATIONSHIPS AND PEOPLE

To be able to talk about people *and* relationships, we shall have to change our approach. In the previous section, we tried to assign part of behavior to the person and another part to the relationship; but it was not clear how a relationship could cause behavior. Nor was it obvious that persons in isolation were causes of behavior in relationships. So instead of trying to find what is caused by the person versus what is caused by the relationship, we shall try to find what human beings take to be expressions of the person and what they take to be expressions of relationships. An experiment and some examples will illustrate the difference in approach.

E. E. Jones, K. E. Davis, and K. J. Gergen ("Role playing variations and their informational value for person perception") found that we are not confident in attributing behavior to a person unless the person behaves *counter* to situational norms. For example, if a person applies for a job expressly requiring extroversion and if the person claims to be an extrovert, we cannot determine whether he is or not. But if he claims to be an introvert, we are confident he is. That is, if the person sticks out above the situation, we take the behavior to be his.

A similar claim may be made about relationships. If a person sticks out above the relationship, we take the behavior to be his. For example, it is appropriate for a teacher to fairly evaluate the performances of his students. If he does, he is not cruel, heartless, or indifferent to their feelings; he is merely being a teacher. Nothing can be said about his personality. If the teacher is fairly evaluating his students' performance, we do not attribute this behavior to the person—or to the role. The person-teacher distinction is not made, just as the self-other distinction is not made in the primal relationship. It is nonsense to say the person fairly evaluates his students' performance. Teachers do that; just plain people don't (they don't have students, for one thing). It is equal nonsense to say the teacher rather than the person evaluates. Teachers are people. Sometimes the distinction is made, however. If it is said that the teacher rather than the person evaluates, it implies that the person would rather not evaluate but does, perhaps to keep his job. In ordinary circumstances, however, we think of teacher-persons.

Similarly, if Joe kisses Mary, we can ask if he did so because of his nature or because kissing is part of Joe and Mary's (love) relationship. The question, "Did you kiss me because you wanted to or because we have a love relationship?" asks for a distinction that is not usually made.

While the normal case may be undifferentiated unity, the balance may be upset. If Joe kisses lots of girls, then Mary may take Joe's kisses to be his rather than the relationship's (he likes to kiss girls). If Joe kisses only Mary and has never had interest in kissing anyone else, Mary may take the kisses to belong (solely) to the relationship rather than to Joe. Usually, people prefer to be kissed by people. If the kissing is too dependent upon the existence of the relationship, Mary may feel that Joe isn't "much of a man." Similarly, students want their teachers to be people also. That is, they prefer qualities such as enthusiasm and interest in the material, even though there is no reason for a teacher as teacher to have such qualities. If the teacher presents the material well, what does it matter if he enjoys himself while doing it?

The person can stick out above a relationship or the person can be swallowed up by a relationship. The stereotypic teacher loses his preteaching personality, and becomes a hollow shell or sometimes a comic but beloved, devout pedant. If Joe and Mary have been married for many years, kissing may become habitual. Joe may be unsure if he kisses Mary because that is part of their relationship or because he wants to. That is, people can become less and less significant in the undifferentiated unity of the person-relationship.

The relationship can also become less significant; but it does not vanish after the members have left it. Much of what Joe and Mary do after a divorce will be expressions of their relationship. Joe will avoid intimate relationships not because he is the kind of person who distrusts such relationships, but because his relationship with Mary has made him distrust his normal gregariousness. Eventually, he will either recover his gregariousness, or his avoidance of intimate relationships will come to be (taken to be) a fact about him. Yet many people are fond of relating their current problems and personalities to their relationships with their parents. When does the statute of limitations run out?

No factual answer can be given. Some people believe that relationships that would seem to be long dead can exert an influence on the present. Mary may believe that Joe drinks because of what his mother did to him, but many impartial observers would claim that by now, this is a cheap excuse. If Joe drinks too much (for Mary), she may become one of these impartial observers.

The preceding discussion has illustrated that we do take it to be the case that *relationships cause behavior.* Under normal circumstances, we do not attribute power to relationships while excluding or deemphasizing persons, or vice versa. Most of the behavior of people in relationships is most appropriately considered a function of the person-relationship, an undifferentiated unity much like the primal relationship. Under some circumstances, we see the individual over and above the relationship; under others, we see the individual vanish into the relationship. It would appear that we think people, relationships, and people-relationships cause behavior.

Traditional Topics

This section discusses two traditional topics in the psychological and sociological study of relationships. I first discuss similarity between members of a relationship and demonstrate that it is impossible. I then discuss some experimental evidence favoring conflict and show that it cannot be generalized to include real life.

Similarity

A major focus in the study of interpersonal attraction for many years has been the relationship between similarity and attraction. It has been repeatedly found that people of similar age, race, religion, social class, geographical location, educational achievement (and other variables) tend to affiliate and get married. There is evidence that marital happiness and stability are a function of degree of similarity on these variables.

Much of the strength of these relationships is probably a by-product of the strong effects of proximity on attraction. We tend, it seems, to like people with whom we come in contact. But we tend to come in contact with people we are like. The guest for dinner who is of a different race can safely be assumed to be a doctor.

To some extent, of course, pressure towards homogeneity is exerted by parents and society. Also, to some extent, people prefer people of their own race, religion, educational achievement, and social class. There should be fewer sources of conflict once the relationship has been formed (although there may also be fewer sources of interesting variation). Friendship and love are bound to be easier (which is not to say better). If one leaves one's stratum, one may have to learn a new way of life to make a friend or find a spouse.

Having offered these explanations, there is not much more to say about these sociological relationships. It is a fact that similarity on sociological variables is related to the establishment of long-term relationships. It is not a fact that advances our understanding of interpersonal relationships, for it is not sufficiently detailed. It is a fact that serves as a circumscription of the scope of this book; it deals with relationships between sociologically similar people. Relationships between dissimilar people require special treatment. We should need, for example, to understand the problems faced by the son of the town drunk when he marries the daughter of the town banker (not to mention the problems faced by the banker's daughter). This kind of problem is more properly the province of the sociology of deviance. A deviant is no more and no less than a person considered noxiously different. Sons of town drunks are considered deviant by many people; daughters of town bankers are considered deviant by the radical bohemian friends of the town drunk's son. It may be, true in some abstract sense that we are all human beings, but we don't act that way. So, while interesting, similarity on sociological variables is not a topic relevant to our major concern here, the details of human relationships.

Psychologists have studied the relationship between attitudinal or personality similarity and attraction. Most of these studies have been laboratory simulations. As members of a leading research group said in 1970 (the situation has changed somewhat since) : "... the laboratory study of attraction is limited in its time span and hence might legitimately be labeled the study of first impressions. Whether the determinants of first impressions are precisely the same as the determinants of prolonged friendship, of love, or of marital happiness is an empirical question." (D. Byrne, C. R. Ervin, and J. Lamberth, "Continuity between the experimental study of attraction and real-life computer dating," p. 157.) Since it is not a question that has been answered, we must ignore this deficiency or dismiss these studies. It will be more interesting, however, to first milk them for more flaws.

These psychological studies are carried out against a background of sociological similarity. That is, usually college students from one college serve as subjects in a particular experiment. Thus the finding that attitudinal and personality similarity is related to attraction is not as trivial as it might at first seem—similarity accounts not only for the variability in attraction across social strata, but also for variability within a stratum. The variance of such similarity would seem to be smaller, perhaps more random, and harder to detect. We might have expected that within a given stratum not only would people be quite similar in attitudes and personality (as the sociological approach to social reality suggests) but would be (therefore) not particularly choosy about whom they would associate with within that stratum. This does not appear to be the case, however, although studies in this area do not specify the homogeneity of the environment of their subject pool. It is true that several studies have found that similarity of belief is more important than similarity of race in determining liking (Stein, Hardyck, & Smith, 1965). Other studies have shown, however, that the order of importance is reversed when abstract liking is changed to concrete expressions of liking such as "marrying one." Furthermore, race is but one of the major sociological variables. The issue has not been resolved; in any event, similarity or dissimilarity in social psychological studies is probably assumed by most subjects to involve those in the same situation. To the extent that this is the case, psychological studies attempt the difficult task of accounting for small amounts of variance.

That people attempt to present themselves in a socially desirable light has been known for a long time. There is remarkable agreement, even by deviant populations such as criminals and schizophrenics, on the desirability of various personality traits. Agreement on some attitudes may be less strong in the population as a whole, but, particularly within a stratum, agreement is high.

The usual study of the relationships between attraction and similarity begins with an assessment of the attitudes or personality of the subject (in such a way that he does not connect this assessment with the later experiment). Later, the subject is confronted with a manufactured other (who often exists only on paper, but who may be a preprogrammed stooge of the experimenter). This other is either similar or dissimilar to the subject. People who are similar to the subject are liked more than people who are dissimilar—that much can be said without qualification. By now there are scores of studies in this area which have investigated many aspects of this phenomenon; they need not concern us. Let me suggest an alternative explanation for the basic phenomenon.

Given that people attempt to portray themselves in a desirable light (regardless of whether they are desirable or merely wish to appear so), dissimilar people are *of necessity* also bad, undesirable people. They are anxious, cold, stupid; they hold dangerous attitudes. Given the goodness of the portrait of the average man painted by the average man, anyone who is dissimilar is sufficiently weird or frightening to be disqualified as a candidate for a friend.

In fact, studies have investigated how well we like people who are like us but who have just come out of a mental institution or have otherwise shown themselves undesirable. One theory is that we should dislike such people very much because they are threatening. If it could happen to him (who is so much like me in so many ways) it could happen to me, so I hate him for suggesting the possibility. The question is not yet resolved. What is interesting is that social psychologists have recognized that desirability is associated with liking and undesirability with disliking, but they have not yet attempted to simultaneously deal with the fact that most people either are or pretend to be desirable.

Another major difficulty arises when one considers the problems of defining similarity and dissimilarity. Roger Brown has suggested that "Cognitive domains that are close up are more differentiated than are remote domains." (R. W. Brown, *Social Psychology*, p. 317.) If Joe and Fred are friends, it is not only likely that they have similar sociological backgrounds, but that they have similar interests, personalities, and attitudes. Similarity is rewarding, says one theoretical explanation of the similarity-attraction relationship. It allows people to define social reality. Since there is no "right answer" to the problem of the death penalty, let's you and I decide it's wrong, refuse to listen to anyone else, and in our little democracy of two, our side wins, 2–0.

But if Joe and Fred are friends, they will necessarily be "close up" to each other. Fred will seem highly differentiated to Joe. This means that Joe will not see Fred as a uniform or consistent person. Walter Mischel has argued, with a good deal of supporting evidence, that the mind functions "... like an extraordinarily effective reducing valve that creates and maintains the perception of continuity even in the face of perpetual observed changes in actual behavior. Often this cognitive construction of continuity, while not arbitrary, is only very tenuously related to the phenomena that are construed." (W. Mischel, *Continuity and Change in Personality*, p. 1012.) If we perceive people correctly, Mischel argues, we will see that they are not consistent in their behavior; and it is precisely this kind of inconsistency that we would expect friendship to allow. Whether people who call each other friends perceive this lack of consistency or not is not really important.

The point is that correct perception of people is hardly the way to go about constructing a stable social reality. Furthermore, of course, Fred cannot be similar to Joe—Fred is too variable.

Friendship is not a frightened huddle. Friends delight in the discovery of differences which, compared to the massive differences in social class in our society, are not large to outside observers, but which are of much importance to Fred and Joe. The differences have little or no significance except in the context of the massive similarity. It is neither surprising nor interesting that a person in another corner of society does not agree with me that the death penalty should be retained. But if someone who should be like me disagrees, then finding the reason is important and valuable. I differ from some people on so many sociological variables that isolating the cause of our difference on the death penalty is impossible. If a friend and I are very similar, however, the probability of finding the essential cause of our difference is high. Debate of this nature is a much more important part of the construction of a social reality than the presence of similarities. Differences are figural; similarities are the background. If the members of our society were all white and from one ethnic background, would we know we were similar on those very important sociological variables?

Turning to another kind of relationship: Joe and Mary are in love and everything is perfect. Except for one thing: Joe likes it cool and Mary likes it hot. Joe suffers when it is hot, but Mary basks comfortably. When cold, Joe feels invigorated, but Mary can't get her feet warm. A minor difference against the background of massive sociological similarity; but will Joe enjoy the heat more because the tormentor who turns off the fan is the same religion as he is?

Joe and Mary both believe children should receive occasional spankings. Joe does it slightly more often than Mary, and Mary thinks he is too restrictive. Mary threatens without delivering more often than Joe does, and Joe feels this is very poor training. If they weren't so similar, they wouldn't be able to disagree. If Joe favored spanking and Mary thought it a crime, they would be too different to talk to each other about it. They would never have married. Yet the fact that an objective (in this case, distant) observer considers them similar is of no value to them. As far as they are concerned, they are different— just as different as they would be if Joe liked spanking and Mary hated it. Will Joe approve of Mary's false threats more because she still believes in spanking?

No matter how similar two people are, they will be different in important respects. When people differ in important respects, the similarities are unimportant. In fact, as suggested, they are often not perceived or are taken for granted.

Thus similarity is not operative in relationships. People who are similar *may* have fewer disagreements. But similarity is the background on which dissimilarity plays a highly figural role (and what appears to be similar from five miles up looks different from one mile up). Dissimilarity *is* operative in relationships; similarity is a description placed on the relationship by (relatively) distant observers. Similarity may allow people to get together, but it takes them no further.

Other reasons for ignoring the empirical study of the relationship between similarity and attraction pertain to almost all laboratory study of human social behavior. These need not be detailed here, as the arguments presented thus far prove that a vast research tradition is of no value to us.

Experimental evidence favoring conflict

All the arguments and evidence presented in this book favor the position that interpersonal conflict is at best of no value and usually harmful. Much of the experimental work on aggression also favors this position. Yet a possible value of conflict is suggested by an interesting contrast effect from social psychology. An examination of this effect provides an excellent example of the danger involved in generalizing from laboratory studies of human social behavior.

E. Aronson and D. Linder ("Gain and loss of esteem as determinants of interpersonal attractiveness") found that a person who initially gives a subject negative evaluations and changes to positive evaluations is liked more than a person who gives continually positive evaluations. Similarly, a person who starts with a positive evaluation and changes to a negative evaluation is disliked more than a person who is consistently negative. This study has received wide attention. While there have been some failures to replicate the findings, it is a reputable and interesting finding. Let us see if it has applicability to conflict between human beings.

The implication is clear: People should sometimes do things to keep satiation from the door. If Joe does not have to work for his rewards, he will not like Mary as well as if she mixed up her behaviors (in some as yet unknown proportion of good to bad behaviors). Because the evaluations Aronson and Linder's subjects received were not based on real quality of performance, but were preprogrammed, we are really comparing the value of random behavior with the value of an even disposition and unconditional positive regard. Should Joe sometimes fly off the handle, get stinking drunk, beat up on Mary, or pick fights? Does the occasional appearance of such behavior place his good features in pleasing contrast? Without occasional displays of mindless rudeness, will Joe's good features not blend into a bland background?

Perhaps the reader is reminded of brainwashing techniques. Against a background of total misery and deprivation, the slightest kindness is said to be enough to reduce the prisoner to a slavering, happy, and willing source of information.

Clearly, then, the results of Aronson and Linder's experiment have no relevance to love relationships. The prisoner is a prisoner. In the experiment, subjects had to listen to the negative evaluations. They could not "leave the field," although they were not under the same kind of control prisoners are. Aronson and Linder's results seem to apply if and only if the subject is under control. The more control, the more marked the effect (if it is assumed brainwashing produces a stronger effect than the experiment did). In real life, people do not always wait out the bad part. They can and do leave.

Some people are locked into relationships (by children, for example) and do not *feel* they can simply walk out on unpleasant behavior. Prisoners, however, *can't* leave. Subjects in psychological experiments are, while wary, usually resigned, and at any rate lack legitimate reasons to leave (anybody who can't take a negative evaluation in the name of science is overly sensitive). People locked into relationships may have the illusion they can leave if they have to. In addition, unlike the prisoner and the subject, they have easy access to a community which will help legitimate the reasons for leaving and derogate the spouse. With the help of parents and friends they can leave the field mentally and fight back in whatever ways are available. Thus Aronson and Linder's experiment does not generalize even to couples who maintain relationships despite their dislike of them.

Furthermore, *happiness* refers to both a state and a trait. If Joe is suddenly released from misery, he will feel great, and will rate his happiness ten on a ten-point scale. Similarly, the subject who suddenly finds himself thrust into the high opinion of the stooge experiences relief. If Joe has been happily married for ten years, however, exaltation is not appropriate. If exaltation is required for a ten, Joe should honestly give his happiness a seven. Thus, Aronson and Linder's results apply only to sudden changes in state. Joe's rating of seven does not mean he is unhappy. It merely reflects the fact that traits are less extreme than states.

But in order to keep love alive, shouldn't a couple make each other miserable now and then? *Love* refers to both a state and a trait, but the state is much more valued than the trait. If Joe and Mary make each other miserable and then suddenly release each other for those pleasant surges to ten, won't their relationship remain forever young?

There is evidence that *misery increases love*. R. Driscoll, K. E. Davis, and M. E. Lipetz ("Parental interference and romantic love: the Romeo and Juliet effect") found that love correlated with parental interference for unmarried couples. But the couple did not make each other suffer. While a man's love for a woman might increase if he suffered at the hands of someone else, there is nothing to suggest that his love would increase if she were the source of his torment. According to the Aronson and Linder paradigm, subjects would probably like best of all, someone who liked them after *someone else* had evaluated them negatively.

In conclusion, an evaluation of the methodological status of the psychological experiment, with particular attention to the freedom of the subject, demonstrates that generalization to love relations is not warranted.

Advice and Rules

One thing people know how to do is give advice and make up rules for living. Homilies pervade our society, often contradicting each other. Books written by people with advanced degrees tell us how to do almost anything. The evidence of logic or data is unnecessary; it is the authority that counts. Most of us have advice to give on a variety of topics.

It is the purpose of this section to demonstrate that advice and rules are almost always pernicious.

Traditional "talk" psychotherapy of all schools is theoretically tailored to the individual. Its effectiveness has, however, been repeatedly questioned, by logic and data. If such psychotherapy is of questionable value, there is no reason to expect a set of directives expressly designed for the largest possible audience to be of much use to any particular member of that audience. If a writer is sufficiently vague, he can issue directives that could conceivably be followed by the entire human race. Everyone *could* follow the directive, "Be yourself," but the advice is worthless—it doesn't tell you how to do it.

Let us consider some directives from the best-seller, *How To Be Your Own Best Friend* (M. Newman and B. Berkowitz, p. 31). "So when you do something that makes you feel bad inside, ask yourself whether that's the way you want to feel. If not, stop doing what makes you feel that way. Instead, do the things that make you feel good about yourself." This directive could be followed by everyone. It could even be followed by John, who feels bad inside when he holds a steady job and spends his free time with his wife and children, but very good when he is on the streets drinking and molesting children. Or consider what Newman and Berkowitz say on page 81: "It takes thought and effort to shake free of bad habits." What kind of thought and effort? How does it help one shake free?

The vagueness of advice tailored to the multitudes, however, is not the major problem. The major problem is common to all advice, no matter how specific and accommodating. Advice and rules are helpful only to people who can, want to, and probably already do follow them. Consider some advice from *Best Friend,* with the responses of a hypothetical but realistic neurotic:

Best Friend: Instead, do the things that make you feel good about yourself (p. 31).

Neurotic: But there isn't anything I do that makes me feel good about myself. Everything I do makes me feel lousy about myself. I think I'll knock myself off. It's lousy knowing there must be some people who do feel good about themselves.

Best Friend: One fundamental thing is to meet your own expectations (p. 32).

Neurotic: But I learned from Mom and Dad to expect to be best at everything always, and I just can't make it.

Best Friend: We all love praise, but have you ever noticed how quickly the glow from a compliment wears off? When we compliment ourselves, the glow stays with us (p. 28).

Neurotic: Ok, I'll try it: "I love you George, because you're great." Bullshit you do, and quite right too, you worthless scum.

Best Friend: Enjoy the experience of being in charge of yourself (p. 32).

Neurotic: I wish I could, but me plus a bottle equals me drunk plus an empty bottle. I enjoy that feeling a lot more than me sober.

Best Friend: Why don't you think about the times you were wise and kind? Why remember and dwell on defeats instead of victories? (p. 38).

Neurotic: What times? What victories?

Best Friend: Getting rid of [bad habits] takes a lot of perseverance. It's not enough to want to change. You must want to want to. You must want to even when you don't want to (p. 82).

Neurotic: But that's just when I don't want to the most.

The book is written by two practicing psychologists with a good many well-known clients and it is not as simplistic as many similar books. But the neurotic is no caricature, nor is he excessively low in self-esteem. He simply cannot, or doesn't want to, follow the advice.

In addition, *Best Friend* focuses on attitudes toward self rather than on more substantial personality traits, which are probably more difficult to change. If the neurotic has been unwilling to be intimate quickly, advising him to open himself to experience is not much different from telling a clumsy weakling to hit a home run or a German to speak English. It is also insulting, for the advice assumes it is bad to be unwilling to be intimate quickly. Most neurotics of any standing have developed what are often called "defenses." In this case, the neurotic might claim that quick intimacy is not real intimacy and that extroverts spill themselves into the environment as soon as there is anything to spill and are therefore not really people. If the neurotic hasn't developed a defense like this one, the advice will do him more harm than good. It may make him feel more inferior.

Thus, attempts to change personality traits involve noxious implicit judgments as to which traits are desirable. But surely everyone should feel good about himself—nothing insidiously pernicious here! No value judgments lurking.

To show that even feeling good is bad, we must take up the other major function of this genre, which is to give comfort. *Best Friend* gives two nice examples:

1. The Questioner is responding to an answer which explains that we do not have to be adults all the time: "That's very nice to hear, very reassuring. I do feel better knowing I don't have to be a super adult" (p. 63). (The threatened neurotic replies, "How childish of you to believe everything you read.")

2. The Questioner says, "Accept the messiness and the mistakes? But I thought the point was to stop making them" (p. 83). The answer is, "If you do, you'll be the only one."

Comfort comes in two major forms, illustrated by the two examples. The first shows that what we do is "okay." To be sure, we are
not given *carte blanche*: "Of course, people can come up with all kinds
of crazy notions about what they think they want to do or be, but they
are just that—notions, and not genuine impulses" (p. 44). (The
downtrodden neurotic sneers, "So I can't rape old women, just when I
had my foolish heart set on it.") No, if you feel that you can give up
doing your housework that day because you would feel better doing
something else, do it: "You may decide to write a poem instead" (p.
32). The boorish neurotic cannot prevent himself, despite having read
this uplifting book, from making the gratuitously vile marginal comment, "How about writing nasty names for oppressed minority groups
on the walls of public toilets instead?" Few of us want to or can write
poems; only a few more feel like writing nasty words on walls. Most
behavior is very much in the middle, and can only with difficulty be
subjected to glorification. Yet most behavior is not particularly evil,
and it is nice to know that; which we will if we accept the word of the
writers; which we will if we can, want to, and already do.

The second example shows that we are all in the same rotten boat.
No matter what we do, "We will still be beset by real problems and
suffer real defeats. Life is not a picnic—or a rose garden. The world is
not run for our benefit. There is no escaping the human condition,
which involves pain and difficulty and loss" (p. 89). Shades of Szasz'
inherent disharmony; but Szasz offers arduous and time-consuming
psychoanalysis as a possible source of relief, rather than the reading of
a short book (although, to be fair, one well-known devotee, Neil
Simon, claims on the cover of the paperback edition that he reads it
"twice a day with a glass of water").

Let us assume that our neurotic is placated and comforted, even
that he feels wonderful about himself. If his low self-esteem had *any*
basis in reality; if there was *anything* about him he should have
changed; then he has been misled.

He feels good; but there is no conclusive evidence that feeling
good is of any use whatsoever. A good shot of heroin would have made
our neurotic feel even better, and it would have been just as much
help in solving any real problems he may have had. There is no point
in feeling better until whatever problems one has have been faced and
solved. Then one will be "healthy," and not in need of feeling better.
One will be ready to start enjoying life or whatever it is one wishes to
enjoy. One will not need books to get one through the night. Anyone
who profits from advice books has problems; anyone without prob-

lems doesn't need advice books; anyone with problems can't be helped by advice books. Q.E.D.

A different sort of advice book is represented by George Bach's *The Intimate Enemy*. Books of his genre purport to teach couples how to argue in a way that will minimize the harm or change the conflict into a meaningful learning experience. The rules make good sense and are hard to disagree with. For example, married couples are urged to wait until the children are in bed before fighting it out. Thus if Joe makes Mary mad, she may pick at Joe during dinner so indirectly that the children can't pick it up. Joe will be angry, but he will be doubly angry if he threatens *sotto voce* to blow his stack and Mary sweetly reminds him that they promised to abide by the rules suggested by the eminent authority on marital conflict.

In addition, such rules can be followed only by those who can, want to, and probably already do. A person who becomes extremely aroused during an argument will not magically turn into a calm philosopher when told that it is better to be calm. Nor is it necessarily better. As with changing personality traits, value judgments are involved; and if the person has not acquired defenses, a list of rules he cannot follow may make him feel more inferior.

Any interaction between Joe and Mary which is conducted according to Hoyle is not properly termed an argument or fight; arguments and fights are not mannered interchanges. It is probably wonderful if a couple can avoid arguments and fights, but they may be able to do so only because they don't care enough to get mad; are dull, moribund, or stupid; or have "better ways" of getting at each other.

Perhaps arguments and fights can be conducted according to rules. Sporting events are: but all sporting events have referees. Referees are constantly subject to abuse, but never by the side their decisions favor. That side usually believes the referee made a good call. Neither side is accused of lying. It is understood that one team can see it one way, while the other team sees it the other way.

Let us assume that a couple has agreed to fight fair. Joe: "You can't bring my mother into it; she's irrelevant to this subject." Mary: "Your mother isn't irrelevant to *anything* you do." Real disagreement is possible on such a topic. The foulness of a batted ball is more palpable than the irrelevance of a reference to Mother; the gratuitousness of a blow after the bell is more tangible than bringing up the claims of the ex-husband. With no referee, we should expect nothing but anarchy in relational contests.

The most potentially dangerous aspect of such rules of conduct is that they encourage the codification of problems. If a couple has a means for handling conflict and disagreement, they should use it. If Mary minds going to Joe's parents' once a week, but only a little bit, and only because she has an inchoate feeling that Joe is too involved with his parents, she may not bother to complain. Nevertheless, if she and Joe have a vehicle for solving problems, why not use it?

What good can come of using it? Either Joe is ready to let loose the apron strings or he's not. Making him aware that other people are aware of his attachments can produce resentment, panic, insecurity, *or more attachment.* It will be harder for him to let loose those apron strings when he is ready because he will be unable to tell if he is letting them loose because he is ready or because he doesn't like Mary knowing he is weak. Her knowledge may make him feel inferior and he may try to retaliate. Going to his parents' will be uncomfortable even if the visits decline in frequency, for he will suspect that each visit is the result of renewed insecurity. Furthermore, now that Mary thinks about it, she has indeed put up with unnecessary self-restraint, and Joe owes her for it. Her consciousness is raised. In what other areas of their relationship is Joe passively controlling her? How could she have missed it: Joe is always calling up his old friends.

What of all the understanding that can grow between Joe and Mary, the understanding Szasz calls a burden? Joe understands what? That Mary is keeping a sharp eye on him. Mary understands what? That Joe is insecure and furthermore that his insecurity is depriving her of her rights.

What are people's rights? A factual answer is impossible if we are being psychological rather than philosophical. What is important is what people take to be their rights. In relationships, the more rights a person has, the more often his rights will be violated. Furthermore, rights spawn rights. If Mary has the right to have a husband independent of his parents, why shouldn't she have the right to have a husband independent of old friends? The possession of conflict-resolving rules is likely to produce conflicts that may or may not be resolved. I do not suggest that everyone should take everything lying down, but that rules are made not only to be broken; they are made to be played by.

As mentioned previously, all the arguments and research in this book suggest that arguing and fighting and raising problems are at best of no value and usually detrimental to a relationship. I therefore conclude this section by advising everyone to eschew arguing.

SEX, MONEY, THE PAST, AND OTHER SCAPEGOATS

Books on marriage and the family usually give detailed discussions of sex, money, in-laws, and other common problems that plague marital and similar relationships (for example, R. K. Kelley, *Courtship, Marriage, and the Family*, 2nd ed). Such books are used in courses on marriage and the family. This is yet another kind of discussion that is of little value, for the following reasons:

Sex and money problems are especially varied and specific to the individual relationship; therefore general discussions of them are not of much use.

Furthermore, divorce lawyers and divorced people to the contrary, I do not believe sex and money are the major causes of divorce. Nor do I take a psychodynamic position that they are symptoms of underlying problems. Underlying problems are by definition in some way removed from the present and the relationship. A common type of underlying problem is early relationships with parents. R. Seidenberg's *Marriage Between Equals* is largely an attempt to trace pathological marriages to pathological childhoods. Such historical approaches cannot or do not explain precisely why the pathology survives into the present relationship. Furthermore, the value of such approaches is nil: people are stuck with their childhoods (if they so choose). As we have seen, whether present behavior will be taken to be caused by a relationship that existed in the past depends to some extent on considerations of logical coherence, but also on perfectly legitimate political grounds. You may be stuck with your childhood, but there is no reason why I should be stuck with it also. After all, almost everyone has had a childhood that could be described as pathological, as anyone who has engaged in a bout of self-pity knows. Either your parents forced you to do too many things or they deprived you of opportunities to learn. They shoved you out the door or they gave you no independence training. So, as with rules for fighting, why bury our heads in *that* sand?

If sex and money are not the major causes, nor their symptoms, why have they received so much attention?

Both are quantifiable. One can count orgasms and measure genital organs. One can compare incomes and weigh the possibility of a new color television. Both are concrete, visible, and unambiguous. If a couple has a "problem in living," it is easy and nice to attribute it to a source that is not only clearly present or absent, but present or absent to a specifiable degree. As people look around for the causes of their vague feelings of dissatisfaction, unhappiness, and frustration, they have little choice but to seize on what they can see. Sex and money are things we know how to see, much as we can see people but not relationships, harm but not intent. We make do with what we have.

Sex and money may be major problems. When they are simply that, there is nothing general to be said. Books have nothing to say; therapists of specific relationships may. In many cases, however, people talk about sex and money because they have nothing else to talk about; sex and money are *scapegoats* for unnamed or unnameable problems. Once scapegoats, they become problems; they become the locus of arguments; they become the arena in which further escalation will take place. Once the couple decides the problem is a bad sexual relationship, all attention can be diverted to the sexual aspect of the relationship. It is to be expected that the couple's sexual problems will increase. Sex does not seem to flourish when it is simultaneously gauged and engaged in. Furthermore, all the couple's dissatisfactions can now be blamed on their sex life. "No wonder I'm so tired; no wonder I can't think up good slogans for toothpaste; no wonder the dog is barking so much at night: I've got a bad sex life."

Sociologists have pointed with alarm at the excessive burden placed on married people by the nuclear family structure as it exists today. The husband must be provider, father, companion, lover, and protector to his wife; she has a similar wide variety of often contradictory roles. Many people have placed their miseries and hopes in sex, but it is a fragile vessel that cannot be expected to hold all the problems in the world. Money cannot be expected to solve all these problems either.

Furthermore, sex and money are not initially felt to be important. Love conquers all—until after marriage, when it is suddenly reduced to impotence by all the problems it indulgently laughed at before the vows. Since most couples say they are in love when they get married, and continue to say so through many problems, a much more important problem than any of those discussed in this section is what happens to love. Does it become impotent? Does it vanish? Was it an illusion? Or did it seem strong only because premaritally the other problems were dormant? Chapters to follow are directed at this and other problems.

2
Love

IF IT IS true that the course of true love does not run smoothly, it is equally true that nobody is quite sure what true love is. Rather than attempting to describe it, this chapter will explain *why* nobody can be sure what it is. Along the way, however, an attempt is made to describe the first phase of love, usually called "romantic love." A general description of this phase is possible.

Two different descriptions of this phase will be offered. Romantic love may be viewed as a preadaptational state with respect to the loved one, an unwillingness and inability to treat the loved one as an instance of anything else. Romantic love may also be viewed as an attempt to act out, with the loved one, fantasies that *could not* be realized in this world. From either view, romantic love is unstable and unsatisfactory. This chapter details the problems inherent in romantic love, and is thus a prelude to the extremely pessimistic chapters three and four. However, it leaves open the possibility that we can and do treat people as novel objects (as themselves) and that we may do so more in the future; in addition, it leaves open the possibility that our impossible fantasies *can* in fact be fulfilled in a relationship with another person.

Most people are willing to admit that something goes on between people, which many call love. But this vague concept is sometimes positively and sometimes negatively valued. The negative evaluations are often accompanied by two types of comments:

1. "Love is nothing more than sex."
2. "Love is nothing more than the way a person feels when his needs are being fulfilled at a minimum of expense. There is no such thing as disinterested love."

In order to discuss romantic love, we must dispose of these common and rather persuasive comments. The first part of this chapter accomplishes this task.

LOVE AND SEX

Sex is possible without love, but is usually considered "better" with it. Love is possible without sex, but the word most commonly describes what participants in heterosexual relationships report they feel for each other. So perhaps love is "better" with sex.

In most cases, however, it is not. Parents and children normally love each other, but sex between parent and child is taboo in almost all cultures. Friends are also often said to love each other, although it is not common for them to say so. Instead, they say they are friends. References to emotions are excluded. This is a valuable rabbit hole, and may be explained in at least two ways. One I shall discuss in detail later:

Briefly, if Joe loves Mary, Joe is withholding something from Mary. The presence of emotion indicates there is something Joe would like to do with Mary that he is not doing (for a variety of reasons). The damming up of this ardent desire leads to the experience of emotion, which is called love. Married and other long-term couples do not experience the emotion called love as often or as intensely as they once did because they have transformed many of their desires into behavior. Thus they are sometimes tempted to feel their love has gone, and in a sense it has. It has gone from the person into the relationship, in the form of relational behaviors. Friendship is the most open and direct of the relationships in this culture because there is little love dammed up—it is all expressed in the relationship.

Or is it? For the second explanation holds that same sex friendship is really latent homosexuality. Emotion is rigidly repressed for fear it will lead to overt homosexual behavior.

Absurd and old-fashioned? Let us look closely.

Lillian Hellman's *The Children's Hour* is about Martha and Karen, who together run a school. A child claims she has seen them together as lovers. Nobody, not even Karen's fiancé, really believes they are not lesbians. Karen correctly feels it would be beneath her dignity to formally and publicly deny the charges, especially since they are not made explicitly or overtly. Her reasons are not strategic, but her behavior is good strategy: if I tell you that I don't beat my wife, you wonder why I tell you, since you didn't ask. Eventually, the child is made to confess she lied, but it is too late: Martha hung herself because she came to believe she did feel "that way" about her friend.

The story illustrates some points: if two people of either sex are close friends, they can deny there is physical feeling between them, but that is like saying I don't beat my wife. You may believe I don't *beat* her, but the fact that I brought it up leads you to believe I do something similar, like pushing her around. She may consider that beating but I (would rather) consider it something else.

To deny physical feeling is also somewhat unfriendly. Ask me if I have physical feelings for male friends and, especially in the company of a friend, I will deny it with excessive emphasis: "Hell no, he's too ugly," or "I never did like blondes." I deny it, but soften the denial by denying I am serious. As far as I know I don't have sexual desire for male friends, but denial goes too far—it seems to imply that they are unattractive, undesirable, and unlikeable.

It seems to be the case that people who like each.other touch each other or feel the desire, need, or impulse to. One *could* ask why. But then again, one could ask why not. In fact, we have many potential and common answers to the latter question: they're both males and not homosexuals, she's married to his best friend, he's her son, he's the teacher and she's a student, or (between a male and a female who are eligible for a love relationship but don't have one) "they're *just* friends." (My italics.)

We also have answers to the former question, but they are tautologies: that's human nature; they love each other; people have bodies and therefore use them. It appears that not touching needs substantive, specific explanation, while touching requires only general tautologies. Not touching is problematic, while touching is "normal."

If two people like each other and don't deny sexual or physical feeling, then perhaps it is there. It is difficult to determine if it is or not without being arbitrary (by insisting, as some psychoanalytic theorists do, that it is, or as other theorists do, that it isn't). There are no obvious criteria if the people don't touch each other sexually. And so if someone asks you *why not?* touch your best friend of the same sex, if you say "I want not to," that implies a revulsion; if you say "I don't want to," your questioner can simply repeat *why not?*, for you haven't answered the question. We don't have good answers to the question; at present our defenses against charges of homosexuality are weak (hence *The Children's Hour*). It is hard to deny sexual feelings without denying feelings. If we feel strongly towards someone of the same sex, it is difficult to determine that there is no sexuality in the strong feeling. If there is any, then the whole feeling is tainted.

Freud is not the culprit here; he is the savior. By proclaiming that everything is sex, he made it possible for us to say that we do have sexual feelings for our friends; it just doesn't happen to be the kind of sexuality associated with a male and a female who love each other. Unfortunately, Freud equated sex with the body. There is no reason for this restriction; mental or social activity can be libidinal also, and so the social intercourse of friends can be described as a sexual kind of intercourse.

But most of us equate sexuality with the body, and old habits die hard. While I often touch my male friends, I am very careful not to touch my female friends. And that *is* because I don't want sexuality.

I don't not want it either, for then my relationship with my female friends would be platonic. By connotation a platonic relationship is sterile, dull, and tired; such relationships are not friendships.

Is love without sex possible? Not if sex is taken to be as broad a term as Freud should have meant it to be; not if "sex" is similar to "life force," as Freud and others have claimed it is (without including the life of the mind). If sex is that broad a term, then, all activities can become sexual in the way that heterosexual love is and incest, homosexuality, and necrophilia begin to appear rather tame perversions. It is not that man just naturally wishes genital sexual intercourse with whatever happens to be around. It is merely that *why not?* is a question that cannot be answered except with such prohibitions as it's against the law, it's unnatural, or it's disgusting; to which anyone can again inquire "why?" The only answers to this question have the status of tautologies. Thus the sexuality in my feelings toward my female friends must be kept under control precisely because sex with females is quite normal for heterosexual males. I would hypothesize that homosexuals avoid physical contact with male friends more than they avoid it with female friends.

Why avoid sex if it's there? Let me use an analogy to answer this "in" question. I am a very unsentimental person and yet I am a very sentimental person. I do not usually express my feelings about people; thus, few of my relationships would be characterized as "warm." When I take leave of a person after a period of time together, I tend to feel very sentimental and, working very hard to keep it under control, I am colder than usual. Why not give way to sentiment if it's there? I could say, "We don't have that kind of relationship," or, "I express my feelings in behavior, not in empty symbolic gestures." In fact, the welling up of sentiment is the experience of unexpressed behaviors. I can no longer behave normally, because I am taking leave. The normal behaviors dam up and try to spill over in tears. So it is not quite correct to say I feel sentimental about the person. I am mourning my behaviors as much as my friend. In fact, it is most accurate to say I am mourning the relationship, that is, the interaction.

Overtly sentimental relationships are different from unsentimental relationships; similarly, sexual relationships are different from nonsexual relationships (using *sexual* in the narrower sense). If I have a relationship I like, why would I want to change it into another kind of relationship in which I would feel uncomfortable—in my case a sentimental relationship? Why enter a (narrowly) sexual relationship with someone whom one doesn't feel comfortable with sexually? Different relationships have different functions and values. Who would want only one kind of relationship? Furthermore, we like our relationships to be unique. If they are not, each seems like a borrowing from others, and it is impossible to determine whether we act as we do in response to a specific personality or to a mode of interaction borrowed because we do not know how to adjust to another person.

Still, the sex is there, or the relationship would be merely platonic.

Thus the common and ancient distinction between sexual and nonsexual love does not mirror reality but is a magical attempt to order chaos, in this case to *create* a love without sex, as a haven. There is no nonsexual love, and yet most love is nonsexual (so there is no real need for a haven).

A similar move—saying that love has a sexual *component*—also fails to mirror reality, because it is an attempt to make sex something that could be excised. Although the move is motivated by a desire for cleanliness, it makes dirt. The "component," compartmentalized, cannot be "sex as life" but must be "sex leading to genital orgasm." Thus "sex" implies "genital orgasm," and must be removed from "life." Most relationships, however, are not characterized by a desire for the kind of sex that leads to genital orgasm. Relationships that do include genital sexuality do not *also* include other relational behaviors. Sexuality pervades the relationship (when it doesn't, the relationship is considered deficient). Sex is integrated into the relationship; nonsexual relational behaviors are integrated into the sexuality. It is true, of course, that some relationships have a sexual component separate from the rest of the relationship; other relationships have had the sexuality excised. In both cases, the operation is a success and the patient is dead. These are not (taken to be) normal relationships.

Love and sex are not inseparable; that would imply that they were two different things. They are not one thing either. Energy provides an analogy. Energy takes many forms, such as electricity and heat. Both are forms of energy, but to say they are the same is to overlook functional differences. Similarly, friendship and sexual love relationships are both sexual in the broad sense of the term, but they are functionally quite different.

Having dealt with the sexuality of nonsexual relationships, we can now deal briefly with the possibility of a purely sexual relationship. Brief encounters or sexual relations with paid partners are marginal relationships. In fact they are sometimes sought, not for sex, but for sex without personality or relationship. Relationships exist that some would call purely sexual, but the participants might legitimately say, "But that is the way we show our love for each other." Such people might feel contempt for "purely" intellectual relationships, while people with the latter relationship might feel contempt for what they consider purely sexual relationships. Neither contempt is warranted. "Purely" sexual relationships are love relationships that tend to ignore minds and personalities; "purely" intellectual relationships are love relationships that tend to ignore bodies.

To conclude: In this area of experience, ordinary language is a poor guide. The traditional distinction between sex and love is poor, dishonest, and has a good word for nobody. It makes nonsexual love dead and sexual love crude. So why does ordinary language make the distinction, then? I contend it does so in an attempt to impose order on chaos. We hope to keep sex out of most of our relationships by words that magically establish that there is love on one hand and sex on the other; and that neither hand should know what the other is doing. The motivation for the distinction is not necessarily affective (anti-sexual); it may well be cognitive—a desire for clarity and simplicity. Nevertheless, the uncertainty and chaos will continue. Friendships will continue to bear a discomfiting resemblance to love relationships (or they will be castrated). This discomfiture is not necessary. Sex will change form as energy does—sometimes inappropriately, as in incest. Incest is not the fault of sex, however, but of the person who commits it.

Unfortunately, modern society seems to have been engaged in a systematic attempt to desexualize behavior, even sexual behavior. This will be described in chapter five.

GIVING AND RECEIVING

Another distinction made by ordinary language (and accepted by its users) is that between love as giving and love as receiving. A related and similar distinction is that between love as a strong need for the other and love as an active love for the other, i.e., between passivity and activity. These distinctions will now be examined.

Behavior exchange theory (K. J. Gergen, *The Psychology of Behavior Exchange*) and similar theories based on an economic conception of human relationships are widely used today. For example, Joe is said to have a good (or satisfactory, or rewarding) relationship with Mary when his rewards in the relationship exceed his costs. Introducing a conceptual nicety to this, the behavior exchange theory, Joe's net profit must exceed his "comparison level"—what he expects to receive from this kind of relationship. Joe may also take into account his "comparison level for alternatives"—what reward-cost outcome he could expect if he broke off his relationship with Mary.

Problems arise when one attempts to specify what functions as reward and what as cost. Money and approval are the rewards usually employed in laboratory experimentation on behavior exchange theory, and their loss or withdrawal are the usual costs. This experimentation is not of much use for the present purposes, due to its conceptual simplicity. The following discussion reveals interesting ambiguities.

We observe Mary knocking herself out on a hot day to cook Joe his favorite dinner. We assume this is a cost. Let us ask Mary, however: "Oh, no, it is a reward; his happiness is mine; it makes me happy to see him happy." Joe comes home, wolfs down the dinner, thanks Mary perfunctorily, and sits down in front of the television. Is Mary miffed? If not, we are tempted to describe her as a slave. Our implicit theory is that Mary is happy to make Joe happy only as long as Joe acknowledges that Mary is the source of his happiness. If Mary is satisfied with no recognition, we tend to treat her behavior as an aberration in need of specific explanation.

Assume now that Joe is properly appreciative. Mary feels gratified. The reward Joe gives (appreciation) easily exceeds the cost of spending hours over a hot stove. Accordingly, Mary often cooks Joe wonderful meals. Eventually, however, the joy goes out of it for both of them. They become satiated—Joe with meals, Mary with apprecia-

tion. The phenomenon of satiation is accepted by experimental psychology and the literature suggests some ways to avoid it: Joe can give
different kinds of rewards—simple approval will not be indefinitely
rewarding. Mary can put Joe on a schedule of variable ratio intermit-
tent reinforcement. Joe will get good meals sometimes. He knows this,
but he cannot predict when they will be. This kind of "schedule of
reinforcement" has been shown by experimental psychology to be very
good for maintaining interest.

Now let us assume that Joe and Mary have worked things out
with the consultation of a behavior exchange theorist and a specialist
in behavior modification. Their relationship is a model of satisfaction.
Each has the other on a schedule of reinforcement that keeps interest
and hope high, so that every reward is maximally effective. Rewards
do not follow too soon on the heels of each other, nor has the delay
been so long that apathy has set in. Costs are rewarded in such a manner that they seem less like costs than like work done towards a reward.

Two questions: First, is this how people operate—trying to give
and receive good reinforcement schedules? Obviously some people do,
to some extent; but not everyone does so always. Second, is it love? No.
People in love may reward each other properly, but love is more than
a felicitous interchange of reinforcements. What else is it?

Sex is often used in relationships as a reward. Withdrawal of sex
is a common punishment. Joe says to Mary, "How about it?" Mary
says, "Yes, you deserve it." One hopes Joe says, "Forget it." Doing
something because one wants to differs from doing something because
one has to. If Joe thinks Mary's behavior is given as a reward for his
good behavior, Joe will probably conclude that Mary is not doing it
because she wants to, but because she perceives that the balance of
payments dictates it or because she wants to build a good credit rating.
So Joe is not rewarded. He is punished. Therefore, theoretically he
will stop doing what led to the punishment. So giving sex as a favor is
a punishment in love relationships.

Another example: Mary likes Joe to bring her flowers. But if Joe
has sinned and then brings Mary flowers, she recognizes the flowers are
not necessarily a "gift of love" but probably also a gesture of appease-
ment. We do not feel as rewarded by a gift given with obvious ulterior
motives as we do by a freely given gift.

A general principle suggests itself: In relationships supposedly
motivated by love, rewards given not out of love but to obtain approval, to even the balance of payments, or to make up for past sins
are not rewarding and are in many cases punishing. On the other

hand, in relationships supposedly motivated by profit, rewards given freely ("because I felt like it," "because I love you," "oh, what the hell") are often not rewarding and are in many cases punishing. As told by movies and television, if Joe offers Fred a deal apparently beneficial to Fred, but not to himself, Fred is suspicious until Joe "lets on" to his nefarious motives. Fred then smiles happily, slaps Joe on the back, and says jovially, "You devil you." This process is at least partially motivated by Fred's real desire to assess Joe's true potential profit. But it is also an affectionate interchange. The more disguised and voracious Joe's profit motive the more delighted Fred is. It is as if displays of affection must be denied by an equal quantity of greed. Hence the more greed, by implication the more affection.

In relationships that are *prima facie* and formally neither strictly business nor strictly love (especially friendship) it is *de rigeur* to constantly reaffirm one's essential selfishness. As a corollary, one must constantly deny that one gets any pleasure from the "mere presence" of the other. Thus friends usually enjoy each other while nominally engaged in something they "really enjoy," e.g., drinking, gossip, games.

To explain this, let us return to love relationships. Are flowers in and of themselves rewarding to Mary? Perhaps. Some people like flowers. Probably, though, Mary is rewarded by the fact that Joe gave her flowers rather than by the fact that she received flowers. That is, Joe's love is rewarding, not what she gets from it. What is the reward of the gift of love? Not much if you are looking for substance. In fact, *the less substantial the reward, the more it is proof of love.*

Mary is very beautiful. Joe and Mary are about to go out. Mary appears, and Joe gets wildly excited about her beauty. This substantial display does not demonstrate Joe's love of Mary but his love of beauty or of the status of being seen with beauty. Similarly, if Joe gives Mary a present she is too happy about, Joe feels left out. Mary is not appreciating him; she is appreciating the present and she has no time for him. So Joe should not give Mary costly gifts. Not only will he feel rejected if she likes it too much, but she will be unable to tell if her reaction is to the present or to the fact that Joe gave it to her. Thus Joe's behavior can lead her to wonder if she loves him or his gifts. Furthermore, she may wonder why he spent so much money when a bauble would have done as well or better. The rich man who gives a woman an expensive present knows that he is required to say, "Just a bauble I picked up at the five and dime, my dear." But he knows he had to bring her an expensive present; he is saying this to try to indicate that their relationship is based on love rather than money.

Norman O. Brown (*Life Against Death*) hypothesizes that in earlier stages of civilization, gift giving was straightforward atonement for real, imagined, symbolic, or fantasy sins. That is, gifts were originally fulfillments of obligation. They still are. Most gift giving in this country is obligatory. We give people gifts at certain times— Christmas, birthdays, weddings—and we are obligated to do so. Good friends often avoid gift giving, especially at the proper time. Gifts between friends are unnecessary. There is no guilt to be removed nor have the friends been sinfully polite to each other. Giving a gift to a friend is an admission of guilt that the friendship is not strong. Such gifts, since they signal the punishing loss of friendship, are far from rewarding.

So why are gifts given in love relationships? And why must they be freely given and for no obvious reason? Perhaps because people in good love relationships do so much for each other in the economic behavior exchange sense that they must demonstrate they are not staying together merely because of felicitiously meshed reinforcement schedules. It might be assumed that free gift giving indicates that the relationship is so good that there are spontaneous overflows of good feelings. Apparently, though, free gift giving is a way of getting rid of guilt—guilt that the relationship gives so much for so little. Gifts are a return of one's excess rewards. But the giving must appear to be a spontaneous overflow of good feeling; otherwise the economic conception of the relationship would be emphasized rather than deemphasized. Gift giving is an attempt to deny that behavior exchange is the basis of the relationship and to affirm that there is more to life and to the relationship than narcissistic enjoyment of ripped off rewards.

Friends insist on a purely economic concept of the relationship because only under such a concept can people take pure pleasure in the company of others and in themselves. Joe can relax and enjoy himself with Fred if he knows Fred is getting something out of it but is not dependent on Joe (he could buy it elsewhere). Hence the pretext that they are *really* having some drinks (and so Fred *could* buy it elsewhere). Friends avoid giving gifts to avoid the emphasis on dependency that gift giving suggests. If Joe gives Fred a watch, Fred might not *merely* appreciate the watch, but might appreciate Joe giving it to him. Then Joe might feel that Fred needed him for his happiness. This would not be fair to Joe, for then he could not relax and enjoy himself. He would feel pressure to try to make Fred happy. So if Joe in a moment of weakness gives Fred a gift, Fred should have the presence of mind to jokingly downgrade the gift and imply, for example, that it was given because Joe had an extra.

I have claimed that love is more than a felicitous interchange of reinforcements. I have not as yet specified what else it is. I have shown that people in love resist the behavior exchange concept of human social behavior precisely because their exchange is so valuable in the behavior exchange sense. I have also demonstrated that friends *exploit* the behavior exchange concept. Friends can relax with each other precisely because they prey on each other. But they really prey on each other's temporary self-sufficiency and indifference to the environment as a source of reward.

So love and friendship involve denials of the total applicability of the theory that man attempts to maximize his gains and minimize his losses—love by involving spontaneous overflows of good feeling, friendship by involving a mockery of the game. Now that it is clear that people tacitly reject this theory, let us try to find out what they propose instead.

In an advance capsule summary, we shall see that people are attempting to establish the possibility of altruism, despite the fact that altruism is conceptually impossible. Human beings do things for reasons. Behavior is motivated. Behavior is intentional. It is an attempt to accomplish something. If Joe does something for Mary and explains, "I wanted to help her," we are tempted to request an explanation of what he was trying to accomplish by means of helping her. Social practices, as defined by P. G. Ossorio (*Persons*), are things done with no further end in view. Can we not imagine that Joe could help Mary with no further end in view? Apparently not, for many people seem to be engaged in a teleology of motives, which usually involves a search for what are called "ulterior motives." Ulterior motives do not coexist with motives which have no further end. Ulterior motives supplant the simple "altruistic" motive, which is invalidated by the discovery of the ulterior motive.

But: I am drinking a cup of coffee. You ask "why?" I tell you I want to wake up. You again ask "why?" I tell you I want to be as effective as possible during the day, and that is about as far as we can go without getting into my philosophy of life. By proceeding cleverly you could get me to admit that the reason I drank the coffee to wake up, to function more effectively, to impress the boss, was to get more money; and you would have traced my innocent act of drinking the cup of coffee to its selfish origins. Yet, what if I planned to spend the money to buy a huge house in the country for which my wife had been whining for years? My motives are not unselfish, but it sounds queer to call them selfish.

When we have our morning cups of coffee are we really planning to build empires (or escape the whines of those we love)? Introspect: at the most we are trying to wake up; as yet not even the thought of functioning, effectively or otherwise, has entered our minds.

And so when Joe leaps into a burning building to save Mary and says "I wanted to help her," why not admit that Joe was, if not altruistic, at least short-sighted or stupid? How could he have had a further end than saving Mary in mind? If he had, he would have stayed out of the building. A man his age should find better routes to glory and ego enhancement than running into burning buildings. Clearly, he simply didn't have time to think of anything except what was right in front of his face (just as a child can see only the harm; just as we can see only people) : Mary's danger. But we often are neurotic about motives:

After the rescue, Joe had better avoid feeling good. If he doesn't, he demonstrates that he didn't rescue Mary solely for her sake, but at least partially for himself. He is permitted happiness that Mary is alive, but he would be wise to avoid expressing it, for it is hard for observers (including himself) to distinguish that kind of happiness from happiness that *he* did it (this is always a problem with relationships and interactions—whatever Joe does for Mary is also something he did and therefore deserves credit for).

We do not usually do things for ourselves; we do things. I drink a cup of coffee in the morning. Am I doing it for myself? I suppose so, but it is a queer question because it implies there is an *I* who is acting on behalf of a *myself*, who is receiving from *I*. I feel good after having drunk the cup, so I guess *I* was not behaving altruistically with respect to *myself*—which isn't surprising, since they are one and the same person, as far as I can tell. But I have not been selfish (both *I* and *myself* got the coffee) nor have I dishonestly tried to sneak altruism in (*I* admits to *myself* he really did it for *I*). Z. Rubin (*Liking and Loving*, p. 85) has extended this pseudoescape from behavior exchange and selfishness to dyadic relationships: "By helping one's partner, one is helping the *partnership* and thus helping oneself as well. Here again there is a reward involved, but it is . . . a reward gained by and for the collective unit." Under those circumstances one could safely feel good. But under *any* circumstances, why feel *bad* after helping someone?

Our bizarre approach to altruistic behavior is further illuminated by the ease with which we accept the enslavement of children to the desires of their parents. "Why are you going to medical school?" "Because ever since I was femur high to a grasshopper my parents have been telling me I'm going to be a doctor so they can have someone to take care of them in their old age." "Do you want to become a doctor?" "No, not really, all things considered I'd rather be in Philadelphia." "So why are you going then?" "Because I am afraid of disappointing my parents. I would feel guilty; they worked so hard for me."

This person is going to medical school against his wishes, to please his parents. Altruism. No, we think it isn't altruism if the person is *forced* to do it.[1] This force is quite insubstantial; but we do not act as if we think so. When Joe devotes his life to helping the underprivileged for no obvious reason we may grant him altruism if he keeps his face in the proper position (no joy but no suffering and not even determination, for that would suggest he was forced, if only by himself). When he says, "I think somebody has to help the underprivileged, and it might as well be me," however, he cannot be altruistic. It is his moral duty that is forcing him, just as it is *I* that is drinking the coffee for the *myself* in me.

In short, we must act like mindless robots to be considered altruistic. Altruism is not possible for a human being, according to the way we think about human behavior. Either choice is selfishly motivated or forces operating on the person allow him no choice. Behavior we call altruistic is functionally similar to behavior engaged in out of a sense of duty or obligation. It does not constitute a special case of intentional action, separate and isolated from normally selfish behavior. Altruism appears to be a holding category for behavior for which we have not yet found an ulterior motive or force. Altruistic acts are done for no reason in the same sense that a drowned man has no name (so they call him John Doe). Behaviors, however, have explanations as inexorably as people have names. Accordingly, we look for the behavior's explanation. When we find it, we can remove the act from the category of altruistic acts. If we can't find it, the behavior is a freak.

We need and sometimes use the concept of a relationship to think less neurotically. When I do something for myself, the distinction between self-interest and other-interest disappears. It is not selfish, for both *I* and *myself* get it. The self-other distinction is not present in the primal relationship; it is blurred in many adult relationships. In any interaction, the giver must receive (at least awareness of his own behavior) and the recipient must give (at least in the sense of being ready and willing to receive). Also, we often must and do distinguish

between behavior with and behavior without a further end in view because the two kinds of behavior are overtly different:

A person is practicing the piano. The person is young and very
good. We wish to distinguish between two states of affairs: (1) he is
practicing to get that particular piece in shape; (2) he is practicing
to become a famous concert pianist. The following dialogue could
result from either:

Q: Why are you practicing?
A: To get this particular piece in shape.
Q: Why do you want to get this piece in shape?
A: To present it to my teacher.
Q: Why do you want to present it to your teacher?
A: So he can help me make it better.
Q: Why do you want to make it better?
A: What are you, some kind of nut?

There are many similarities between behaving with and behaving
without further end in view. As the above dialogue reveals, the pene-
tration into motives will reveal approximately the same sequence.
Most good young pianists would have no objection to becoming a famous concert pianist; but while many good young pianists behave as if
they have that end in view, others do not. Those who do might be expected to adopt a histrionic rather than an appropriate or original
interpretation; to daydream more than other good young pianists; to
feel contempt for their teachers for being not much more than teachers; or to choose music that contest judges and audiences like.

The person about to consume a piece of steak is not necessarily
fighting the never-ending battle of survival; nor is a parent helping a
child with mathematics necessarily trying to produce a brilliant child
who will reflect favorably upon the parent. We can determine by observation and intervention what a person's goals are. Eaters fighting
the never-ending battle for survival should savor their food and eat
with more intensity than the merely hungry. The ambitious parent
will have less patience than the merely helpful. The person who drinks
coffee in the morning to become famous will be more fastidious about
the procedure of coffee drinking than the merely groggy. In all cases,
the distinction between behavior with an end in view and behavior
with no end in view is worth making from the point of view of dis-
tinguishing overt behaviors. When we ask questions of a person of the
sort we asked the pianist, we move across the line from psychology,
which is concerned with behavior, to philosophy, which is concerned

with ultimates. The line is located differently for different people. One pianist may practice merely for the fun of it; another to get that piece in shape; another in preparation for an imminent concert; another to become a famous concert pianist; another to avoid boredom. Each pianist will practice in a different way, appropriate to whatever end is in mind (although we might have to try to deduce the differences, for example, by asking the pianist to go out for a beer). I drink my coffee to wake up, to work well, to make money, to buy food, to eat, to survive; but to argue that my behavior is ultimately motivated by the desire to survive is to engage in philosophy, not in a psychological discussion of what motivates my coffee drinking. The latter kind of discussion must take into account the fact that I, now a stereotypic cartoon slob recently removed from the womb of sleep, don't care if I live or die as I drink my morning coffee.

Regardless of where the line is drawn, the dialogue is the same. The location of the line must be established by observing overt behavior.

The critics of behavior exchange theory are attempting to establish that people can act with no further end in view. They are not attempting to establish that people can behave altruistically or unselfishly, for that smacks of sacrifice, which is unwelcome in love and in friendship. We have demonstrated that it is necessary to make the distinction between behavior with and without further ends in view, and that the latter kind of behavior is neither random nor freakish. It merely has looked less into time.

The relationship is the "explanatory fiction" usually employed to satisfy flagitious teleologists of motivation. If Joe brings Mary flowers for no obvious reason, the first *why?* elicits the dead-end relational attribution, "He loves her." Love is understood to be blind, irrational, self-immolating, extravagant, and fanciful; and it is accepted as an explanation. We accept the statement that certain relationships exist (most notably love, friendship, and blood) as reasonable explanations of unreasonable behavior even though the relationships are known to be unreasonable. It is as if such relationships are institutionalizations of the insane, just as mental hospitals have been provided for people who don't behave rationally and do so without a relationship. We cannot stand the lack of order produced by behavior that has no obvious motivation, so we invent relationships into which to throw such behavior; if we can't find the relationship, we throw the person into a mental hospital.

This is not, however, the intention of those attempting to maintain their right to behave with no further end in view. The man who brings his wife flowers out of a spontaneous overflow of good feeling is not fighting for the view of man as capable of doing things with no further end in view. If he were, he would be behaving with a further end in view, and thus would be defeating my philosophical description of his purpose.

We have examined the love-sex and the give-take distinctions and have found them wanting. Some attempts have been made to clean up around the confusions they cause. In the next section, I develop a description of romantic love which integrates its features and relates it to other phenomena, especially to the developmental history of love relationships. The description is, to some extent, an ideal or paradigm case of romantic love. The description is also empirical—I will draw on "popular notions," the works of Proust, stereotypic situations, and platitudes as examples and as evidence.

ROMANTIC LOVE

Romantic love is described from two related points of view; the two descriptions will eventually be integrated. The first is Piagetian: romantic love is described as a refusal or inability to adapt to the loved one. The second is psychoanalytic; romantic love is described as a refusal or inability to translate emotionally saturated fantasies into overt behavior.

The first description employs Piagetian concepts. An introduction, brief but more substantial than that offered earlier, borrowed largely from Flavell (*Psychology of Piaget*) is therefore presented first.

Flavell defines a schema as "a cognitive structure which has reference to a class of similar action sequences, these sequences of necessity being strong, bounded totalities in which the constituent behavioral elements are tightly interrelated" (pp. 52–53). To grasp an object is to *assimilate* it to the schema of grasping. Initially, an infant has an undifferentiated grasping schema; that is, he cannot accommodate to the object. When the infant can grasp objects somewhat in accordance with their shapes, he has developed a "class of similar action sequences" that are "tightly interrelated" in that all are instances of grasping. To grasp a pen with a hand open wide enough to grasp a baseball is not only unaccommodative: the infant cannot be said to have assimilated the pen because he has not grasped it. The infant comes to be able to assimilate the pen in part through accommodation

—through contact with the pen. The infant comes to be able to accommodate to objects in part through assimilation, trying one schema and then another.

All behavior is an attempt to adapt to the environment. Adaptation is accomplished by assimilation and accommodation. Piaget considers assimilation and accommodation the two aspects or modes of adaptation, and although they are "distinguished conceptually, they are obviously indissociable in the concrete reality of any adaptational act" (Flavell, *Psychology of Piaget,* p. 46). Any act of assimilation is also an act of accommodation. To treat an object as an instance of a particular concept associated with a schema is to display perforce an implicit theory of the peculiar nature of the object. To grasp an object (or to attempt to grasp it) is to treat it as a graspable object. Similarly, any act of accommodation is also an act of assimilation. To behave with respect to an object is to treat it as an instance of something. To engage in sexual intercourse with an object is to assimilate it to the schema of sexual behavior—to treat it as a sexual object. To stare with a puzzled expression at an object is to assimilate it to the schema of unfamiliar objects, which does not have significant action sequences.

Behavior is intelligent when it is adaptive, and behavior is most adaptive when assimilation and accommodation are in *equilibrium,* in balance, making equal contributions. To accommodate to an object is to behave with respect to it in a manner that takes the peculiarities of the object into account. Since it is to *behave with respect to it,* accommodation must of necessity also involve assimilating it to an exisiting schema. Since the existing schema must be sufficiently differentiated to take into account the novelties of the object, modification of an existing schema may take place. This is accommodation.

We must have a theory (an assimilatory schema) if we are to enter the world of evidence, but we must modify our theories to fit this world of evidence. This process is in equilibrium when we modify the existing theory to fit new facts rather than develop new theories. This latter process is adaptation out of equilibrium, with accommodation in the ascendancy. On the other hand, we must modify the theory rather than rigidly attempt to force the facts to fit it. That latter process is adaptation out of equilibrium, with assimilation in the ascendancy. Modification of existing theories is not as difficult as it sounds, as long as the theories are somewhat in accord with reality. For example, as we have seen, one major form of modification is differentiation. The infant says, "I thought there was one way to grasp, but

I find there are two—one way for pens, the other for baseballs." Adaptation can never be slavish accommodation to the environment. The grasping comes from the infant, after all, and the sexual activity comes from Joe.

Imitation and play would appear to be maladaptive, and are indeed activities during which assimilation and accommodation are not in equilibrium. Play is pure assimilation. Objects are assimilated to whatever schemata the person desires to put into action, regardless of their nature. However, most play is at least somewhat accommodatory. A child can play at being Mommy by wearing Daddy's clothes, but Mommy's clothes are preferred. Play serves adaptation: the child can try out schemata he is not ready or able to try out on the real world. Imitation is pure accommodation; it involves taking the form of the environment. Conformity resembles imitation in this sense. Assimilation is nevertheless involved in imitation. Imitation serves adaptation, the child can try out new roles or points of view, and thus develop new assimilatory schemata. Also, any attempt at imitation must proceed from existing schemata. The child cannot perfectly imitate his mother because his schema of grasping is not sufficiently differentiated to allow him to pick up objects with her efficiency. The child shows through the imitative attempt. Even great actors have styles.

Imitation and play, then, are not maladaptive. Beginning encounters with new objects are maladaptive in the sense that they are preadaptive and in the additional sense that assimilation and accommodation are at cross-purposes.

A person cannot assimilate a novel object; it requires too much accommodation. The person will attempt to apply existing schemata, but how does one *grasp* a *word*? And is that what one should do with it? Attempts at assimilation will be inappropriate. One must have some concept of the nature of the object before one attempts to assimilate it. If one is attempting to come to grips with a person, one may apply existing schemata created through experience with physical objects. For example, one may grasp the person; but one does not get a grip on what a person is by grasping the person physically.

Part of the problem of assimilating a novel object is that the object's "real' nature will reject the assimilatory attempt. If the person is aware of this, he is on the road to finding appropriate assimilatory schemata. Initially, accommodation, conceived of here as the nature of the object, interferes with assimilation by rejecting poor efforts. Joe does not learn much from his attempt to assimilate Mary to his schema of sexual behavior if she merely walks off in a huff.

Totally new schemata can be formed for new objects. This is an attempt at accommodation. Such schemata must be vague, global, undifferentiated—empty concepts of the object. They cannot be action schemata—any attempts to behave with respect to the object must be applications of existing schemata, which will be inappropriate. Thus, assimilation interferes with accommodation, while accommodation without assimilation creates an empty schema. Being empty, it is full of infinite potential. Because the object has had a brand new schema created especially for it (an original), it is necessarily a brand new object (as, of course, it is). That is, it does not resemble familiar objects of schemata sufficiently for it to be described in ordinary language.

A person can adapt to an object very well on one level without comprehending other levels. An infant may adapt to his rubber ring very well for purposes of living with it in his crib—he can grasp it, suck it, and shake it; but the thought of rolling it has never crossed his mind. The child may be able to assess harm done very well without ever having thought of entering intention into the guilt equation. A person may relate to another very well sexually without ever having "realized" that there is a personality attached to the sex object.

The initial adaptations must be mastered before the later ones are possible. More complex adaptations are dependent on earlier ones. The child cannot roll the ring until he can grasp it. Can a person deal with another's personality without having mastered the other's body? Or does the personality need to be mastered before the body? In such cases perhaps one dimension needs to be mastered before the other can be dealt with. In other cases, it is clear which dimension is basic and this is a common theme. Painters are "supposed to" know how to draw horses and hands before "expressing themselves" in abstract paintings. Writers are "supposed to" know how to write a "simple declarative sentence" before writing poetry. Unless the earlier adaptations are mastered, the later adaptations will be travesties, pseudoadaptations. For example, the obscurity of my adolescent poetry reflected the confusion of my thinking rather than the complexity and profundity of thought that forces great poets to uncommon juxtapositions. An "abstract" horse drawn by a novice does not look like a horse, but much of the lack of resemblance reflects the artist's inability to draw. If one wishes to depart from a realistic picture of a horse, one must modify existing schemata.

In addition to being travesties, premature attempts at assimilation are often impossible. If Joe does not have an action schema for women his own age and tries to treat Mary as he treats his mother, Mary will

tell him to get lost. The peculiarities of the object prevent inappropriate attempts at assimilation. Similarly, inappropriate accommodation
(the development of a vague, global, and undifferentiated schema for a
novel object) is not merely pointless, but often impossible. If Joe takes
Mary to be something new under the sun, he will be unable to direct
behavior at her (shyness and hesitancy, characteristics of romantic
love), in which case she will get lost; or he will neglect to assimilate
Mary to schemata she should be assimilated to; for example, he will
"forget" that one does not talk too much about oneself with new acquaintances, which is what Mary is.

Part of being unable to assimilate or accommodate involves what
I will refer to as being on the "rim of the circle," a phrase based on a
Piaget diagram. Piaget (Flavell, *Psychology of Piaget*, p. 62) says:

> *Intelligence thus begins neither with knowledge of the self nor of*
> *things as such but with the knowledge of their interaction, and it is*
> *by orientating itself simultaneously toward the two poles of that inter-*
> *action that intelligence organizes the world by organizing itself.*

The rim of the circle is where organism and environment first meet;
there is consciousness only of their interaction. This is the "primal
relationship."

The infant differentiates the environment and differentiates it
from himself by experiencing objects in a variety of contexts, and by
assimilating them to a variety of schemata. In the beginning we are on
the rim of the circle, and experience is a flow undifferentiated by
schemata. When the child interacts with ball-being-grasped, ball-being-
squeezed, ball-seen-in-crib, and ball-seen-on-floor, he has the raw ma-
terials for forming the concept of ball. The concept is not pressed
upon him immediately—there is no reason why the child can't have
four concepts instead of one, especially since on the rim there is no
memory to force juxtaposition of the four concepts. On the rim there
is only consciousness of interaction. The details of the process need not
concern us here, but eventually the child develops the concept of ball.
By the same process, he differentiates himself from the environment.
"The principal uniting relationship between two hitherto separate
schemas is called *reciprocal assimilation,* that is, each schema assimilates the other" (Flavell, *Psychology of Piaget*, p. 57, emphasis his).
By reciprocal assimilation—the precise details of which need not concern us—the child comes to place a subject, the same one, in front of
each of his schemata, and they are united:

I: —grasp
     —squeeze
     —see

In simple terms, the child comes to recognize that there is something common to each of these activities. The more contexts the self is seen in and the more schemata it participates in as subject, the more detached it is from specific schemata. And so the "self-concept" develops. Sometimes it becomes so detached from the world that the self experiences loneliness and alienation. I call this process of detachment "retreating into the pit," again based on Piaget's diagram. In the pit, there is a stable self observing the world. It is possible to be on the rim and in the pit simultaneously—people often report observing their own very involved behavior with astounding detachment—but usually a person is somewhere in between.

The preceding introduction to Piagetian concepts is over-simplified, but sufficient for the discussion to follow. This discussion will begin with a Piagetian definition of romantic love:

Romantic love is involvement on the rim of the circle, in interaction with the loved one; it is unwillingness or inability to make a balanced adaptation to the loved one. The loved one is a novel object for whom a brand-new schema has been developed. There are attempts at assimilation which interfere with this schema, and are in turn interfered with.

To reciprocally assimilate the two aspects of the definition, romantic love is the preadaptational state of relation to the loved one. First I shall attempt to describe what it means for two people to be on the rim of the circle with each other. This is best described in terms of reciprocal romantic love, although it is possible to be on the rim with someone who is not on his own rim. The implications of this description of romantic love are best taken up separately and from the position of one person.

One important respect in which real life love differs from the description given here is in its extremity. Most love is somewhere in between. During the phase of romantic love vacillations between the rim and the pit are most extreme. As adaptation approaches equilibrium vacillation decreases.

On the rim of the circle, there is only consciousness of interaction. Therefore, if Mary is in love and on the rim with Joe, she doesn't know if Joe's behavior is a result of his personality, his response to her personality, or expressive of the interaction, that is, what is unique to

Joe and Mary's relationship. Nor does she know if her behavior is a result of her personality, her response to Joe's personality, or, again, the interaction. The interaction is the relationship, and appears to have a life of its own, since Joe and Mary do not exist as separate entities. They are lost or caught up in the interaction.

That this state is preadaptive is obvious. Joe and Mary don't mind; there is nobody home to mind. This is one of the joys of romantic love—it functions as a powerful drug. If the interaction is to stay on the rim, it must be smooth and well-coordinated. When it isn't, people emerge and begin to observe. Detached observation is antithetical to romantic love. Joe doesn't want Mary to leave a part of herself out of the interaction to observe it. He wants her as completely caught up in it as he is. If she is not, it is like kissing someone with one's eyes closed and opening them briefly to find oneself looking into a cold stare.

The process of retreat from the rim to the pit is initiated by hitches and starts in the interaction. If Joe waits too long before responding to Mary, he is clearly thinking inside himself, and the concept of separate selves is reborn. If Joe responds too quickly, he is clearly running on his own track and is not in interaction with Mary. Again, the existence of selves is implicated. When Mary observes Joe, she is detached from the love relationship. The love relationship retreats into people, who are then in the pit. Love can be located either in the interaction or in the lovers. In the case of rim love, it is in the interaction, and no selves exist. In the case of pit love, it is stuck in the people, and whatever interaction there is is not loaded with love.

It is possible to distinguish between rim interaction and pit interaction, and to do so sets forth the major features of rim love. The distinction is most clearly made with the help of some analogies from sports.

In basketball, a player passing to another player who then scores is sometimes credited with an assist; other times, he is not. If the pass seems to lead directly to the score, the player is perceived as having assisted. If the time interval between pass and score is too great, or if the scoring player has to do too much after he receives the pass, the passing player is not perceived as having assisted. Similarly, Joe and Mary can appear to be assisting each other if Joe's statements lead directly and quickly to Mary's statements and if Mary doesn't have to do too much once the conversation is turned over to her. If Mary responds to brief questions with long stories, Joe is credited with an assist no more than the player who passes to the star and watches him dribble the length of the court for a brilliant twisting lay-up. On the other hand, if Joe has to work overly hard to elicit a response from Mary, it is like the star dribbling all over the court to set up a poor player standing under the basket. While the star deserves an assist, there has been no interaction, for the poor player doesn't deserve the score.

When a score comes from a true assist, it does not come from the individual players, but from their interaction. Neither one should receive all the credit, but to divide the two points in half is to create an artificial dichotomy. (It is somewhat like giving separate checks to an obviously married couple.) The prize should be given to the relationship. (The box score should list Smith, Jones, and Smith-Jones.)

A relationship is different from the sum or arithmetic average of the parts. In tennis there are champion doubles teams made up of players who are not champions in singles. These teams can beat a pair of champion singles players. While it is a cliché that there are interactions that produce better results than would be predicted by a sum of the abilities of the individuals, the notion that relationships exist is substantiated by the fact that there are also interactions that produce poorer results than would be so predicted. Relationships between two otherwise decent people can be awful; the "interaction" between star basketball players can lead to a very poor team.

There is a difference between an assist between two players who know each other well and an assist between two good players who don't know each other. The latter assist will surprise the players, and they will have to wait longer for the next one than the players who know each other. Similarly, romantic love on the rim is unstable. Because the "players" do not know each other, there are many potential intrusions into the interaction. For example, Joe may be habitually late (he doesn't mean it personally, but is simply unable to get anywhere on time). Mary does not know if this is Joe or Joe's response to her. The interaction is likely to be shattered.

Romantic love on the rim, then, is an unstable state of total involvement in interaction. Joe is *not* involved in *Mary*. If he were, his responses would be unimportant to him, Mary would be dissatisfied, and the interaction would be shattered. This demonstrates that worship is not appropriate to love. Joe is not involved in himself either. If he were, Mary's responses would be unimportant to him, Mary would be dissatisfied, and the interaction would be shattered; this demonstrates that self-love is antithetical to love. On the rim, at least, love of self or other destroys the smoothness and coordination of the interaction.

There is nothing else to describe. The details of the interaction are unimportant (people returning from an evening with the one they love report they don't know what they talked about, they were so enraptured). If they were important, it wouldn't be romantic love on the rim: The importance of the details would shatter the interaction. There are no general rules for facial expressions. While people in love are usually pictured in the movies and on television as smiling, that is because the world needs to know they are in love. Any expression is acceptable as long as it is appropriate—as long as it doesn't shatter the interaction. A smile at the wrong juncture can break up an interaction as easily as an unexpected frown.

Let us leave the preconceptual rim and examine some of the features of romantic love when the lovers are closer to the pit. Some of these features are attempts to regain (or sometimes merely gain) the rim; others follow from the preadaptational status of love.

Romantic love is said to be blind. This follows directly from the proposition that the lover won't or can't assimilate or accommodate to the loved one. The lover is unable to see the faults (or virtues) of the loved one because the lover does not take the loved one to be an instance of any familiar concept. The lover makes a pseudoaccommodation by taking the loved one to be an instance of him- or herself, by forming a new but necessarily vague concept.[2]

Being nothing in particular allows the loved one to be anything, as Proust points out:

> But the infinitude of love, or its egoism, has the result that the people whom we love are those whose intellectual and moral physiognomy is least defined objectively in our eyes, we alter them incessantly to suit our desires and fears, we do not separate them from ourselves, they are only a vast and vague place in which our affections take root.
> (M. Proust, *Remembrance of Things Past*, II: 730)

That is, the relationship has infinite potential and no constrictions; however, it is not a specific relationship with concrete characteristics.

That lovers are defined as having a *gestalt* of the loved one allows an explanation of the normal blindness attributed to romantic love, the failure to notice faults. Specific assimilations are washed out by this sense of the whole which is greater than the sum of its as yet undefined parts. When assimilations do occur, they are often (to an outside observer) inappropriate. Hence the paradox that the lover cannot only overlook faults, but cherish them:

> [*Swann*] *tried not to contradict (Odette's) vulgar ideas, that bad taste which she displayed on every possible occasion, which all the same he loved, as he could not help loving everything that came from her, which even fascinated him, for were they not so many more of those characteristic features, by virtue of which the essential qualities of the woman emerged, and were made visible?*
>
> (M. Proust, *Remembrance* I: 188)

As lovers often say, the loved one is loved for him- or herself. Yet the lovers must be vague as to what the essential self is. Specifics are not the essence, nor do virtues contribute to the essence: "I do not love Joe for his money, his Purple Heart, his Nobel prize, his kindness and tenderness, his beautiful body, his rugged handsomeness, his brilliant mind, nor for any other externals; I love Joe for himself." What is this thing called Joe?

Among other things, Joe is Mary. He is "a vast and vague place in which (Mary's) affections take root," and Mary does not separate herself from Joe, to paraphrase the quote from Proust. Proust suggests another answer:

> "She?"—he (Swann) tried to ask himself what that meant; for it is something like love, like death (rather than like those vague conceptions of maladies), a thing which one repeatedly calls in question, in order to make oneself probe further into it, in the fear that the question will find no answer, that the substance will escape our grasp— the mystery of personality.
>
> (M. Proust, *Remembrance* I: 237)

If Joe's essence is his personality, it is indeeed a mysterious personality, largely created by the lover and often invisible to everyone else. Proust often juxtaposes the lover's perception of the loved one with that of society. This juxtaposition is the cause of the common comment, "I don't know what he sees in her."

Furthermore, this mysterious personality is not one the lover is satisfied to describe in words. No specific assimilations in the form of ordinary trait names are satisfactory, as we have seen. This is not to say that love is merely blind and mute. Just as words in one language are untranslatable into another, so the loved one is untranslatable into the language of everyday life. What is the language of love, and what is its relationship to the language of ordinary life?

Psychological research into generative-transformational grammar suggests that the sentence has psychological reality. We do not even begin with the sentence; we begin with its "deep structure." The following quote is helpful (N. Chomsky, *Language and Mind,* p. 25, emphasis his).

> *We can distinguish the* surface structure *of the sentence, the organization into categories and phrases that is directly associated with the physical signal, from the underlying* deep structure, *also a system of categories and phrases, but with a more abstract character.*

The deep structure is categorically and qualitatively different from the surface structure (which is a sentence). We apply transformations to the deep structure to produce sentences. Some sentences require fewer transformations than others. For example, *Joe is beautiful* requires fewer transformations than *Joe is not beautiful,* but, the implication is, both can be said to come from the same deep structure. They are closely related because the latter sentence is merely one transformation away from the former.

Perhaps love is analogous to the deep structure of language, which is not a language, but the source of language. Like love, the deep structure is mute yet fecund. We are born with the deep structure, and later produce specific sentences. We approach experience similarly: first it is present to us as an undifferentiated flow and then, by assimilation and accommodation, we analyze it into its component parts of self and other. Romantic love can be seen as an attempt to recapture people as they are experienced before analysis, before they are familiar, externalized, pinned against the wall by words and categories (even favorable ones). Love is not blind so much as it is developmentally prior to analysis.

Naturally, then, we should examine the love of children for their parents. It is similar to romantic love. Children know they love their parents, but they do not know why, and find the question meaningless. They have not subjected their parents to analysis as a chemist subjects a substance to analysis, to find the component parts. They cannot even describe their parents except to say that they are their parents. We come to adult knowledge of things by experiencing them in a variety of contexts; initially, the child's mother exists in only one context—in her relationship with the child. Later he may know her as cook, comforter, and companion. But perhaps that is *our* (adult) analysis. Perhaps the child only experiences Mom. Mom doesn't do various things or function in various roles. It is not "Mom does X, Mom does Y." It is *"Mom* does X,Y." Everything Mom does is dominated by Mom and rendered equivalent by Mom's presence. At first the child has an undifferentiated schema for Mom. Later, "differentiation has the consequence of dividing the originally global schema into several new schemas, each with a sharper, more discriminating focus on reality" (Flavell, *Psychology of Piaget,* p. 57) .[3]

Romantic love, having been equated with the child's love for his parents, should not be considered a regression. It is, in a sense, but it is in good company. The experience of music, art, and literature is often initially similar to that of romantic love; categories are unimportant and do not apply to the work of art. It is common to lose the ability to experience works of art *directly* (on the rim) ; to simultaneously understand them and feel their mystery. People can devote their lives to one of the arts and yet experience it only through a welter of jargon. Such people are often called pedants, but the word does not emphasize the sterility and futility of this kind of scholarly endeavor. It is perverse to assimilate a novel by relating its events to similar events in the life of the novelist. Yet this kind of activity is the preoccupation of many teachers of English. I have seen the romantic poets reduced to their life histories, and it took most of the romance out of them. Paintings have been reduced to the influences of various schools. Even the oenophile has suffered some strange displacement of accent, some sickness of the soul, for he does not enjoy wine as Dionysus does; nor does he approve of such indelicate gulping of the precious fluid (does he think it is considered precious because of its *taste*?) .

Most critics of the various forms of art spend most of their time disliking that which they claim to be inspired by; only the best can inspire them, but the more they know about what is good (the more they retreat into the pit) , the less of it there seems to be. They come to vent their frustration at being unable to feel by spitting out petty detractions and reductions. As they move from experience to analysis, they come to negate the experience. One would be wise to resist the move from deep to surface structure for then the negative, but one transformation away, is born as a possibility. Before analysis, the negative does not exist.

The negative has a peculiar power once it has been born. Research in attribution theory has shown it to be stronger than the positive, that is, *Joe is not beautiful* is more believable than *Joe is beautiful* (D. E. Kanouse and L. R. Hanson, *Negativity in Evaluations*) . *Joe is beautiful* is not a correct translation of *Joe,* for it is not a description of a direct experience. It is a description of experience mediated by language. It is surface structure.[4]

Romantic love is a primal mode of experience; the loss of the ability to love is as sad as the loss of ability to appreciate music, art, literature, nature, wine, or simple sensory experience—it is the loss of ability to experience people directly, without mediating, negating categories. All categories are negating—they imply the object hasn't the strength to stand on its own. Hence Mary refuses to love Joe's "positive qualities." He does not need to be beautiful. He is sufficient unto himself and needs no props or plugs.

We will now juxtapose a less exalted aspect of romantic love against the romantic description given thus far.

People in love often report self-other confusions. They feel a part of their loved one and that their loved one is part of them; they are together forever, even when physically apart; they are a unity; they have always loved each other; they were made for each other.

The blurred self-other distinction follows directly from the definition of romantic love. To have no schemata with which to assimilate an object is to have raw contact with it; to over-accommodate to an object is to engulf it. To have no concept of an object is to be unable to disentangle it from its effects (interaction) on oneself.

On the rim, this blurred self-other distinction is at worst merely regressive. In the pit, self and other blurring takes bizarre shapes, as some examples demonstrate.

In Proust, romantic love inevitably means jealousy, possessiveness, and a consuming frantic passion to know everything about the loved one. This partially reflects the fact that Proust's loved ones, a class distinct from the lovers, always appear to be in search of assignations. Thus it *appears* that the lovers are correct, but it is never completely clear. Proust faithfully captures the perceptual ambiguity produced by love by often refusing to give us an "objective" view of the "facts."

This kind of possessiveness can be almost invisible and not very disturbing (if two people are in love, each is a major part of the other's existence; having no separate existence from the lover, the loved one is no threat). Nevertheless, might not all romantic love contain, as a potential, the deranged possessiveness common in Proust? It is hard to tell from Proust, for love in *Remembrance of Things Past* is presented in only one context—it is always nonreciprocal. We cannot tell what he thinks of reciprocal love; but let us assume his descriptions are appropriate to romantic love whenever the lover is sunk rather deeply into the pit.

Upon hearing an unimportant description of how Odette looked at a particular time, Swann becomes upset:

> *This simple outline reduced Swann to utter confusion by enabling him suddenly to perceive that Odette had an existence which was not wholly subordinated to his own; he burned to know whom she had been seeking to fascinate by this costume in which he had never seen her; he registered a vow to insist upon her telling him where she had been going at that intercepted moment, as though, in all the colourless life—a life always non-existent, since she was then invisible to him—of his mistress, there had been but a single incident apart from all those smiles directed towards himself; namely her walking abroad beneath a Rembrandt hat, with a bunch of violets in her bosom.*
> (M. Proust, *Remembrance*, I: 184–85)

This is a description of the first interruption of interaction on the rim—the first time Joe looks across the table at Mary and wonders what she is really thinking. But in reciprocal love, the loved one would nip this kind of thinking in the bud. If Swann had "confronted" Odette with the evidence and if she had claimed that she did not in fact have a separate existence, had worn the costume in the hope of meeting him and had, at the moment she had been observed, been thinking of Swann, he would have been comforted. Odette does not always deny him such comforts; he seems to deny them to himself. His love affair with Odette is carried out more inside his head than in interaction with Odette, and so he does not confront her. Thus the fact of her separate existence blossoms. In an attempt to capture her existence, he becomes voracious in his search for knowledge:

> *At every other period in his life, the little everyday words and actions of another person had always seemed wholly valueless to Swann; if gossip about such things were repeated to him, he would dismiss it as insignificant, and while he listened it was only the lowest, the most commonplace part of his mind that was interested; at such moments he felt utterly dull and uninspired. But in this strange phase of love the personality of another person becomes so enlarged, so deepened, that the curiosity which he could now feel aroused in himself, to know the least details of a woman's daily occupation, was the same thirst for knowledge with which he had once studied history.*
> (Proust, *Remembrance*, I: 210)

Once more, gossip and spying:

> *All manner of actions, from which, until now, he would have recoiled in shame, seemed to him, now, to be precisely on a level with the de-*

*ciphering of manuscripts, the weighing of evidence, the interpreta-
tion of old monuments, that was to say, so many different methods
of scientific investigation, each one having a definite intellectual
value and being legitimately employable in the search for truth.*
(I: 210)

Note that in attempting to assimilate a novel object the usual relationships between parts are disturbed. Swann now considers gossip and
scientific evidence equally valuable.

The separate existence of the loved one is frightening because it is
mysterious. Swann suspects, but cannot feel, that:

*the world inhabited by Odette was not that other world, fearful and
supernatural, in which he spent his time in placing her—and which
existed, perhaps, only in his imagination, but the real universe, ex-
haling no special atmosphere of gloom, comprising that table at which
he might sit down, presently, and write....*
(I: 228)

It is not surprising, then, that Swann would wish respite from that
love which transmogrifies ordinary existence into a vague but powerful mystery:

*But in his morbid state, to tell the truth, he feared death itself no
more than such a recovery, which would, in fact, amount to the death
of all that he then was.*
(I: 230)

It is common for a husband to die shortly after his wife does. Suicide
also often follows such deaths. The cliché here is that life is not worth
living without the loved one. Here we can see that love, an attempt to
put all of oneself into interaction with another, may swallow up the
individual. When one person dies, the other is already dead, having no
behaviors not "tied up" in the relationship. Swann senses the slow
death of his autonomous self in his new pleasure in society:

*And in the small extent to which this detachment was not absolute,
the reason for this new pleasure which Swann was tasting was that he
could emigrate for a moment into those few and distant parts of himself which had remained almost foreign to his love and to his pain.*
(I: 237)

The cure for love, when it comes, is provided by descriptions of
Odette as an ordinary human being:

> *To compete with and so to stimulate the moribund feelings that*
> *Swann had for Odette, Mme. Cottard ... had grafted among them*
> *other, more normal, feelings of gratitude, of friendship, which in*
> *Swann's mind were to make Odette seem again more human (more*
> *like other women, since other women could inspire the same feelings*
> *in him), were to hasten her final transformation back into that*
> *Odette, loved with an* undisturbed *affection. ...*
>
> (I: 289, emphasis mine)

In other words, Odette is seen through ordinary language rather than the nonlanguage of love. Nevertheless, ordinary language cannot have been the cause of the cure. Only a little earlier, Swann had been hunting for Odette's essence in the rubble of ordinary information. While such details are relevant to thinking about people when they are ordinary, they are irrelevant to the essence of Odette. This essence is on an entirely different level than her self as it appears to society. Swann is attempting to incorporate Odette by collecting details of her daily existence. To be slightly metaphorical, attempting to catch an empty schema with details is like trying to hurt a ghost by throwing rocks at it. Attempting to become one with Odette by knowing details of her existence is like attempting to understand *Hamlet* by reading about Shakespeare's life. Another quotation from Proust illustrates the untranslatability of the two modes of experience:

> *... but his love extended a long way beyond the province of physical*
> *desire. Odette's person, indeed, no longer held any great place in it.*
> *When his eyes fell upon the photograph of Odette on his table, or*
> *when she came to see him, he had difficulty in identifying her face,*
> *either in the flesh or on the pasteboard, with the painful and con-*
> *tinuous anxiety which dwelt in his mind.*
>
> (I: 236–37)

We have seen that we begin developmentally with that which is the most concrete and visible. Hence Swann's attempt to capture the essence of Odette with concrete details.

The quotation illustrates another difficulty in the attempt to possess another person's essence. As we have seen, the person Swann is trying to perceive is a creature largely of his own construction. Furthermore, he has projected himself into Odette. Swann is trying to find himself in another person, and it is not surprising that he cannot always make her correspond to his emotional needs. Although "we alter [people we love] incessantly to suit our desires and fears" (II: 730), reality is not completely plastic, nor can we completely overlook the peculiarities of the environment. The attempt to unite self and object is again inappropriate. Swann is trying to unite himself with—what? Himself. The vague and cloudy schema has as much of him as it has of Odette. If he looks to either himself or to Odette for the essence of the schema, he will fail; the schema contains them both.

Two other problems involved in striving to merge self and other are illustrated by the following two quotations from Proust, again concerning Swann and Odette:

> As a matter of fact, she had never given him a thought. And such moments as these, in which she forgot Swann's very existence, were of more value to Odette, did more to attach him to her, than all her infidelities.
>
> (I: 227)

> ...he was leaving behind him Odette, transformed into a brilliant stranger, surrounded by men to whom her glances and her gaiety, which were not for him, seemed to hint at some voluptuous pleasure to be enjoyed there or elsewhere ...which made Swann more jealous than the thought of their actual physical union, since it was more difficult to imagine.
>
> (I: 228)

When Swann is not in Odette's mind, to the extent that he has put himself into her, he ceases to exist. In addition, the infinite but non-specific potential that is Swann's special schema for Odette gives her magical powers over him. Sex, a familiar schema, does not worry him nearly as much as what he fears Odette could do, although of course he has no specific idea what this is.

In summary, when romantic love is nonreciprocal, as it seems from the vantage point of the pit, attempts to merge self and other are, while understandable in Piagetian terms, highly unsuccessful and somewhat bizarre. Lovers in Proust's novel do not know how to go about merging self and other. Their very efforts doom them, for they are efforts of the solitary self. The simpler loved ones have no difficulty getting to the rim; but they do not love either. They are trapped in interaction, with no self to lose in love. Love, an attempt to *become* trapped in interaction, is impossible for those who begin that way. Some people stay in the primal interaction and never develop a concept of a separate self. Others do, but then lose the self in love. Just as the lack of self makes love an impossibility for those who never got off the rim, having a self precludes love for those who did get off the primal rim. Swann is always present, observing himself, observing

Odette. The more he observes, the deeper he is driven into the pit, and the more indirect and symbolic are his attempts to find unity. Marcel, the narrator, tries to obliterate the self-other distinction by keeping Albertine in familiar surroundings. The attempt fails because Albertine conspires with Marcel's brilliant imagination to fill the most familiar situations with threat of her separate existence. When he does succeed in having her present or captive in a safe place, he is (often) bored with her. He cannot see his love *for* her *in* her.

A major theme in literature has been the dichotomy between people who can (or have no choice but to) live on the surface of existence and people who are trapped in self-consciousness. By implication from Piagetian theory, these people are also trapped in other-consciousness. They find action difficult (*Hamlet* and *Notes from Underground* provide good examples). An unself-conscious life on the surface is treated as both a cowardly refusal to face selfhood and a courageous attack on life's problems; as subhuman and divine. There are few examples in literature of successful attempts to bridge the dichotomy. Bloom in *Ulysses* and Kierkegaard's Knight of Faith in *Fear and Trembling* are examples, but their focus is the rim rather than the pit. It is active, driven, and yet cheerful and secure. Bloom and the Knight of Faith are caught up in their intellectual activities much as a lover should be caught up with his loved one.

Bloom and the Knight of Faith are also absurd, and the absurd is an important modern concept. To simultaneously recognize the inherent ordinariness of existence, and attempt to transcend it, is *absurd;* but that is what romantic love, as described thus far, is.

In Proust's novel, objects of love must be people on the surface of existence, which is after all what the lovers wish to capture. Swann says,

> *To think that I have wasted years of my life, that I have longed for death, that the greatest love that I have ever known has been for a woman who did not please me, who was not in my style!*
>
> (I: 292)

Lovers in Proust's novel love noncontemplative types. This theme is common in modern literature, especially in the work of D. H. Lawrence.

It looks as if we have priced love out of the market. It looks as if love is the province of great minds and profound souls, while us simple types are doomed never to experience its joy and terror. Yet love is not at all uncommon among the young; nor does it require difference of social class or personality; nor is the love so clearly an escape from an oppressive self. What is it that makes people approach other people as novel objects? It is puberty that makes Mary, whom Joe has known for years as the kid next door, an entirely different and mysterious Mary—Joe's puberty. It is Mary's puberty that will change Joe for Mary. As time goes on, however, love should be increasingly difficult. Adolescents become aware of the nature of other people and of themselves. After his fourth love affair comes to a bitter end, Joe should finally learn that he is a neurotic clinging vine with a peeling veneer of independence; he should be unable to make the Knight's leap of faith that will enable his personality to be swallowed by interaction. He should know that *he* will always be around to destroy the interaction.

Still, people fall in love throughout life. It is possible and even likely whenever a change occurs in the life of the *lover*. Everything is seen from a novel angle. That recently divorced people are likely to run headlong back into marriage is usually taken as a comment on the stupidity of human nature; but the adaptation from a habitual existence where nothing is seen, to a new life with a new point of view, makes love highly probable. Romantic love *is* a preadaptational relationship. To the extent that old schemata for assimilating people have been invalidated by a change in perspective, love is a prerequisite for adaptation.

While defining love as either maladaptive groping or blissful unconsciousness, this discussion has presented love as intentional and serious rather than as frivolous and random. Love has been described as an attempt to know and interact with the essence of another person. The discussion has been vague on the nature of this essence. In the next section, an approach to it is offered. But love does not always reach the barrier beyond which lies the essence. Sex and marriage may be within the barrier, and this is often as far as love gets.

If love is an attempt to approach the essence of another, it is also an attempt to approach essence of self and the essence of the relationship between self and other. Sex and marriage are often premature, leading to inappropriate assimilations of self and other. Most people know how to engage in sexual behavior; most people know how to get married. Most people are disposed to assimilate their relationships into these common schemata; but these schemata may not produce the sort of relationships that some people would like to have. These schemata have much psychological and cultural power; it is difficult to avoid them. We tend to attempt to assimilate objects to schemata we already possess, especially if the object accommodates our attempt. If we don't have a schema, we don't have an object. If we don't have a word or short phrase in our language for something, it is hard to recognize an instance of it when it comes along. When "things" require long individual descriptions, the description seems designed for the thing; it has no separate existence, having been "applied" to only one thing. Just as objects attain independent existence by being observed in various contexts, so descriptions attain independent existence only by being applied to various (but similar) things. The description initially has only a parasitic reality. Similarly, a "thing" with an insubstantial description is also shadowy.

Why are we uncomfortable with an undefined relationship? People do not seem satisfied to remain on the rim of the circle. (To remain there forever *is* to remain frivolous and random, but that does not explain why people tend to retreat somewhat from the rim.) Assimilatory schemata (descriptions in this case) serve as guides. People may simply proceed ("You know, man, love. Without always talking about it. Dig?") without guiding schemas, but their movement is likely to be random. They will respond to nonessential stimuli and to different kinds of stimuli at different times. That is, they will behave as children do at a certain stage of development when sorting objects into categories. These children will first put one object with another because they have the same color. They will add an object resembling the second, but not the first, in shape. The fourth object will resemble only the third, in texture. Without a guiding concept present throughout the task, the category will contain a motley collection of objects.

This is no way to run a relationship, much less capture essences; so let us assume something like a *need to know*. Without it, human behavior would be random (granting that much of it is) .

At first, assimilation and accommodation will be at odds. The description of the nature of the relationship will change as the relationship changes; accommodation will destroy schemata as fast as they are created. Assimilations will pull back on necessary accommodations. Description and thing are as inseparable as self and other in love interactions.

Through the mists of a globally conceived and therefore undefined relationship, sex and marriage beckon with all the volume and melody of fog horns. It is easier to give in to them. The mystery of personality, that which is unique to the particular person, remains unsolved (there is no guarantee that the mystery will turn out to have been worth solving) . Joe and Mary treat each other as barren outlines.

Joe is a husband, Mary is a wife—and that is the end of their search for themselves.

Thus, sex and marriage are often premature assimilations, schemata employed because they are there. The drunk looks for his money under the light because it is easier to see there. In this case, he is likely to find it; this kind of money is attracted to lights like moths. Strong and familiar schemata have considerable guiding (pulling) power: once Joe tries to assimilate Mary as a wife in the schema of marriage, she is likely to accommodate herself to the schema. Psychological reality is more plastic than physical reality.

Premature assimilation causes another kind of problem. As discussed, adaptations are often dependent on the success of earlier and "easier" adaptations to the same object. If not, the adaptations will be pseudoadaptations. While, as suggested, love is easiest between the young, young love is often clumsy, shy, hesitant, and prone to brief periods of excess. These periods may lead to lasting damage, as in shotgun teenage marriages. This is likely if, as is often the case, the sexes have little to do with each other before puberty (or, as is more commonly the case now, they begin behaving towards each other as sexual objects well before puberty). While it may be true that Mary becomes brand-new when Joe reaches puberty, his adaptation to her will be less imbalanced and confusing if he retains the old schema as well. Similarly, practitioners of many skills return to the "basics" when they find themselves performing badly. The golfer practices his swing by merely hitting balls rather than trying to hit them onto the green close to the flag—he neglects accommodation and focuses on assimilation. The baseball player tries to swing for contact rather than home runs, the typist returns to the quick brown fox, the pianist to scales, and Joe to the fact that Mary is the kid next door.

We may now pursue the essence further. The preceding discussion has demonstrated that we will not find it here, for the essence is not general; however, the search will reveal another important view of love.

An Emotional and Psychoanalytical View of Love

Consider the elderly and venerated "frustration-aggression" hypothesis. Frustration, as the hypothesis originally went, leads to aggression. If Joe wants Mary but she won't let him have her, Joe will want to be aggressive. If he also wants his relationship with Mary to continue, he cannot aggress against her, so he may take it out on his roommate. This is called *displacement* of aggression. Or he may find another girl to give him "relief," which is called displacement of sexuality, although a Freudian might predict that such sexual behavior would have aggressive overtones. Or Joe may simply continue to want Mary, and this is called stewing in one's juices, or *feeling the emotion of frustration*. Let us zero in on this process.

I am about to eat a hot dog. It is 4.5 cms. from my mouth. Suddenly a man in a white coat snatches the hot dog from me and asks me if I want it.

"Yes, of course I want it. Why do you think I was about to eat it, you ass?"

"But did you consciously want the hot dog during those seconds before it was about to enter your mouth?"

I will have to admit that I didn't, that I felt no desire for the hot dog, probably because it was, I thought, in the bag.

He then asks me, "Did you have an unconscious motivation for the hot dog during those fateful seconds?" And I will have to admit that I didn't, for, the phallic symbolism of hot dogs aside, eating is nothing I am ashamed of and I do it all the time.

So he concludes, "So you didn't want it."

"No, I guess not, but I sure do now. Gimme."

"Hold but a moment as I state the paradox clearly. You didn't want it until you couldn't have it but now that you can't have it you want it." As an afterthought, the afterthought that arouses my pride and therefore my cognitive apparatus, he adds, "Just like a spoiled child who never wants anything until you mention you're about to have something, when suddenly he wants all of it for himself."

At this point, I must point out to the psychologist that while human behavior is motivated, it is not a jerky series of states of desire followed by states of movement towards the attainment of that desire. Closing the door to my study is an intentional action and in that sense motivated, but I do not want to close my door and then close it. I close my door. I eat my hot dog. The last two sentences are descriptions of intentional actions with motivational statements deleted because the motivational bases of the actions are nonproblematic and of no interest to normal people.

Behavior can, however, be broken up into jerky series of states of desire followed by movements toward the desired goal by interrupting the action in midstream. *Eating a hot dog* is a usually acceptable and not overly parsimonious description of *one* intentional action. Only the psychologist in the white coat would break it up, while most people would want to break up and expand *I killed my wife*. If someone takes the hot dog from me just as I am about to consume it, suddenly I become aware of the fact that I want the hot dog. My behavior has been made jerky.

At first, I will merely want the hot dog, and I will be content to say "Gimme." Then, suppose the psychologist wants to talk more about motivation, and suppose further that I am restrained and cannot grab the hot dog back. Instead of wanting the hot dog, I am now likely to *experience* desire for it. I am on the road to feeling emotion. If the break between desire and goal attainment is short, I will want my goal. The longer the break, the more conscious I will become of my desire. I will no longer *want the hot dog*—wanting is an active state of an organism—although I may have other desires in the form of active wants, such as the desire to break the psychologist's neck. If my desire is blocked, I am aware that I had that desire. If my desire cannot be expressed in behavior, it will "back up" in consciousness. In noninterrupted behavior, there is no backup and therefore no consciousness of desire. With slight interruption, there is some consciousness of desire; but there are attempts to translate the desire quickly back into behavior. When desire cannot be expressed, I am alone and quiet with my desire, and that is emotion.

Thus we feel emotion when we cannot get what we want. Emotion is the experience of desire. Emotion is that which has not been translated into (goal-directed or diffuse) behavior.

Therefore, emotion should arise when (and only when) we are frustrated and can find no acceptable substitute activity. This assumes that frustration precedes emotion; but, phenomenologically, this is not always the case. We often experience emotion with no immediately known cause. Anxiety neurosis, to take an extreme example, is characterized by "free-floating" anxiety, anxiety with no known source. The anxiety neurotic is afraid of something, but doesn't know what, and he is therefore doomed to experience intense emotion. He cannot flee, for not knowing the source of his fear, he might flee right into its arms.

Paradoxically, fleeing, especially successful fleeing, is insurance against emotion. Only when we have just missed having an automobile accident do we experience fear; but in such cases we are made conscious of our flight only by the interval between desire for safety and its attainment. Successful fleeing is the normal state of affairs when driving. We make thousands of minute adjustments and perceptions which are absolutely necessary for our survival, so we are always in flight from danger, but rarely feel the emotion.[5]

Thus the anxiety neurotic should try to flee. In order to flee, he will need to find a cause. It is interesting to note that many forms of psychotherapy attempt to find the sources of psychopathology in childhood and adolescence. This is a nice move: the adult is not likely to run into his childhood. Since the anxiety neurotic is anxious, he will likely accept the first plausible cause offered to him. As long as he flees he should be free of anxiety; but what if he runs into the real source in escape from a false source?

The question contains the implicit assumption that there is a real source. The anxiety neurotic may be seen as searching for his source of anxiety. In this search, the neurotic may accept premature assimilations. There is, however, nothing specific to catch the fleeing anxiety neurotic; there is only the nebulous cloud waiting to be precipitated into a form. Once it has been condensed, there is nothing left. Some forms are better than others, and some will be vaguely dissatisfactory. A global schema requires further adaptation: varieties of assimilation are needed to differentiate and sharpen the content of the schema. Since it is initially an empty schema, it can be given many specific concrete forms. Since the schema does concern *something*, this differentiating and sharpening assimilation must be accommodatory. If it is not completely accommodatory, the adaptation is not a *complete* failure. In fact, no adaptation can be completely accommodatory (if an object is so novel that we are completely unable to assimilate it to existing schemata or suitable modifications of existing schemata, we cannot adapt to it. So the anxiety neurotic can be wrong without being so wrong that he finds out how wrong by running into the true source of his fear. Just as Mary tends to become a wife if she is treated as one, so will the anxiety neurotic's source of fear tend to become similar to the source upon which the neurotic and his therapist decide (now that we can cure snake phobias, snake phobias are becoming common).

Thus people can have emotions without knowing their cause. In addition, there is no guarantee the cause will be correctly chosen.

Let us assume P has an emotion and does not know its cause. Let us assume the cause is not fear; P wants something he doesn't have. He will search for what it is he wants. He can sample various things either concretely or symbolically, in his mind. He can try apples, Italy, homosexuality, and exercise. Suppose he has a hypothesis on the basis of this sampling. Suppose further that his hypothesis will remain correct if and only if he does *not* get what he wants concretely and in real time. Stephen Dedalus (James Joyce, *Portrait of the Artist as a Young Man*) thinks he wants to be "something in religion." Fortunately for him, he is able to sample symbolically. He subtracts his religious emotions from his image of the actual daily existence of a member of a religious order and finds it commonplace and dull. Similarly, one of Proust's common themes is that if we subtract our love from our loved one, we are left with an ordinary person—at best a wonderful ordinary person —describable in ordinary language.

Thus, some emotions seem to be caused by something, but are not. Stephen's religious emotions are not caused by, and could not be elicited by a religious existence. Symbolic sampling reveals to Stephen that religion causes his religious emotions only if the emotions suffuse his image of a concrete religious existence. If such an existence expressed those emotions in behavior, it would no longer be the existence Stephen imagines would express (satisfy) those emotions. So that existence, barren of the warning of emotion, could not cause the emotion.

It is but a short step to imagine emotions without cause—emotions with no real life objects or events whose lack is sufficient to cause the emotion. Thus in some cases the attempt to translate an ideal image suffused with emotion into a concrete existence is impossible. In such cases, people are forced into fantasy existences, activities that are not satisfactory translations of an emotion into behavior, but which are symbolically similar to the true one. The emotion simultaneously shrouds the inadequacy of the symbolic substitute and serves as a constant reminder that there is a backup, a frustration.

The notion of an untranslatable emotion is but a step or two along the dimension we have already defined. We have established that there are emotions without immediately obvious causes and that some translations of these emotions will be more satisfactory than others. We are now merely suggesting that some emotions will lack *any* satisfactory, concrete translation, and that the solution to this problem is to find a symbolic substitute and imbue it with the untranslated remainder of the emotion.

An example will help clarify this: near a famous university there is a bar, once frequented by Jack Kerouac, that some years ago was inhabited by two young men who were sons of well-known writers. These young men aspired to be writers, except that they did not yet write. They used the bar to "gather material," as one of them put it. This definition of the situation was accepted by all (save those who were spitefully envious), partially because these young men were sons of well-known writers, but also because writers can and do gather material by observation, and bars are good places to observe. Writers also write; but these young men preferred to frequent the bar to the exclusion of writing. Why?

Since they have not been heard from, and since their fathers are sufficiently famous that if they had written anything it would have been well publicized, one must assume they could not write. They lacked either motivation or ability. There is, however, a third possibility.

Being a famous writer no doubt has its moments of glory, but they are the by-products of being a writer. *Writing* itself is not a glamorous occupation. There can be no audience applause, one must be sober, avoid the distractions of company, get plenty of sleep, and eat right. Also, most writers find it hard work (the blood, sweat, and tears image).

On the other hand, the occupation of *being a writer surrounded* by admirers, cigarette smoke, and beer is a glamorous occupation in and of itself, and not a very difficult one. It *is* an occupation, although an entirely different one than the occupation of writing.

If one wishes to be a *writer surrounded,* one *can* get there by having been a mere writer for a number of years. But the daily existence of writing does not stoke the image of being a writer surrounded. The only daily existence that does is being a writer surrounded (the glamour), but one cannot have that existence without having been a writer (unless one is the child of a famous writer, then only for a year or two). This is a frustrating thought for those who want to be writers surrounded. There is no daily existence that nurtures the emotion of being a writer surrounded.

We need not accuse these young men of being meretricious. They merely aspired to have what their fathers had. As young boys trying to discover what their fathers were, they were trying to assimilate with inadequate schemata. They had not mastered the necessary earlier adaptations, just as a novice painter cannot paint good abstracts. This kind of behavior on the part of children is well known and an established form of humor. The child of the surgeon says his father cuts people open and takes pieces of them out and then sews up the hole again. We would expect children to select the most concrete and visible dimension of their fathers' behavior (as the child of the surgeon does), but what is concrete and visible about putting words on

paper? To children, books are *there*; they are not written. But television appearances, name in the papers, and public recognition are
concrete and visible.

Norman O. Brown, in *Life Against Death,* has traced the developmental history of what he has psychoanalytically demonstrated to
be man's constant and only desire: to become one with the environment. This is an ambiguous notion. On the one hand, the desire appears to be regressive. In Freudian theory, such unity is found only in
the womb or perhaps in the first few years of life. We have seen that in
Piagetian theory the self and the environment are merged during
infancy and whenever new objects are encountered or the self changes
positions substantially. In Freudian theory, primal unity is pleasant;
in Piagetian theory it is frustrating, because it is a state of ignorance
and impotence. The infant, not having the prerequisite adaptations, is
not frustrated by the words in a book; the four-year-old is. Until one
knows it all or declines to see further novelty in known objects, periods of frustration are inevitable. Primal unity would seem to be
aversive.

On the other hand, being one with the environment can also be
equated with the pit. The child comes to terms with the physical environment by gaining the ability to represent and manipulate it internally. He is not one with it in the concrete sense, but in a more abstract sense he has it in him. Also, knowledge is power and control,
which reduces the separateness or at least the independence of the
known objects.

Therefore, "being one with the environment" has at least three
meanings: A pleasant state of ignorance, an unpleasant state of ignorance, or a not unpleasant state of knowledge.

Why does man desire unity with the environment, according to
Brown? Because his infancy is prolonged, he has a long period of unity
before experiencing frustration. Therefore, confronted with lack of
unity, he experiences *strong emotion,* much stronger than an organism
less attached to unity would experience. If emotion increases with delay between desire and attainment, it also looms large as a function of
the degree of initial fusion of desire and attainment.

But what is the unity the infant, and later the man, desires?
Brown's *Life Against Death* is a history of attempts to create symbolic
unity—to create an illusion of a unity no concrete state of affairs could
adequately embody. The infant cannot gain unity with the environment by controlling his eliminatory behavior, but this is what Brown
with much wit calls an infantile "project." It is eventually abandoned

as unsatisfactory, because it is too far from the real cause of the emotion to contain the frustration (that the true lack has not been removed) as it mounts.

The implication is that strong frustration produces emotions with no possible concrete embodiments; and that frustration, therefore, leads to approximately what the emotion desires. That approximation is simultaneously suffused with the emotion to make it seem adequate, and shrouded by the emotion to hide its inadequacies.

A simple example of the proposition that frustration produces emotions with no concrete embodiments: First I want my hot dog. Then I experience desire for my hot dog. Then I become angry at the psychologist and desire to kill him so I can take my hot dog. By now I am so angry that my stomach is churning and I am no longer hungry. As my anger at the psychologist grows, murder would be too good for him. I plan slow torture. Soon, the torture would have to last all of my lifetime, and then two dozen lifetimes would barely suffice, and we have an emotion with no possible concrete embodiments.

We must explain why man, unlike other animals, does not merely abandon his desires, but lets them blossom into emotions so powerful that the originally desired object is no longer satisfactory. (Why, for example, didn't I let the psychologist have his lousy hot dog and his points about motivation and walk off?) Then we must explain in a more general fashion why powerful emotions lead to rejection of the original object. It is not necessary to explain why man wishes to become one with his environment. As we have seen, the concept is vague and has several possible specific meanings. It can refer to knowledge or feeling from the rim or the pit, or points in between. Let us, then accept the obvious. Man desires control and mastery of his environment somehow, be it by returning to a safe womb or by knowing all there is to know. What kind of man would it be who didn't?

Man may not be the only animal with social behavior; he may not be the only animal with language; he may not be the only animal that has wars and kills his own kind; but he is the only animal that falls into romantic love. He is not the only animal with an institution like marriage, and in fact is far from being the most faithful or monogamous animal. Romantic love may be all we have that is unique; it may be the direct result of the snake in the garden, man's intelligence.

Consider a wolf cub. In the wilderness with his mother and father and siblings, he is trying to survive. One day he wanders too far from the fold and becomes hungry. Naturally, he whimpers and then howls for his mother. But she cannot hear. Eventually, the wolf cub stops howling and begins sniffing around. Perhaps he finds something to eat; perhaps he finds his mother; perhaps he dies. In any case, he has accepted frustration—he has no other choice.

The human infant in a similar situation differs in two important respects. One, he can delay the time interval between the awakening of desire and its abandonment, generally speaking, by developing *internal* projects designed to attain the goal. Such projects are beyond the cognitive ability of the wolf cub. That is, the human infant can remain in the frustrated and active state of desire longer than the wolf cub. On the other side of the coin, the human infant does not have the motor development to seek food or even to wander aimlessly. He cannot experience the relief of fleeing. Hence the human infant experiences passivity and separation from his environment more strongly than the wolf cub; he is the prisoner of his brain. So his incapacities for motor discharge of emotion and development of internal plans both result from the same aspect of the human infant. He is intelligent and therefore slow to develop.

In Brown's account, it is at this impasse that the infant begins to symbolically attempt to recapture unity. He accomplishes this by imagining that his mother's breast is present and later by having fantasies of consuming his mother so that she will be always there. In Brown's theory, man is too deviously clever to accept separation and aloneness (which eventually accounts for our fear of death and other strange reactions to the ultimate separation). Symbolic satisfaction is not real satisfaction, however, and frustration builds. As it builds, so do new emotions and desires: the infant can hate his mother's breast for treating him so badly. Hence when he next encounters the breast in the flesh he has an old score to settle. He also must drink; and so he bites while drinking. He also fears his mother will bash in his skull for this, yet another emotion.

This demonstrates another reason why the buildup of emotions eventually precludes concrete satisfaction. The infant wants happy sucking on his mother's breast; he wants to bite it; he wants to consume it to keep it always around; and he fears for his health due to his desire to bite the breast. What concrete set of operations could possibly correspond to such a complicated, contradictory set of desires?

In addition, planning to remove separation is a flight from reality. The wolf cub may have the capacity to imagine his mother's breast, but this will not satisfy him, and that is as far as he can go, and he turns to something concrete, whatever sources of food may be lying around. But the human infant conceives the "project" of consuming the breast so as to always have it on hand. *And this move makes the breast itself of little or no value.*

"It is all very well and good," says the infant to his mother and himself, "that the breast is here right now, but you and I know that there will be times when it will not be here. Its presence has the status of a historical accident, while I am planning for all time."

So the curse of humanity is not, as Brown suggested, prolonged infancy, but the unfortunate ability of man to symbolically deny separation in order to symbolically recapture unity. He devotes his life to an attempt to find a concrete expression of the emotions aroused by frustration. The projects become more and more grandiose as the number and intensity of emotions grow. Concrete satisfaction becomes more and more impossible, causing more emotional buildup, causing more elaborate fantasy gratification: a vicious circle.

The details of the developmental sequence are not necessary for this account. The project of consuming the mother's breast is complicated enough. The infant later has and abandons the desire to capture unity by controlling his feces and then by killing his father and sleeping with his mother. Each time the project itself engenders emotions which lead to its abandonment, just as the infant feels afraid of his desire to consume the breast for fear of retaliation by his mother.

I think psychoanalysis is an attempt to apply adult reasoning to child development. It is a good description of how it would go if the child had adult mentality. It is a projection. For example, the crucial reason for abandoning the Oedipal project is the discovery that there are two sexes, which arouses what Brown calls the horror of sexual differentiation. It is hard to see why a child of three or four or five should find the fact of two sexes particularly horrible. The vast majority of children do not seem put off by this fact; neither do the vast majority of adults. I think psychoanalysis is trying to find a concrete cause for adult horror of sexual differentiation. What is this horror, and what is its source? Imagine how a boy must feel when he discovers that little boys don't want to play with dolls. Imagine how a girl must feel when she discovers she can't play baseball anymore. Imagine how a man feels when he discovers he must not cry, or how a woman feels when she is made to feel uncomfortable when she yells "fuck you" at an irritant. The confinement of various activities to one of the sexes is another separation, another lack of unity. Thus psychoanalysis reflects adult mankind's horror at disunity. First, however, let us switch the cameras from the infant conceiving complicated projects to a child of six trying a typical Piagetian problem, so that we can illustrate our claim about the psychoanalytic account of child development.

The child confronts two full glasses of water of the same size and shape. One is poured into a tall thin glass, the other into a short fat glass, and the child is asked which glass has the most water. The tall one, since it is taller, he says, or the short one, since it is fatter. Not until he is older can the child solve the problem. And this is the child who could symbolically imagine eating his mother as a way of attaining unity?

Or consider the child of two, beyond Freud's oral stage. He sees an object. It is put behind a screen. He demonstrates that as far as he is concerned it no longer exists. He behaves as the wolf cub does with respect to his mother.

Piaget and others have demonstrated quite convincingly that children do not until the age of two attain even the rudiments of the capacity to represent and manipulate images in the mind. Only an intelligent adult could dream up the logic of the child's breast project; the child in the oral stage cannot even form an image of a breast—when it is not present, it is not present.

The dynamics of emotion suggested by psychoanalytic theory, while inapplicable to child development, will help us understand Piagetian love.

The End of the Essence

That sex signals the end of romantic love is an idea that appears in various forms throughout history. For example, recently in this culture men were supposed to lose respect for any woman with whom they could have sexual intercourse. As we have seen, the schema, "having sex with it," is often a familiar one. To have sex with a person is to treat the person as a familiar object. It is not necessarily to render the person harmless and commonplace. Marcel, the narrator in *Remembrance of Things Past,* had sexual relations with Albertine, but they did not lessen his love for her, for her love for women (or his suspicion of this love) made her unassimilable. He could not understand this attraction of hers for other women and she remained mysterious until long after she died.

As an attempt to assimilate an object, sexual behavior will sometimes work no better than hitting a typewriter with a hammer as a means of making the typewriter work. One can play *Jingle Bells* on a piano, but that does not exhaust the resources of the piano, nor would many people consider it "really" playing. Sex is more like playing *Jingle Bells* than like playing a piano concerto. We do not know what it means to play a piano concerto on a person. We have made beginnings. The body, the most concrete and visible aspect of a human being, is reported by pornographic books and sex manuals to be an instrument mastered by some. Adaptation to other aspects of humans is a less developed concept. Understanding is passive rather than active. We do not know how to employ it except in tolerance, playing whatever music we are handed, or manipulation, which is analogous to playing advertising jingles. Furthermore, humans are more complex than pianos. They do not sit still for a concerto, but "play back."

The love affairs in Proust remain beautiful to the lover, but to us they appear seamy or ridiculous from the outset. Furthermore, lovers are so insistent that their love resembles an intrusion, and cannot be reciprocated. The loved one needs to defend against the intrusion and has no energy left to return love. Romantic love may be an attempt to adapt to a person, but it is taken as an intrusion by the superficial people who are loved in Proust. The lovers in Proust should not be considered quixotic. They are not trying to open the human race to its essence. Ironically, they remain opaque and constantly employ subterfuge in their attempts to penetrate the opaque disguises of their loved ones. Thus, they do not make themselves available for adaptation. Only when the lover begins to love with tireless probings does the loved one need to withdraw. Thus Proust's view is that two people cannot adapt to each other simultaneously. The highest form of romantic love described in Proust is of one person (opaque) for another (also opaque). We cannot play a person as a piano unless the person sits still for it.

From this point of view, the emotion of romantic love is a consequence of the lover's inability to adapt to the loved one. When two people are on the rim with each other, they are not present to assimilate or accommodate. When the interaction is interrupted, the failure to adapt causes emotion to back up. Love is frustration.

But what is the source of frustration? If man has a need to master and control, romantic love should appear only when society is weak or broken down. If a man is to become only a husband, and a woman a wife, there should be no frustrating uncertainty and mystery surrounding anyone, and romantic love should not exist. Nevertheless, it has existed, even in well-programmed societies, throughout the centuries, all over the world. Mace and Mace (*Marriage East and West*) point out that throughout the ages societies have known that some young people would sometimes be violently attracted to each other to the exclusion of all other considerations, and they have almost invariably understood that this kind of love was dangerous.

Psychoanalysis implies that the loved object fulfills a symbolic function. Therefore, the loved object is more satisfactory (in one sense) before adaptive (particularly accommodatory) movements are made toward it. Such movements will be frustrating to the extent that the loved object is unlike that which it symbolizes. Before the attempt is made to translate fantasy into reality, the object has what appears to be infinite potential. That the object is known only in fantasy is, however, frustrating. Hence another definition of romantic love:

Romantic love is that infinitesimal moment between fantasy and reality, when the lover is finally moving into reality; when he is freed of the frustration of knowing it is only a dream, albeit a beautiful dream, albeit a vague dream in which the loved object, being nothing, is everything; when the lover has not yet had to face the fact that the loved one is not all the fantasy desired, because anything experienced in time and space must be limited.

Of what is the loved one symbolic? Not of anything in particular, for that would be a limitation. There is no concrete translation of the fantasy—*as yet*.

Let us consider the tentative proposition that the loved one is symbolic of everything and nothing.

An analogy will be useful. Education, to the extent that it is successful, should produce people who are romantically in love with life. Therefore, it is a good thing education is usually not successful.

J. Kerouac's *On The Road* has a plot consisting of an unrelated series of events, most of which are banal, mundane, ordinary, and boring. But it is clear that Kerouac means these events to have extreme significance. They are to be taken to be merely the performance of intentional actions which achieve something else. It is not clear what. When one writes a letter to a friend, that is a *means* of reestablishing contact. When one takes a sacred drug, that is a *means* of attaining unity with the unknown. The achievement is more than the performance. Racing from New York to Denver to say "Wow!" and racing back again to say "Wow!" again is a performance which is a means of achieving . . . ? Everything. And therefore nothing.

Kerouac tells us that an event was exciting (or some other superlative—it doesn't matter which) or that a person was beautiful (or, etc.) but we must take him on faith. He does not supply the details the reader would need to draw his own conclusions. And to say why a person is beautiful is to delimit the beauty and leave room for the possibility that someone might think the person was not beautiful. For example: "His hair was long and soft, as was his beard." "He" will not be perceived as beautiful by readers who believe males should not have long hair and beards. And Kerouac remains sufficiently vague so that as long as the reader does not disapprove of a little sex and drugs, he will have no grounds for disagreeing with Kerouac (nor will he have grounds for agreeing with him). Kerouac loves life as Mary loves Joe.

Kerouac is unable or unwilling to translate his perception of the excitement surrounding the events he relates. That is because the events are not possible embodiments of such diffuse excitement. A related story is Norman Mailer's "The Time of Her Time," which is a detailed description of a sexual relationship that is a good deal more than just a sexual relationship. That is, the story is about more than sex; it is an attempt to say what sex is besides sex.

Thus if one has read Mailer's story, one cannot but hope or desire that sex will have additional, surplus significance. It need not have the specific significance Mailer's story gives that particular relationship, but, one hopes and perhaps eventually expects, it will be a complex, dynamic encounter between complex, dynamic people who make a general statement about life. One cannot go from that story to a meat-packing plant and a wife and three kids at home without feeling that one is not receiving all that life has to offer. Kerouac's characters do nothing of particular significance, but everything they do is of vast but also of vague and unspecified significance; if only one could see one's own life as Kerouac sees his. Kerouac is more possible for most of us than Mailer. Kerouac resembles Kierkegaard's Knight of Faith, who would work in a meatpacking plant believing and acting as if it was the most important and exciting occupation in the world. And yet the chasm between style and content in Kerouac demonstrates that unless one transforms mundane events like sex into something specific, as Mailer does, they will remain mundane no matter how often one says "Wow!" The reader of Kerouac sees a model case of a discrepancy between one's own perceptions and the perceptions of society (one of Proust's major themes). The educated person will then recall from Kierkegaard's "Diary of a Seducer" that in order to make an event more than its mundane concrete details, one must retreat from the rim of the circle to the pit; in order to experience a beautiful affair, one must make sure one does not experience it.

Suppose Joe has read these and other works and has thought these and other thoughts about love and then meets Mary. Joe can either

accept his limitations and have an "ordinary relationship" with Mary
or he can attempt various "projects" with her. These projects need
have nothing to do with the infantile projects mentioned above, nor
need they have the aim of mastery and control. Joe may merely wish to
see if he can make Mary sweat the sweat of the sea rather than the sweat
of the gym, the project of Mailer's hero. The educated Joe will have
many and often conflicting viewpoints concerning what he wants from
Mary and they will interfere with correct accommodation to her. What
is correct accommodation to Mary? If she is simple, opaque, and exists
only on the rim, it is not a qualitatively different process than correct
accommodation to the piano. The educated Mary will, however, be
loaded with contradictory, vague, exciting schemata concerning what
she wants from Joe.

And so romantic love is Joe and Mary trying to apply schemata to
each other in a sufficiently vague way that neither feels the essential
nature of either is violated. The fantasies are schemata and the sense
of infinite potential is the sense that any or all of the schemata will be
applicable and applied.

Romantic love has spread like wildfire mainly in the West and
particularly in the United States, the country with the heterogeneous
population and little or no tradition. As humans become less programmed, the sense of infinite potential grows. Emotion arises when
behavior is blocked. Therefore, emotion arises whenever there are
several equally attractive alternatives. Emotions tend to spawn new
emotions—an internal dialogue. We seek outlets, modes of behavior
that embody our emotions. Human beings are the most complex objects available; relationships with people therefore have the greatest
potential for becoming the concrete embodiments of complex emotional states.

Humans, particularly in wealthy cultures, spend much of their
lives preparing for life. It is no wonder that when we get ready for life
we are full of vague plans and have no concept of limits. Education
theoretically should make real life less livable by providing us with
more projects and less tolerance of particulars. Emotions, whether
produced by formal or informal education, build up vertically, demanding immediate discharge; but life is lived horizontally. Daily
existence is likely to seem dull and empty of significance unless we can
suffuse it with emotion. The function of flooding daily existence with
emotion, however, is to simultaneously make it seem worthy of our
desires and to conceal the fact that it isn't.

On the rim romantic love, while preadaptive, is (by definition) the total expression of all one's vague emotions in interaction. In the pit romantic love, which develops when rim love is interrupted, is the attempt to recapture total expression. Because time and self do not exist on the rim, the limitations of daily existence cannot be perceived there. While everything can happen, nothing has happened yet.

Still, it is a start. The pile of emotions must be shaken down and given concrete behavioral expression. This transition from romantic love to love cannot be given precise description, for it is not general. It is a complex process, for it is an attempt to adapt to another human being. One must make the other satisfy one's needs while being sufficiently accommodatory to the other and to oneself.

The question of what the loved one symbolizes can now be given as final an answer as is possible. The loved one symbolizes whatever he or she becomes in the relationship. The loved one initially symbolizes infinite potential and nothing actual. In the complex process of adaptation, the loved one *becomes* him or herself. That self is what the lover desired. There was no way to find out in advance what it was, for it was not yet there.

Thus ends the description of romantic love. Everything further is specific and peculiar to the relationship; for love is the interaction, internal and overt, between two people who have translated all emotions toward each other into concrete behavior. It is horizontal rather than vertical. It is most essentially particular—interaction designed expressly for the two people involved.

This sounds vague and idealistic despite the invocation of uniqueness and particularity. Nothing is perfect, the slogan goes. Nor can two people expect to find a relationship (interaction) that allows for the expression of all their emotions. Many sociologists have blamed the divorce rate on the excessive expectations people have for their marriages. One should not expect one's spouse to fulfill fantasies that deal with children or friends. Furthermore, the interesting observation that romantic love has often been confined to and expected only in same-sex relationships (Seidenberg, 1973) can be brought into focus. Male-female relationships have not been in a state of equilibrium. Males have usually over-assimilated. They have treated women as instances of general categories rather than as unique human beings, and so they have behaved in gross and undifferentiated ways. Females, on the other hand, have had to overaccommodate themselves. Neither sex, then, has adapted well to the other. Love can only exist between people who regard each other as equals, for then the desire to assimilate the other into desired shapes will be exactly balanced by the desire to know the essence of the other.

A unique pattern of interaction designed expressly for the two individuals involved.... The discovery of a concrete daily existence that expresses the ineffable thundercloud schema each of us builds during the prelife periods of childhood and adolescence; a schema directed only vaguely towards life in real time.... The mystery of personality discovered.... I can hear people who know me well:

"Come *on,* George. Will you cut the *crap?* Pretty soon you'll come out in favor of self-actualization. I have no idea what you're talking about."

Nor, of course, do I; and not just because of the impossibility of generally characterizing perfect translations of what is by definition untranslatable. I would have to confess that I haven't seen this kind of love. Of course if I had, it wouldn't have appeared to be love, and probably the people who had it wouldn't have been aware of it either. To feel the emotions of love is to have not completed the translation. Perhaps it exists and perhaps it doesn't. What, then, has been the point of the whole discussion?

Piaget has demonstrated that physics went through an Aristotelian phase when Aristotle was alive. Children go through the same Aristotelian phase as they develop. The human race had to adapt to the physical world, and it took time. But the earlier adaptations were not mere aberrations and stupidities. They were the kind of adaptation necessary for later and more complex adaptations—children must go through the Aristotelian phase before they can come to the Newtonian and Einsteinian.

In what stage of adaptation (to human beings) is the human race? I do not know. Nor do I know the future any more than the infant knows he will eventually be able to roll the ring. I do know that romantic love is the beginning of a more complex adaptation than is characteristic of well-programmed societies in which the sociological view of human relationships is applicable. Personality is a mystery and therefore is somewhat more suspect as a scientific causal entity than a social role; but that is only because we do not understand it yet (and "it" is not out there to be discovered—we are in the process of inventing "it"). We don't know where we are. We don't know where we are going.

Note, however, that we have returned to the beginning. On the rim romantic love is a totally involving interaction, without adapting selves. We retreat to the pit to digest the fact that Joe is a person. We return to the rim—to interaction—when we translate empty schemata into concrete action. That is love. It is interaction, and it is involving; but it has also incorporated the seemingly inescapable fact that there are two personalities involved.

3
Process Models
of Relationships
Going Bad

THIS CHAPTER CONTAINS several process models of love relationships going bad.[1] The next chapter details reasons why, having gone bad, relationships do not formally dissolve. Bad relationships are too variable to be susceptible to general characterization. However, as a fitting conclusion to this chapter and introduction to the next, a partial and merely suggestive list is given of ways in which relationships can be bad.

Many of the process models described here assume that the relationship has become an institution. Marriage and cohabitation are common forms of institutionalization, but it is not necessary that the couple share living quarters. What is required is that the courtship stage of the relationship give way to a stage when the relationship is acknowledged by both participants, not necessarily explicitly, to exist and to have causal power. It is now acceptable for the participants to make claims based on the existence of the relationship, for example, that one person can't or shouldn't do something to the other.

Institutionalization is not necessarily a rite of passage, nor is the transition from courtship to a more formal stage always clearly demarcated. Marriage can be considered a rite of passage, but in most cases in this society the relationship has become an institution prior to marriage and even engagement. Therefore, no distinction between marriage and other kinds of relationships will be made. It appears that physical rather than legal separation is experienced as traumatic (W. J. Goode, *After Divorce*), and that young couples living together value and demand sexual fidelity more than older married couples (J. Bernard, "No news but new ideas"). One does not need to be married to experience the emotions attributed to married people.

Chapter two has made explicit some reasons why relationships might be or go bad; for example, bad translation of emotion or premature assimilation. The forces leading to failure given in this and the following chapter are not necessarily direct failures of romantic love as described in chapter two, but do infringe upon romantic love. The major purpose of this chapter is to explain why relationships, most of which began with at least some romantic love, go bad; it is therefore only partially a direct extension of chapter two.

This chapter and the next deal with relationships going bad and then *staying* bad. Thus the process of relationships going downhill has been divided into two sequential, smaller processes. The division reveals a relatively more specific and detailed description of the total process. Similarly, each of the process models in this chapter details divisions which reveal more detailed and specific descriptions of this part of the total process.

The process models are almost completely content free. We may all run from A to B, but will do so in different ways. None are inevitable. If they sound as if they are, it is because no attempt has been made to list process-stoppers. Again, we may all stop on our way from A to B, but will do so in different ways. Individual relationships are too specific in content for a general account; hence the term "model." Clothes are separate; leaving the models naked places certain forces, which operate on relationships, in stark relief often hidden by clothes.

PROCESS MODEL I: MARRIAGE VS. MARRIAGEE

In our society, people want to get married or have boy and girl friends. This desire is inappropriate and detrimental to the success of relationships.

Let me approach this proposition slowly and somewhat indirectly.

It is said that people need love.[2] What does this mean? It could mean that a person needs a love relationship. It could mean a person needs to be in love. It could mean a person needs the kind of love young children receive from their parents—unilateral unconditional positive and constant approval and attention, nearly instantaneous satisfaction of needs, with no payment required except gurgles or other expressions of satisfaction.

Let us first consider the need for parental love. It is possible for an adult to obtain such love from another adult. But the "child" must trust the "parent." So must the parent trust the child. Inappropriate or unwanted parental behavior is considered condescending and insulting, even by adults acting as if they were children. The development of such mutual trust takes time. The person who wants to act as if he were a child will not immediately become passive and helpless, lest he be humiliated. He will approach his goal slowly and indirectly, often by pretending to act as if he were a child. Eventually, the attainment of his goal will be a *fait accompli*—it will require very little more childishness than his previous position, which has been already accepted. In addition, the potential child will have been observing the potential parent, not just to make sure he is being adequately parental, but to make sure he is not overdoing it.

In this situation, "mutual trust" is not enough. Regression is not free.

Payment is of two sorts. In many adult interpersonal relationships, both members feel free to act as if they were children, but it is understood that the child of today will have to play parent tomorrow and that one member of the relationship cannot hog the show.

The child may pay for the privilege by allowing the parent to play parent. If one member of the relationship needs to play child much of the time, the other must be allowed to play parent. This constitutes payment because parents have their privileges too, the major one being control over the child for the child's and often for the parents' good. This privilege occurs in normal parent-child relationships, but there the parent has a right *and* an obligation to exert control. Most adults do not like to be controlled, or at least they resist it (as children often do for that matter; why should we expect adults to be more pliant than children in this respect?). Nor do most adults like to or want to exert control in intimate personal relationships. The proof of this proposition lies in its examination in the context of normal parent-child relationships: A parent should control his child, but to like or want to is inappropriate and perhaps pathological. Children need a certain amount of control, but the person who needs to control can be expected to exert more control, given the opportunity, than the child needs. Needs are narcissistic and not much interested in their effects on reality. Either the parental adult pays by having to play parent (to a no doubt recalcitrant child) or by being encouraged in his neurotic need for control.

In summary, parental love may be obtained in adult relationships; but one must pay for it. Either one must become a child to a

greater extent than one wanted, or one must agree to play parent as
often as one gets to play child. The latter solution is not likely to be
satisfactory to a person with a chronic need for parental love. A person
who needs parental love is by definition not an adult when the need is
operative, and is not likely to be interested in a pattern of reciprocity.
The pattern of reciprocity must develop from an adult love relationship; it is, in fact, modeled on one. The person who needs parental
love by definition wants a nonreciprocal pattern.

Let us examine what it means for an adult to need nonreciprocal
parental love. We begin with an examination of what it means for a
child to need nonreciprocal parental love. A child is picked on by bullies and comes home to mother. The child needs a parent. Children
often signal that they need nonreciprocal parental love by crying. If a
child comes home obviously unhappy but trying hard to conceal it, he
is trying to be a "big boy" about something. At this point, the parent
has a choice. The parent can ignore the not quite convincing stoicism,
believing, perhaps, that the child "really" needs love but is "being
defensive" or "trying to be too old too fast." Alternatively, the parent
can ignore the "latent" tears, believing, perhaps, that the child will
never become a "big boy" unless amateurish performances are allowed
to pass as professional jobs.

The child cannot be said to "really" know which kind of behavior
he wants from his parents. It makes some sense to say he wants both.
We are talking about a child who is trying, although not very success-
fully, to control his unhappiness. Eventually, people learn to control
their unhappiness—or they don't, in which case they become adults
who signal for parental love. Adults cannot behave childishly. If a
young child comes home crying every time bullies beat up on him, he
is merely childish, but if an adult cries every time misfortune strikes,
he is taken to be abnormal or mentally ill. The mentally ill are by
definition people who cannot be reached by ordinary means. We do
not know how to deal with adults who sob hysterically at the drop of a
hat (except to shove them into institutions). If traditional parental
behaviors did the trick for adults who handle their unhappiness in
this straightforward if extreme manner, there would be considerably
fewer people labelled as neurotics than there are. What works for children, however, does not work for adults. Adults are not usually placated by a shoulder to cry on.

The option of control is (taken to be) available to adults. Even
children attempt to control themselves; adults who don't are (taken to

be) mentally ill (and therefore *must* submit to parental control), or they are taken to have chosen not to exercise control.

Children can emit signs that parental behavior is needed or wanted; adults *can* emit signs, but because they are taken to be usually capable of suppressing them, their emission is usually taken as a *request* for parental behavior. Presumably, anyone of sound enough mind and mood to request parental behavior is not a child. Furthermore, a request for control does not allow control (J. Haley, *Strategies of Psychotherapy*). If adult P asks adult O for domination, O complies with P's permission. P is the person in charge; P demonstrates the power to get O to do what P wants.

Therefore, adults who need parental love are logically (and psychologically) incapable of receiving it. Children need and receive domination and control without asking. To ask for domination and control is to ask for control of the situation; it is therefore to reject domination.

We would, accordingly, expect people who claim to need parental love to be uncooperative in their reception of it. What they claim to want is domination and control, and yet they phrase their request in such a manner that they cannot be dominated or controlled.

In conclusion, it is not possible for adults to *need* parental love (although there are adults *in need* of such love). It is possible to request domination by requesting love, but the request makes receipt impossible.

Let us now consider the need to be in love. "In love" here means "being in romantic love," with particular emphasis on the considerable consumption of time and energy that romantic love implies. The present is all that exists and the emotional tone of the present extrapolates in the mind to the past and future. People are said to be swept off their feet, carried off on white horses, or taken away from all this.

While romantic love does not need reciprocity, it must be possible. Otherwise, fantasy love cannot proceed without leaving reality far behind, a situation which reduces the power of fantasy. Not many people really fall in love with movie stars—it is hard to keep up a sustaining fantasy about someone you rarely see. To want this kind of love is to want to progress beyond fantasy. No doubt some people are satisfied to sustain an unrealistic fantasy over the years with no hope of, or interest in, fulfillment. But we would not describe Walter Mitty as needing to be a hero. We would describe him as *having* the fantasies he (would be said to) need if he didn't already have them.

The person who needs to be in love will have to attempt to translate fantasy into reality. But to need to be in love is to want passivity. It is to want to be possessed by romantic love, to be *taken* away from all this. On the other hand, to *be* in love in this sense is to be highly active, especially with respect to the loved one. People in love *take themselves* away from all *this* by getting involved in all *that* (the loved one).

And how is it possible to need to be in love without having someone in particular in mind? It is not possible unless it is an abstract need to be removed from one's boring or unpleasant situation. Thus, we can imagine Joe falling in love with Mary if Mary is receptive to Joe in various ways, but not if Mary is only attentive to her inner needs and feelings. To the extent that Mary is narcissistic or onanistic, she is not lovable. Therefore, to the extent that she simply needs to be in love, her behavior will defeat her purpose.

To need to be in love is incompatible with being in love; the former blocks the possibility of the latter. To need to be in love (with *love* an intransitive verb) can only mean to need a passive but exciting experience; but love is activity, and usually, at least at first, love is pain. People in love report being swept along by their love, but in order to feel helpless or passive in that way, one must be highly active. As we have seen, the "old self" is temporarily unseated by romantic love, when the person is completely on the rim. When it creeps back to observe, it reports the sensation of being swept away, which indicates inability to assimilate.

A formula currently popular in social psychology is that arousal (pleasant or unpleasant plus an appropriate object equals love. If a person is physiologically aroused in the presence of an object that could be loved, the person may conclude that he loves the object. This formula neglects the fact that people do not usually find themselves aroused in situations which have not contributed to that arousal. If they are aroused in such situations by extrasituational factors, there is no reason to expect they will be aroused for extraneous reasons the next time they encounter the nonarousing situation. Unless the love was "at first sight," for instance one-trial learning, it will be extinguished. Nevertheless, the formula illustrates what it is that people who claim to want to be in love really want: arousal. People who say "I wish there was something interesting to do" usually mean "I wish I was interested in something."

Experiments relating arousal to attribution have employed drugs; they give what one might call "pure" arousal. If an experimenter arouses a subject by angering him with taunts of a stooge, and the subject subsequently falls in love with an available and attractive object, it is not clear that arousal per se leads to love. An alternative explanation is that an angry person needs friends or lovers to help him justify or scream off his anger at the stooge. But drugs are content free.

People who use drugs sometimes narcissistically savor their arousal rather than use it to accomplish something. This is taboo. The only legal powerful drug, alcohol, is supposed to be taken socially. What ensues is a relaxed social gathering. People who drink alone are labelled alcoholics despite the fact that drinking alone can help relax a "social gathering" with a book or television show. Furthermore, "drunkenness" is usually defined as that state when the person becomes incoherent and therefore socially useless. No matter how much one drinks, one is not considered drunk if one remains socially acceptable.

People who need to be in love need an injection. Without the subsequent arousal, they will be unable to fall in love. If people enter relationships without arousal, and want the other to take care of the sweeping and taking away, the relationship will be a puppet show.

If people who need to be in love receive an injection (for example, by getting someone to love them), they are likely to savor their arousal. People who want to be in love do not want to be in love with a person anymore than people who "need a drink" wish to engage in social interaction. Thus if Joe needs love and is able to enter a relationship with Mary, Joe is likely to spend more time talking about and savoring the love than doing anything with Mary, and she will feel justifiably cheated. *Like liquor, love is meant to be taken socially.*

In conclusion, the thought of love, like the influence of sex and drugs, creates the illusion of passivity and obliviousness to what before seemed unpleasantly important. It is the thought of love rather than love itself that creates the illusion, which is akin to the awareness of that crumb of self that persists in real life love. In complete involvement, there is no awareness of the state of nonarousal which no longer exists. To want involvement is thus to want a state of affairs which would not be satisfactory to a person who wants involvement, for to want involvement is paradoxically to want passivity; but involvement is contrary to passivity. When one is in love, one is not conscious of how much better it is to be in love than to not be in love—if one is, one's love is not as satisfactory as it might be, because it has not swept one away completely.

Thus people who claim to want to be in love want to be aroused and to simultaneously savor that arousal. This state is best achieved by drugs, when one can be aware simultaneously of one's arousal and of oneself—drugs produce free-floating arousal. The person who wants to be in love would rather not be bothered with other people; they would disturb his meditation.

Wanting to be in love and wanting parental love are not really possible. Wanting parental love turns out to be wanting to be dominated without being willing to be dominated. Wanting to be in love turns out to be wanting to be aroused in solitude. Neither is a desire for anything resembling normal love. Let us now consider a far less abnormal desire, one that seems to be common in our society, the desire for an adult love relationship.

Consider the following proposition: It is counterproductive to want anything other than that which is attainable by one's next move. An attainable goal is one that stands a reasonably good chance of being attained and can appropriately be reached by the kind of move about to be made.

Some examples will illustrate the proposition. In many sports, players insist they plan on playing according to the "game plan." How else can a game be played? Players *can* play as if each play had to lead to victory. In this case, they would want not just what they could reasonably expect to attain on the next play (five yards and a first down) but to win the whole game (a long and risky touchdown pass). This would be counterproductive. If the desire to win the whole game predominates over more reasonable desires, high risk plays are probable. In football, for example, long passes would be thrown often. Not only are these high risk plays (there is a relatively low probability the pass will be caught and a relatively high probability an interception will result), but the defense can easily adjust to a homogeneous offense, no matter how wild. In chess, the player who wants to win rather than to attain a reasonable goal for the next move may get his Queen out too soon rather than develop his pieces. The general principle illustrated here is that the desire to win and the desire to accomplish what is reasonable can become unfused and unintegrated, causing irrational play.

Let us apply this proposition to adult relationships, that one should not want too much too soon. It is possible to "go too fast" (the equivalent of trying to win the whole game with one play). This can be counterproductive in two somewhat different senses. Joe may attempt an intimacy with Mary .that she is not yet willing to accept.

Thus Joe may be rejected. Or they may attempt an intimacy with each other that neither is ready to accept. Consequently, they back off from each other.

If both of them want an adult interpersonal relationship, however, why should they object to intimacies? That is what they want, isn't it?

They do indeed want intimacies; but consider what it means to want an adult interpersonal relationship: it means to want to be *in* one. There is a difference between having sexual relations with a stranger and having sexual relations with a husband or wife. There is a difference between talking intimately with a stranger and talking intimately with a husband or wife. Domestic bliss is fine, but one *cannot achieve* domestic bliss with a stranger (it is not the *kind* of thing one can achieve with a stranger; it is like trying to kick a field goal with a baseball bat). Bliss may be achieved with a stranger, but not domestic bliss. To want an adult interpersonal relationship is to want something one cannot reasonably expect to attain with one's opening move, for the coordination of good adult interpersonal relationships is the result of practice—or dumb luck.

It can and does happen that two people luckily "hit it off," just as it can and does happen that a football team will score a touchdown or win a game on a series of risky plays. If the tenth of a series of risky plays goes wrong, however, the loss will be considerable. Thus the whole series retroactively receives a negative net gain. Most of the time ten less risky plays will yield some positive gain. Similarly, if a couple is hitting it off, but if one of them then makes a bad move, the contrast of the bad with the good will be striking. If, for example, a series of nine moves has been so successful that Mary has become "completely open" to Joe, and if on the tenth move Joe, with all confidence of a success, does something that Mary considers a betrayal, Mary will feel relatively more betrayed because she was so open, and Joe will feel relatively more rejected because he had such a high expectation of success. For example, Joe and Mary might have done very well in the area of personal intimacies; Joe might see only a slight difference of degree between personal and sexual intimacies, while Mary might consider it a large and qualitative difference. Both positions are defensible, and neither need be accused of bad faith, prudery, or lechery. If we assume that Joe and Mary are both reasonable people, in time they could have come to sexual intimacy on terms acceptable to both; but they blow it because they have gone too fast.

The argument suggests that caution, moderation, and deliberate speed are favorable to the growth of love—a decidedly unromantic position. But the position is not yet complete: A great deal of intensity can be concentrated on a very limited move. In fact, employing a simplistic thermodynamic conceptual framework, the more energy given to a distant goal, the less available for the present, which is romantic love's growth medium. Wanting something that must be in the future is bound to be *distracting*. The medical student cannot be expected to concentrate on his books if he is daydreaming about performing magnificent operations. Nor will his books seem as interesting. This example illustrates an earlier point about the growth of emotion and fantasy satisfaction. If that which is desired is a state of passivity or ease (in the sense that great athletes "make it look easy" but also in the sense that sitting in a bar surrounded by admirers is easier than writing), the necessity for slow assimilation of difficult medical material will seem aversive. Furthermore, the medical student will become a bad doctor. From this point of view, romantic love will be intense to the extent that there is no thought of the future, especially of a relaxed, domestic future. But the relationship should still proceed slowly.

Even if one plans to play cautiously, the desire to be *in* an adult interpersonal relationship is counterproductive. If P wishes to be in such a relationship, O is the enemy, the opposition, or, at best, an impersonal foe like a mountain. Every move that P makes with respect to O may be redescribed. An offering of an intimacy is more appropriately described as ... an inducement to O to behave more intimately. P is not being intimate. P is being a hustler. P's intimacies are less likely to be sincere or true, since their presentation will be guided by considerations of the goal of obtaining a relationship rather than by the goal of presenting that particular intimacy.

Thus far, the dangers of proceeding too quickly have been presented, but not the virtues of proceeding slowly and without long-term goals. Here, it is necessary to introduce another dimension, the personalities of the individuals involved.

Love at first sight is associated with the very young. "Young love" is also noted for its instability. Johannes, the seducer in Kierkegaard's "Diary of a Seducer," prefers young girls to young women. From the context, the reason is clear: Young girls may not be innocent, but they are unformed. The Seducer, who represents the search for the interesting, wishes to make the young girl free of clinging, dependent *need* for him (and full only of freely given *want*) so that the seduction will be interesting. To do so he must first shape her into proper form. Having developed into a personality a person can no longer be formed as perfectly. Furthermore, if personality refers to traits—enduring behavior patterns—a person with a personality is less malleable. Two people with personalities can have a "love affair between people" but cannot simply love; extraneous factors need to be dealt with. The continuity of the dialectic of a love affair is broken if your lover has a job, child, other interests, insecurities, or excess of self-confidence. The young girl, on the other hand, has the emotional flexibility, the intensity of attention, and the innocence of future and past, that are needed for an interesting seduction.

Put another way, to the extent that the young girl is unformed, accommodation is unnecessary. She may be assimilated to the schema of pure love, whereas a person with a personality demands modification of existing schemata. To the extent that the young girl is malleable, she can be made to accommodate the schema without misperception of the true nature of the girl by the seducer. Furthermore, the operation of the schema of love need not be interrupted by other schemata—that of moneymaking, for example.

We have seen in chapter two that young people are more susceptible to love because of the changes they undergo as they develop. The present point of view explains why the young are easier to love: The lover may simply love—there is nothing in particular at which to direct one's arousal. It is easier for the young to receive love because there is no particular kind of love they require—a meat and potatoes diet (sex and tenderness) will suffice. Furthermore, if the young are faceless but beautiful, they can be the receptacles for any kind of fantasy; having done nothing they have infinite potential. Love of the young is unstable because there is nothing for it to get stuck on. If Joe loves Mary and she happens to be honest, then Joe may get the idea that he loves honesty in addition to Mary, or that he loves Mary because she is honest. Then it will be harder to fall out of love with Mary, since she *is* honest (even if she has become mean and nasty). It will also be harder to fall in love with someone new, for if the new candidate is dishonest or not particularly honest, Joe will find her less eligible. Similarly, the love of a person without personality will be purer—personality traits interfere. Consider honesty. Pure love is clichéd love; but the young are able to say things like "I love you with all my heart" with ease and without dishonesty, while honest people are not. The love of a self-confident person will differ from the love of a person without self-confidence—but the love of a person who is not yet either is pure love.

Love between people who have personalities cannot exist until they know each other, which takes time. Why?

The more complex a machine or game, the longer it takes to learn to operate or play it. 'In chapter two love was described as interaction between people designed expressly for them. In addition, love followed romantic love by a process of adaptation. To the extent that a person is complex, accommodations will be difficult. Furthermore, simple and general assimilatory schemata will not work; they will have to be modified.

While I do not know what it means to adapt to another person's essence or to develop an interaction appropriate to that essence, it is possible to give an example of the difficulties involved in adjusting to an already present personality trait. Let us see what Mary, who is honest, needs from Joe to avoid feeling like a piano banged on by a child.

Joe should not call Mary beautiful if she knows she is not. Many people have either formed no strong opinion on their looks or are willing to go with the decision of the beholder. Also, many people use the word "beautiful" in a political way; since most people don't mind being complimented on their looks, the word can be used to ingratiate. Mary may not be typical in these respects, and so Joe should proceed with caution. Initially, perhaps, he will tell Mary he likes something as detached from Mary as possible, perhaps her purse. From her reaction to his objective and noningratiating comment on the neutral subject of purses, he can get some information on how she reacts to compliments. He should then select something not much more a part of Mary, perhaps a raincoat, with special emphasis on its efficiency. If she becomes annoyed, he can still claim he is nothing but a disinterested scientist. He would be a fool to immediately tell her she is beautiful if she reacts favorably to his comment on her purse, for she too may make the distinction between personal objects and neutral objects.

It will not be sufficient for Mary merely to tell Joe she is honest. Honesty is too vague a concept. A current debate in social personality psychology is whether behavior is situation-specific or whether traits exist. There is considerable evidence that traits do not—people who are honest in one situation are not necessarily honest in another. People can, however, claim that situations in which they were faulted for their lack of honesty were not situations that called for honesty, or were situations in which honesty was impossible. For example, I believe students should receive evaluations, even of their ability. Sometimes I give them gratuitously and claim I am being honest. Others do not agree with me that the situation calls for honesty, and they therefore consider me nasty rather than honest. Similarly, if Joe asks Mary if she loves him, I do not believe she *can* give him an honest answer, because love is not the kind of thing that either does or doesn't exist.

In summary, Mary's honesty is a complex set of behaviors, which cannot be transmitted by "I am honest." What is required is experience with Mary.

Thus, a desire for a relationship is likely to precipitate overly rapid approaches to intimacy, which will either abort the relationship or produce a nonaccommodatory relationship that will generate friction.

Furthermore, to desire a relationship is to desire a relationship of a particular kind. Whether the concept of the desired relationship is sharp or blurred, a person can tell if a particular relational behavior is acceptable or not. The person with a concept of a desirable relationship will therefore be unable to focus on a developing, real time relationship; he will narcissistically consult his check list rather than attend to the one he hopes to relate to.

Let us suppose that Joe and Mary desire marriage but not so strongly as to activate the various damaging processes described here. They get married and are happy.

When one has finished a meal, one does not wish to eat more. The analogy: to the extent that a person wants to get married, the person will be satisfied, relaxed, and let down once the ceremony is over. To be sure, when one buys a car, one wishes to drive it; but what can one do with a marriage? In fact, what can one do with a person whom one has merely wanted to possess? The engagement ring may be driven all over town, but once everyone has seen it, one can only wear it and hope a stranger on the subway notices it. Since marriage is symbolic, the only things one can do with it are symbolic themselves, parasitic on the symbolic nature of marriage. To the extent that marriage rather than a person has been the object of desire, the person is secondary, and so the desire to deal with the person is lacking. The ability is also lacking, since the desire for marriage tends to force inappropriate and premature assimilation.

This process model predicts that if people want marriage, once they get it they will "go to seed," as the common and well-known phrase goes, and will in addition pay no attention to their spouses. As we shall see, other process models predict similar outcomes, but for dissimilar reasons.

This outcome is common enough, suggesting that those process models have some relationship to reality. People do go to seed after the courtship phase.

This process model demonstrates how people can be inactive or passive in a relationship. In addition, it shows how desire for a relationship may cause *both* individuals to be lost in the shuffle. But they will reappear eventually, demanding their due. The other process models deal mostly with the postformalization stage of relationships. This one is presented first because it is the only one that deals with dissolution inherent in the process of relational formation. In short, this is a model of the process of a relationship going bad *before it has been formed.*

PROCESS MODEL II: ACTIVITY STATUS

Social practices were introduced in chapter two. They are performed with no further end in view; they are intrinsically motivated and rewarding. Social practices do not *exist*. Rather, there is behavior that certain people at certain times *take to be social practices*. A social practice, then, is the behavior someone takes to be a social practice at a given time. In practice it is possible to identify social practices by noting that they are performed without a chorus of queries into their origins.

"Courting" and "hustling" are two of many terms that refer to a ubiquitous activity that is a social practice. People do not usually ask other people, particularly males, why they are in pursuit of the opposite sex. Furthermore, a couple developing a relationship is allowed to want to spend a good deal of their time together. It is even acceptable to want to spend this time alone: being alone with the object of one's affection is an activity with relatively high status in our society, as long as the object is not completely captured. Single people who spend much of their lives engaged in being alone together are admired and envied by married people.

Married couples, on the other hand, are expected to go to parties and other social gatherings. Staying home alone has relatively low status; it suggests that the couple has no friends. Married couples are supposed to have friends, while courting couples are supposed to ignore theirs. Other norms for courting couples are different from comparable norms for an established couple. The difference is even reflected in seating arrangements. A courting couple sits side by side. After they are married, segregation is usually enforced.

"A night out with the boys" is often a status symbol for a married man, particularly if the wife doesn't—or better, isn't allowed to—complain. Prior to marriage or setting up housekeeping extrarelational activities are expected to be kept to a minimum and their value deemphasized. After the marriage both partners may suddenly realize how constraining the relationship is. But the couple is simply remembering how constraining it *has been*. Postformalization relationships usually become less constraining in the specific sense that they occupy less time.

Marriage has many causes and one may be that a courting couple spends too much time with each other and wants to spend less and yet more. Other important activities are neglected, but when engaged in, make the couple feel robbed of each other's company. So the couple decides to make more time for themselves *and* the other aspects of their lives by setting up two timelines. Togetherness is formalized or institutionalized by marriage or setting up housekeeping. A couple is then always together by fiat and social definition. They are now a couple. Even when Joe is in Washington and Mary is in New York. Real time is freed for other activities, including being together. Thus the formalized couple having dinner together is together in two different senses.

The change in status *may* now occur. Why would Joe spend time with Mary if he is already always with her by virtue of the status of the relationship?

This question is often asked, and for rather transparent reasons. During the course of an intense courtship, friends, relatives, and employers of the participants suffer loss of attention. Now that the couple has each other symbolically at all times, they should have more real time for others. The negative connotations that often attach to the image of a formalized couple spending much time together may come entirely from jealous outside parties. Ordinarily, however, courtship involves partial, although usually not begrudged, suppression of activities that have been a part of the participants' lives longer than the other member of the couple has. It is reasonable to expect they would return to their old activities even without pressure.

Furthermore, a married couple institutionalizes not only togetherness but love. Love is thrust out of behaviors and into the formal structure of the relationship. "Of course I love you. I married you, didn't I?" The relationship is by definition a love relationship. Thus the couple may develop a nonintimate manner of relating to each other. Why express in real time behavior that which is formally, explicitly, and unambiguously expressed by the nature of the relationship?

That this process operates in the histories of relationships is attested to by the widely held view that romance does have a natural history, which includes a cooling off period and habituation. Additional evidence is provided by the existence of various bromides: keep your marriage young, think of her as the bride you married twenty years ago, don't take each other for granted, don't let him see you in your curlers, bring her flowers.

This aging process need not operate—in some relationships it simply doesn't—but it is not necessarily bad when it does. There is no reason why a person's relationship with his mate should occupy any particular percentage of his time, nor why intensity should be confined to intimate sexual relationships. Even if the process does occur to a marked extent, the relationship does not necessarily become completely bad. J. F. Cuber and P. B. Harroff in *Sex and the Significant Americans* report that a sizable proportion of the marriages of upper class Americans are best described as arrangements suitable to both parties. It is unlikely that in all of these love has been removed entirely from real time interaction to the institution.

Institutionalization of love and togetherness does facilitate nonintimate relationships that occupy little time and energy. He who would devote himself to love had best not be too successful, as Proust has described. When the loved one is possessed, the lover is calm, indifferent, critical, bored. When the loved one is not possessed, the lover suffers greatly from jealousy and a strong need to be in the company of the loved one. The latter state is love, and it is this state which people find valuable. Swann finds that the "sereness, the depression of the preceding years had been followed by a sort of spiritual superabundance" (*Remembrance*, I: 233) ; however, in the same story mention is made of a potentate who found he was in love with a member of his harem and stabbed her to regain his freedom. Marriage is often functionally equivalent to stabbing.

PROCESS MODEL III: ON AND OFF STAGE

E. Goffman, in *The Presentation of Self in Everyday Life*, has analyzed social behavior using the concept of the theater as an analogy. When one is on stage, one is selling something and so must show deference to the desires of one's clients. Depending on the actor's job, more or less of his integrity is sacrificed. In *Asylums,* Goffman describes the process by which the prisoner of the mental hospital is divested of his autonomous self. He also describes the underground backstage region patients develop to give them what Goffman calls "secondary adjustment." Secondary adjustment consists of activities that allow patients to feel they exist independently of the institution and that they are not *just* mental patients. Backstage one can prepare one's face, relieve the frustration of being someone else's man rather than one's own, relax and be intimate with one's equals, derogate the client, and do other things one would do "at home."

To the extent that the actor must demean himself on stage, a cathartic backstage will be required. Thus, backstage is not always a warm and intimate region. Scapegoating, sullenness, and withdrawal are just as "offstage" as badinage, consolation, and solidarity.

Courtship is conducted on stage. While courtship often has the trappings of backstage, such as casual dress and speech, it is not true backstage. Couples may present their backstage selves but they do so on stage, to sell themselves. Once a couple marries or lives together, the members have sold themselves (there is no double your money back guarantee if not absolutely satisfied). There is no longer a need to "put on an act" with each other.

The first process model was a description of demeaning, groveling onstage behavior. It was a description of people who needed relationships too much to develop them properly. To the extent that that process model is operative, the backstage that follows formalization will be a region of no behavior. There are, however, other possibilities.

If the other "plays" in the lives of the members of the couple are taxing, scapegoating and petty competition may be common. The couple may simply not be able to tolerate being backstage. Recalling Swift, the knowledge that Celia excretes waste products may disgust the formerly ardent lover. If the courtship has been particularly degrading, there may be scores to settle. Alternatively, the couple may settle down to the serious business of getting their bad features accepted.

This latter process may not occur; or the backstage selves may not be unpleasant. Some couples are happy with a relaxed if sometimes snappish atmosphere. Furthermore, some relationships have never been on a stage. A colleague relationship may progress towards intimacy without the typical onstage courting behaviors—and perhaps this absence facilitates the growth of intimacy.

Process Models II and III have much in common. Both involve a more or less sudden change following the change in status of the relationship from provisional to formal. Both are exacerbated by a courtship phase requiring abnormal behavior; both involve sharper contrasts to the extent that courtship is intense.

There is, however, some difference. The second process is at least partially an imposition by society (although the rules are probably internalized). The third results from the inevitable tendency of people to let down their hair at home.

PROCESS MODEL IV: POSSESSIVENESS

Many species of animals establish territories. Having a territory allows the animal to feed and breed. Animals are not happy when their territories are invaded. Humans establish territories also, both around their immediate persons (E. T. Hall, *The Silent Language*) and their living spaces, neighborhoods, and countries. Humans do not like their territories invaded either.

Clearly humans believe (or act as if they believe) that they own what is in their territories. The legal technicalities of ownership are unimportant here. What matters is that humans act as if what is in their territories is theirs. "Territory" here, of course, refers to the psychological life space of the relationship rather than merely to physical territory held in common.

Most couples with formalized relationships share a common territory, although each may have a subterritory that the other is expected to avoid. In addition, one's spouse is part of one's territory. We say, "My husband" or "My girlfriend," and when making introductions we usually use these locutions before the given name.

While clinging possessiveness has a bad name at this time, I think it unlikely that many relationships with complete freedom can last for long. I think it is unlikely because it is not true that people don't own each other.

If a territory is considered an ecosystem, the most powerful organism in the territory, the one powerful enough to have the territory defined according to his movement or named after him, owes a good deal to the territory. If the dues aren't paid, the territory will collapse. A coyote cannot deplete his territory any more than the "breadwinner" can violate the wishes of the other organisms in his territory.

Put somewhat differently, people in a relationship have rights and obligations. People can live together without making claims on each other, but these are arrangements, not relationships; and even arrangements involve rights and obligations, although of a different sort.

From this point of view, claims like "You don't own me" or "You're possessive" are attempts to establish the limits of ownership rather than statements of absolute philosophical fact. Neither claim would be appropriate if there were a total absence of ownership.

The process, then, results from the dialectic between two tendencies to assume ownership of a territory and two tendencies to resist being a territorial possession.

Generally, trouble will arise if one person asks for too much freedom or requires too much obedience. Trouble can also arise if too little freedom is requested (overdependency) or too little obedience is required (the government is *laissez faire* rather than democratic).

Possessiveness may never cause trouble if the couple meshes well; it may be limited by negotiation. In addition, some people are quite happy to be owned. People vary in their territoriality. In this case, as well as in the all-important case of room temperature preferences, similarity is of tremendous importance.

Possessiveness is so commonly mentioned that it can probably be considered a structural aspect of all relationships of the kind under discussion. In some it will lead to serious problems; in some it will cause no problems; in others it will lead to a relationship that satisfies the neuroses of both members of the couple.

PROCESS MODEL V: FAMILIES AND OTHER GHOSTS

In-laws would not be mentioned, it was promised, and the problems caused by families are usually not processes. However, there is one interesting little process involved, and while we are here an attempt will be made to distinguish various forms of familial interference.

There may be direct personal interference on the part of in-laws, who may try to rob the relationship of its autonomy (often by making their children feel guilty of neglect), criticize the spouse, or develop problems of their own to draw the attention of their lost son or daughter. A member of the couple may "borrow" his style of interaction from his relationship with his mother. This style may be entirely inappropriate to the mate. A member of the couple may "play out" a neurotic relationship with a parent and may, for example, act towards the mate as he wished he had acted with the parent. One member may act towards the other as his father acted towards his mother. This too can be entirely nonaccommodatory. Finally, one member may act towards the other as he wished his father had acted towards his mother. For people coming from unhappy or broken homes, the maintenance of an idealized relationship may be particularly important.

As suggested, these problems are not processes. Either bad ghosts haunt the relationship or they don't, however, something seems to happen that resembles Freud's concept of "the return of the repressed." It is often remarked that children become more like their parents as they grow older (i.e., after adolescence and young adulthood). This is not surprising. Most children seek autonomy from their parents, and one way of becoming autonomous is to behave differently from one's parents. However, many children behave differently than their parents solely to gain autonomy rather than because they differ from their parents in fundamental values, morals, and manners. In most cases, parents and children share fundamental values, morals, and manners. Once one has gained autonomy, one can behave as one really should. Hence it may gradually dawn on one or both members of the couple that their mate is gradually changing. The change may be unwelcome. The wife who was the husband's first female drinking companion slowly rediscovers the evils of alcohol. Her mother was right about her father after all, now that she has seen what it is like to see one's husband drunk. The wife's first considerate, liberated male finally understands how his father could come home from a hard day's work and not give a damn about his mother's boring day with her darling son.

PROCESS MODEL VI: INCONGRUENCE AND ITS CHILDREN

The preceding five process models have concrete sociological units (marriage, the family, courtship) as elements. They run parallel to the chronological life history of the relationship. The next three are theoretical and molecular, and have little to do with the facts of daily life. They are processes requiring only a problem, any problem, to be set in motion.

The first of these is based on the work of Jay Haley (*Strategies of Psychotherapy* and *The Power Tactics of Jesus Christ*). It is a process model of a process that goes nowhere. The second two are process models of arguments, which in turn are taken to be models of relationships going bad. Incongruence (Haley's concept) gets nowhere; arguments do get somewhere—usually to the end of the line.

Haley views relationship formation as the process of settling the balance of power in various areas of the relationship. He discusses three kinds of relationships: symmetric, complementary, and meta-complementary. In symmetric relationships there is competition, sharing of expertise, equality, and autonomy. In complementary relationships, one person tells the other what to do and it is done. In meta-complementary relationships, one person *allows* the other a symmetric or a complementary relationship, for example, by saying "You may dominate me."

Metacomplementary relationships usually involve incongruent messages. An incongruent message says one thing on one level and the opposite on another. The traditional example here comes from research on the so-called schizophrenogenic mother, hypothesized by Bateson and others (G. Bateson, D. D. Jackson, J. Haley, and J. Weakland, "Toward a theory of schizophrenia"). The schizophrenogenic mother implores her son to come over for a big hug. When the boy arrives he finds his mother verbally cooing but physically stiff and frigid. He is now in a "double bind." As Bateson realized, no one person is entirely to blame for an incongruent relationship. In presenting the process, however, one must make one person appear to start it; it is formally instigated by an incongruent message.

The wife who requests that her husband dominate her is a stereotypic folklore character; we have seen that such a request is similar to a request by an adult for parental love. It is an incongruent message. If the husband dominates, he is doing it with his wife's permission and in fact under her orders (it is a metacomplementary relationship). Following orders is not dominating behavior. If he refuses to dominate he is still the mouse he has always been. The woman simultaneously demands and rejects domination.

There are three possible responses to an incongruent message. One may "leave the field." But this is difficult. The double-bound boy cannot leave his mother—particularly when half of her displays love. The double-bound husband cannot leave. That is the kind of cowardly behavior for which he was indicted.

One can point out the incongruence. If the boy does, his mother will deny it and wonder how he could say something so horrible to her when she loves him so. The man can point it out, but the woman will point out that quoting obscure theorists is not manly behavior.

Finally, one can respond in kind. The boy can accept his mother's affection with an inappropriate giggle; he can arrange to drool sloppily during his hugs. In short, he can begin to develop the symptoms of schizophrenia, accepting the affection on one level but responding to the coldness on another. The husband can get drunk and beat up his wife. He is simultaneously dominating her and denying that it is *he* who is doing the dominating; he claims it is the liquor.

Thus incongruence breeds incongruence, and all we need to start the process rolling is an initial incongruent message. There is no reason to expect them to be uncommon. They can be expected whenever there is an incongruent attitude. For example, if a woman simultaneously desires and resents dominance, "Dominate me" perfectly expresses her ambivalence. To the extent that women are simultaneously socialized to accept male dominance and to develop into independent human beings, we can expect such ambivalence.

While incongruent messages may perfectly express ambivalence, they do not resolve problems. If the man does begin to be more dominating, we can expect the women to subvert his attempt—she doesn't want to be dominated. When the man ceases his attempt to dominate, we may expect the woman to again complain he is insufficiently manly —she wants to be dominated.

The woman cannot continue this pattern without the man's cooperation. It is not "her fault." It is probable that many men in this society are ambivalent about exerting authority. They should become increasingly insecure as they attempt dominance. This may appear almost as a call for subversion. But as they become less dominating, self-pity is to be expected; self-pity is almost a call for nagging.

Incongruent relationships may end. One member may simply bust loose. But because both members choreograph the dance, it seems unlikely.

Unlike the preceding process models, the two-stage nature of love relationships does not set it in motion. Once in the vortex of this process, however, the relationship will either dissolve or eventually hover in an unhealthy equilibrium.

PROCESS MODEL VII: THE LOGICAL STRUCTURE OF ARGUMENTS

What starts this process model is a behavior on the part of one member that the other member takes to be violative of the relationship. An objection or complaint is raised on the grounds that the behavior is not of the kind that should be found in the relationship. Of course, no such formal declarations are made. One member merely objects, complains, takes exception, or glares.

Let us postulate that P, the violator, does not wish to take responsibility for the behavior. He can accomplish this if he can describe the behavior solely in terms of its situational determinants. If he can establish that he had no choice, then it was not *his* violation and the relationship has not been violated. Attribution theory research has shown that people tend to give situation descriptions of their own behavior and personality descriptions of the behavior of others (E. E. Jones and R. E. Nisbett, *The Actor and the Observer: Divergent Perceptions of the Causes of Behavior*). The motivation in this case is obvious, but there are cognitive explanations also; we need not assume that P is merely trying to escape responsibility for his behavior. The evidence supports the proposition that people *see* it this way.

O may accept P's situation description. It may be perfectly good ("There was an accident and traffic backed up for miles"). It may be pretty good ("Joe was feeling bad about losing the Park Crest account and wanted me to have a drink with him"). It may be lousy ("I stopped at a bar for one drink and don't remember a thing since"). But O has two kinds of reasons for accepting P's situation description: its objective adequacy (what a neutral observer might think about it), and her desire to accept it. P and O both have reasons to want the behavior to not have violated the relationship.

If O accepts the situation description, the relationship remains as it was and no blame accrues to P *personally*. P has defined the situation as one in which anyone, an ordinary person doing what ordinary people do, would have done the same thing. But in the process he has defined himself as an ordinary person. In some cases this does no harm. O would not expect P to drive home on top of the traffic. But people have been known to refuse a drink with Joe, the Park Crest account be damned.

O accepts the situation description. Then P engages in the behavior again. He again attempts a situation description. The probability that O will accept it is now lower. O will be more likely to give a personality description.

It is logical to attribute at least some causality to a person when his behavior occurs in a variety of situations or even when it occurs often in the same situation. P *must* like a behavior if it is his usual response to a situation; there are a wide variety of possible responses, but P always selects one. If P can never resist the constellation of situational forces "making him" elicit the offending behavior, P is at best not trying to avoid the constellation and will more probably be considered the kind of person who wants to engage in the behavior.

If P continues to engage in the behavior (or if his initial situation description is rejected), O will eventually switch to a personality description; this will not be to P's liking. By making the switch, O has rejected *all* of P's prior situation explanations, even ones she accepted before. Now that P has a trait, he had it before, since traits are enduring features of the personality. This trait must have been operating as a causal agent the other times P engaged in the behavior. Therefore, P's situation descriptions were rationalizations.

P has now been cut off from situational determinants and is left *entirely* on his own. The penalty for attempting to keep oneself out of one's own behavior is the eventual receipt of it all back in one's own lap. P may consider this unfair. From an "objective" or "theoretical" point of view it *is* unfair; a well-accepted formula in the social sciences is that behavior is the joint product of the person and his environment. P has ignored this formula by claiming that his behavior was a function of the situation. Now O balances the causal picture by claiming that behavior is a function of personality.

During the course of negotiation concerning the correct description of the initial violation, new violations are likely to be introduced. P, for example, may take O's refusal to accept his descriptions as a violation of the relationship; it is customary to take the partner's word for such matters in such relationships. Thus the initial process may spawn other similar processes. This feature of the logical structure of arguments also allows it to "work" with no more than one initial violation. If P offers a faulty situation description again and again in the course of the same argument, it is as if he has engaged in the behavior over and over; and each time O refuses to accept the description, P feels violated. P may move to a personality description of O (nag, stupid, pigheaded). Thus one violative behavior is enough to cause an escalation to a more serious level of argumentation.

At this point in the process, P may either accept a negative personality description of himself or attempt to negotiate for a more favorable one. In either case, P must cease engaging in the behavior, and, if the personality description is negative, cease having the personality trait. Further behavior expressive of the trait will constitute continued and, by now, intentional violation of the relationship. The switch from situation to personality description thus involves the attribution of full intentionality. While P's intent is not to hurt O, he knows that engaging in the behavior hurts O. If he continues engaging in the behavior, he is intentionally hurting O. It is now *he* who is hurting O, since the behavior has become an expression of him rather than of the situation.

A personality trait attribution is necessarily more damaging to the relationship and more restrictive of P's future behavior than a situation description. Just as there is more than one way to skin a cat, there is more than one way to be hostile or irresponsible or selfish. Some of P's behavior not previously taken to be violative now is because it is an expression of the personality trait. If P previously forgot to clean his shoes before entering the house "because he just forgets now and then," O may now see this as indicative of P's general selfishness. That P's initial violation was selfishness of another sort will make no difference.

Thus trait names function as assimilatory schemata, making sense of previously random experience. To see failure to clean one's shoes as selfish simply requires a slight modification of the existing schema. It is like knowing how to grasp a ring and using this as a base of operations to learn how to grasp a baseball and a pen.

Schemata also operate along the temporal dimension. P's past behavior can be seen as expressive of the trait. Even worse, so can his future behavior: "Don't nag me, I'm not drunk, we're not even at the party yet." "You'll be drunk soon enough, though."

If P does not cease the offending behavior and personality trait, O must move to a damage description—claims based on P's obligations to the relationship. P is intentionally behaving in a manner that he knows hurts or bothers O. O has a right to object and to demand that P stop on the basis of the rights and obligations that are a part of such relationships.

Prior to damage descriptions, P engaged in his behavior to achieve something; a side effect was the violation of the relationship and of O. The damage description redescribes the behavior as more significantly a violation of the relationship and of O; the violation is now the *real* achievement of the behavior. P is no longer drinking to relieve tension. Now he is avoiding "not drinking to avoid hurting O." This is not quite equivalent to "He is drinking to hurt O," but it is close enough.

It is not solipsistic for O to take it personally. If P's relationship with O occupies a substantial portion of his life space, much of his behavior is conducted with that relationship in mind. If it isn't kept in mind, he is either intentionally violating the relationship or implicitly suggesting it has less scope and causal power in his life. A damage description assumes the relationship has its usual causal power; to act as if it doesn't is to violate the relationship.

When a couple gets to the level of damage descriptions, their problems are less likely to be resolved. When O is giving personality descriptions of P, her focus is on P and the relationship. When O is giving damage descriptions, her focus is on herself and her wounds. Damage descriptions are retreats for wound-licking. There is not much P can say to O, for O is focused on herself and her pain and is therefore unable to communicate. O is holding her stomach in pain. To be sure, it was P who hit her in the stomach, but the pain is stronger than the fact that P caused it.

Finally, if P does not honor these claims, O has nothing left to bargain with except the relationship itself. O must threaten that if P does not cease the intentionally damaging trait, O will have to terminate the relationship. If the threat doesn't work, O will either have to terminate the relationship or live with a new one, defined as one in which P can hurt O and get away with it.

Threats to the relationship are redescriptions of it with question marks. O says, "You are acting as if the relationship does not have the causal power I had attributed to it. You are redefining it as a smaller and less important relationship or one in which you have all the rights. My redescription is correct if you ignore my damage descriptions and do not make adequate reparations. Is it correct?"

In summary, arguments have four levels, each increasingly damaging to the relationship, each therefore increasingly indicting of P. Personality descriptions are more damaging to the relationship than situation descriptions because, as assimilatory schemata, they automatically produce new violations. Damage descriptions redescribe the violations "caused by" the trait as intentional rather than incidental. Threats to the relationship redescribe the relationship as smaller and less important than it once was.

Retreat from any given level is impossible. Personality descriptions invalidate all previous situation descriptions. Damage descriptions are withdrawals into the self—the pain blocks further attempts at negotiations. Threats to the relationship invalidate the relationship and therefore burn their own bridges. Damage descriptions are made on the presumption that the relationship is at full strength, but once the relationship has been reduced, the violated rights and obligations O claims have no basis.

This process is theoretical. A chemical process may be isolated in the laboratory and the result of the process will be predictable. In real life, however, many chemical processes are going on simultaneously; predictions are not as accurate. Similarly, while this process of relational dissolution may be isolated, real life arguments will not occur in a pure or linear fashion.

An argument may skip stages. If behavior is sufficiently violative, O may immediately threaten the relationship. If the relationship has been sufficiently damaged by previous arguments, a moderate violation may lead to an immediate escalation to damage descriptions or threats to the relationship. On the other hand, various forces, including fatigue, love, or acceptable explanations, may stop the process at any stage. Thus, again, there is no inevitability. The implication of the model, however, is clearly that arguments are to be avoided.

PROCESS MODEL VIII: A STIMULUS-REPONSE MODEL OF ARGUMENTS

The expression of aggression is cathartic. It makes one feel better. There is, however, evidence that if P expresses aggression toward O, not only will O's tendency to aggress against P be increased, but P's tendency to aggress against O, given another opportunity, will be increased (M. Kahn, "The physiology of catharsis"; L. Berkowitz, J. A. Green, and J. R. McCaulay, "Hostility catharsis as the reduction of emotional tension"; R. H. Walters and T. L. Thomas, "Enhancement of punitiveness by visual and audio visual displays"; A. Bandura, D. Ross, and S. Ross, "Imitation of film-mediated aggressive models"). There are various explanations for this finding. One is based on consistency theory. If P has aggressed against O in the past, either P is an aggressive person or O deserves aggression. The latter choice is more attractive to P. In fact, P may seek legitimate opportunities to aggress against O to relieve his guilty suspicion that he is at fault.

Another explanation is suggested by a process often initiated by arguments. In the context of arguments, participants often find themselves saying things they didn't know they had in them to say. When the argument is terminated, it is customary for P to say that these came out in the heat of the moment and were not meant. Thus O is faced with an incongruent message; "I said you were a blank and I offered reasonable supporting evidence, but I didn't mean it." O is justified in asking just exactly what P did mean and why P sent *that particular message* rather than another. O may believe P did mean what he said. P may come to believe it also. Examining what he has said, he may wonder how he could have missed it before. Thus, a complaint becomes codified and achieves psychological reality. P now has a new reason to be nasty to O (she is a blank), and O now has a new reason to be nasty to P (if she's a blank, she'd better find something wrong with him; or, simply, he called her a blank).

An exchange of information should, no doubt, be part of every relationship; but by the time a complaint comes out in the context of an argument, it is too late for a profitable exchange. In the first place, O has legitimate reason to feel deceived. She did not know P felt that way, and (given the anger with which P delivered the information) P has obviously felt that way for a long time (even though he may not have). In the second place, P has made the relationship worse by codifying a complaint that, had it not been considered in the context of a heated argument, would have seemed minor.

If this description of the course of information exchange during arguments is correct, one might wonder why people continue to say things in the heat of the moment they will later regret. The language of stimulus-response theory is valuable here. Arguments may be described as having a life of their own. Once started, they lead to the dissolution of the relationship.

Again, let us begin with P's violation. O responds. To O, it is a response, perhaps cathartic, but only to the extent warranted by P's behavior. O is satisfied. To P, however, O's response is a (nasty, unpleasant, unaccepting, insulting) stimulus. P responds. Having responded and summed up the situation to his satisfaction, he is satisfied; but O, who had merely delivered an appropriate response designed to settle the matter, is now faced with P's response. To O, it is another stimulus. This will continue until they have called each other every possible name, broken up, or killed each other.

While this structural model of an argument explains the continuation of arguments *despite the wishes of the participants,* it does not directly and specifically explain why arguing is harmful. The langauge of stimulus-response theory in addition allows a specification of various probable results of arguments.

An argument may be considered as one stimulus. People remember them as one unpleasant event. Furthermore, arguments are taken to have significance over and above the significance of their context. "We're arguing a lot" is a statement that indicates a relationship is not going well regardless of the content of the arguments.

At the same time, the specific content statements of arguments may be considered stimuli in their own right. The pairing of a specific content statement that would by itself elicit a hostile response with the stimulus of an argument as a whole will tend to strengthen the hostile response. The responses to the specific content statements, if they should be presented later individually, will be much stronger than they otherwise would have been. Therefore, the response will seem disproportionate. In other words, people can become "sensitive" to negative comments that have appeared in arguments. Now, if P responds to a criticism that seems reasonable to O in what O (but not P) considers a disproportionate manner, O has another reason to be mad at P. In addition, if the response (habit) has been strengthened, it will be elicited by weaker versions of the stimulus, thus increasing the probability of arguments.

Finally, there are several possibilities for stimulus generalization. Just as a personality trait may bring together formerly separate behaviors, O will give her hostile response to behaviors by P that are similar but not identical to the original stimulus. If O initially became hostile only when P was critical, and if the strength of O's hostile response becomes strengthened by the association of criticism with other insults, O may come to give her hostile response when P merely offers advice. The stronger the habit strength, the less similar the stimulus must be to the original stimulus in order for it to elicit the response. Hence O may eventually respond hostilely to P when he compliments her (because compliments can be taken to be attempts to make the recipient continue doing whatever elicited the compliment, and in that sense resemble advice). This sounds extreme, but then so do the stories in the news about the precipitating causes of in-family murders.

Theoretically, *any* stimulus present during the argument may come to elicit the response. O may find herself angry because P is wearing a shirt that he happened to have worn during an argument. There may be stimulus generalization along a temporal dimension. If, for example, the couple has had many discussions, some of which have led to arguments, eventually all discussions will remind the couple of arguments. All discussions will become arguments.

There are other possibilities, and the ones discussed could be more elegantly elaborated. Thus, it appears that learning theory terminology can be profitably applied to the complex phenomenon of relational dissolution. Perhaps couples could be desensitized to arguments by, for example, arguing in pleasant situations. Many couples may avoid discussing their problems out of fear that a violent argument will arise. In fact, such arguments often do arise, but there is no reason why they should always arise, or why they should be as frightening as they often are.

The preceding two process models suggest that a relationship will deteriorate or end if couples fight, argue, or even engage in seemingly inevitable counterrelational behavior. This may or may not be true; it is an empirical matter, and some evidence concerning it is offered in chapter six. Even if it were shown to be true, it is unlikely that more than a few couples would—or even should—restrain themselves from arguing unless they would have otherwise, at least until the dangers of restraint have been charted. As promised, no advice will be offered, not even advice as fatuous as "Don't argue."

PROCESS MODEL IX: FROM ROMANTIC LOVE TO LOVE

The transition from romantic love to love is the process of translation of emotions and fantasies into behavior that is expressive of those emotions and fantasies. The translation can be good or bad. When bad, emotions protrude and there is dissatisfaction with the relationship. When the translation is good, love is no longer solely located in interaction, as it is when the lover is on the rim; nor is it lodged in the person, as it is when the lover is in the pit and unable to get onto the rim with his loved one. It is in the relationship, which is now a relationship between people. It is in the behavior exchanged by the two people. They are not present as detached observers, as in the case of pit love. Nor are they lost or submerged in the interaction.

Love can be very unsatisfactory, and this section details some of the problems that can result if love is reached via romantic love. These problems arise from good translations as well as from bad ones; in fact, this list of problems is based on the assumption that the translation has been good; if it hasn't, the problems would probably be magnified.

When one has made the transition from romantic love to love, one is empty of the emotion and fantasy that has been translated. The infinite potential is gone; it is not that the future is mapped out with deadening certainty, but love is neither blind nor stupid. The loved one and oneself are well known.

Thus, love is not an emotional existence, nor is it a search for the unknown. To the extent that a person feels deprived if he isn't feeling emotions or exploring the unknown, he will be willing to throw away a "perfectly good" love relationship.

Love is not particularly satisfying to the ego. Joe is not wonderful in Mary's eyes. He is just Joe. *Joe* is no longer an empty, global, undifferentiated schema suffused with an emotion as he was when Joe and Mary were initially on the rim. He is still untranslatable, not because there are no specific contents to be translated but because the contents are too specific to fit the categories of ordinary language. For her own purposes, *Joe* is an adequate summary, for she knows what it means, just as the word *Hamlet* communicates the whole play to a person who knows it.

The problem is not simply cognitive. Mary will not gush over Joe. If taken to task for this, she will say, "But I know him, so why should I tell him what I already know when he knows I know it?" If Joe needs gushing and Mary provides it, then they have a parent-child relationship. Love between two adults needs to be between equals—otherwise, one will over-assimilate and the other will over-accommodate. Awe, on the other hand, is a one-down emotion; if Mary feels awe for Joe, the relationship is not between equals.

Why should we need to be told what wonderful human beings we are? I can think of only one reason: we doubt it ourselves. It is true that people pat each other on the back, comfort each other, give supportive psychotherapy, brag and boast, go on ego trips, put others down, and so on. The world is full of this kind of activity; but to assume, as many people do who write and speak about the human condition, that therefore giving support to egos is good and natural behavior, is to go too far. If Joe needs praise, Joe is tacitly admitting he will not and cannot go on without it. When we drive across the country, we must stop for gas. These pit stops do not move us across the country. Cars need gas, but what do humans run on? Books like *Best Friend* assume they run on comfort, encouragement, liking, and approval. Since the book is addressed to people who need such a book, it is clearly addressed to people who do not run on their own gas, who are dependent on the pats of others (or of themselves in their roles as their own best friends). It is clear that comfort and approval are the fuel and not the trip. They are a part of human life in the sense that gas is part of a car trip. They are not, as many assume, part of life itself but things that make life possible. The car doesn't care how it gets its gas—it would be just as happy to receive it while moving, as bombers do. If humans can keep going without stopping for gas, they will be much more efficient and have a more pleasant trip. They can enjoy the scenery instead of worrying if they can make it to the next service station. ("I just had to call, darling, I need a shot of comfort.")

During times of trouble, people in love do help each other. Unless, however, the trouble is great, the help is not visible in the same way harm (rather than intent) and people (rather than relationships) are. Dramatic deliveries of comfort are exciting, but a love relationship is continual comfort. The comfort is integrated into the couple's habitual interaction. If Joe comes home from a bad day at the office,

Mary is there, and they have habitual ways of interacting in which Joe can relieve some of his feelings of inferiority. He will not necessarily be aware of this—the relationship will have adapted to the fact that Joe will often have bad days at the office, and will require support. Practice makes it look easy—comfort will be given without the fanfare and trappings that often accompany it.

We are brought up on visible praise and support, probably for no more profound a reason than that children and adolescents are necessarily unsure of themselves, and, in addition, attend to the more visible aspects of behavior. It is hard for us to "get out of the habit" of taking our comfort with fanfare—it is like switching from vitamin pills (a parent-child relationship) to a balanced diet (a love relationship). We recognize that the person who needs to take tablets is deficient and not self-supporting, but we do not make the analogous recognition in the area of adult human relationships. We are "primitive" in this area. We need to have concrete, visible evidence that we are being supported.

In summary, while love relationships *do* satisfy needs for support and comfort, they do not do so in as obvious a way as we are used to; and so, just as the American public apparently takes vitamins by the pill when it is unnecessary, human beings may ruin "perfectly good" human relationships in the search for that which they already have in a better form. A pat on the back is a *symbol* of support; an interaction which is designed expressly to give support actually gives it. If Mary pats Joe on the back, he is reminded of his weakness. If she naturally, spontaneously, and intelligently hates Joe's boss, she gives him good reasons to feel better about himself and helps create a social reality in which Joe's boss is no good. *That* is support.

Our discussion of love's inattention to the ego seems to have switched from its first thrust, which was that normal adult human beings do not need pit stops. An extremely good love relationship involves people who don't need pit stops. This suggests another reason for the transition to a translated emotion bringing ruin to a relationship.

A recent survey by a psychologist showed that a large percentage of people claim they are shy (P. Zimbardo, "Shyness—the people phobia"). They would find it difficult, then, to begin love relationships. Put another way, the unknown and mysterious is frightening. And if a person is afraid of relationships, whatever efforts they make are likely to be over-cautious. We have seen some of the dangers of proceeding without sufficient caution, but over-caution is just as dangerous. If Joe has been dating Mary and doesn't eventually kiss her, Mary will become frustrated and angry at Joe.

Ironically, having a good love relationship is perhaps the best basis for beginning another. If one is still shy with others, at least one knows one is not stuck in one's shyness. The unknown will beckon more than it will threaten, for there is a solid base to return to. Being on the rim can be a frightening experience, for it involves demolition of the self. When young people fall in love, there is often no haven—as argued, Joe is better off if he has the old schema of Mary as the kid next door. When people who have a love relationship fall in love, they can fearlessly throw themselves into it, as they believe they can return to their old stable relationship. Also, since one already has a relationship, there is no need to proceed too rapidly. So the person with a love relationship is in an ideal position to proceed with the proper speed.

The discussion has tacitly assumed that the only kind of relationship Joe will seek will be another love relationship. That is not necessary, but it is probable, given that we tend to utilize old schemata. If, however, Joe seeks another kind of relationship, then this process is not bad, and does not involve the eventual abandonment of the old love relationship. One *must* master love relationships, and until one does, they will occupy much of one's existence. But once one has one, one is freed to find new and different relationships.

In summary, the transition from romantic love to love can lead to the attempt to form new relationships, which may supplant the old one. We have discussed three reasons why this may happen.

P wants excitement of the more obvious kind. If children like sweets because that is a taste that hits them over the head, some adults like romantic love because it can't be missed; plain old love is slow and steady, and easily overloooked. Furthermore, some adults want to continue to explore the unknown. The irony of this is that the application of old, habitual schemata (love and sex) to new people is not true exploration.

P wants comfort and ego-enhancement of the more obvious kind. The irony of this is that this kind of support is not real, but merely symbolic.

P is in an ideal position to begin a new relationship. The irony of this is that once he abandons his old relationship, he is in a very poor position to maintain his new relationship. Joe may be dashing, confident, and urbane; that is what attracts Susie; if Joe were to divorce Mary, he would be alone, dependent, and in need. No wonder the advice columnists have for years told Susies to avoid Joes. Joe will go back to Mary because Joe's relationship with Susie is based on Joe's relationship with Mary.

PROCESS MODEL X: THE FUTILITY OF PROBLEM-SOLVING

When people have problems, they try to solve them. This section examines three common approaches to solving interpersonal problems and demonstrates that they do not work.

Briefly, the methods are: The aesthetic method, which rearranges a set of facts to fit an explanatory theory; the pragmatic method, which changes the facts; and the cathartic method, which accepts the facts.

Joe and Mary have been married seven years and have two children. Joe is not doing very well in life, Mary is depressed, and under these circumstances the kids seem bratty. A dull and dismal and apparently common situation. What can be done about it?

What would Norman Mailer say? Probably he couldn't be bothered. Mailer is not interested in bourgeois unhappiness. Nor is Proust, although probably because he wasn't exposed to it. Shakespeare's characters are too lively. Cheever demands strange details. Bellow is too philosophical. Updike is obscure. P. DeVries tried it: In *Tents of Wickedness,* a man with a domestic problem tries the styles and therefore to some extent the content of a number of writers in the hope of finding a solution; but it doesn't work. Jack Kerouac!!! Yes, he would come in, talking a mile a minute, saying, "Wow, you got a great pad here, what a nice kid, yes, I can see it now, Wow, wife has red hands from days dishwashing, yes, it's ok, now listen, this is what we gotta do..." Forget him. He's a great guy, willing to bless any scene, but no real help.

One Easter a priest rode the Long Island Railroad praying for the men who rode the trains. He knew they did it only for their wives and children. Do we want him? No, for he accepts the fact that commuting is miserable.

On May 16 in 1974, Mr. Allan, the pseudonym for a fundraiser for an overseas relief agency who was recently divorced, wrote a piece for *The New York Times* entitled "Good-by, Scarsdale. I wish you well." He had learned that "crabgrass and clogged gutters are not the universal problems you thought them to be. There are other things in life." For example, "Brownsville, Watts, Appalachia, Bangladesh, and Rwanda, to name a few." He has also learned that "Commuting was never too tough but once you don't have to do it, it's a pleasant experience." Mr. Allan, in this article, is trying to switch the focus from what happened between him and his wife to irrelevancies. This solution is cowardly. The aesthetic method requires facing the real problems. Even if the method is a failure, it has more dignity than Mr. Allan, who name drops the locations of atrocities to make his divorce look small and unimportant.

Joe and Mary sit in a bar with Fred and Susie, two old friends whom they have not seen in five years. They have a horrible evening because Mary is depressed and quiet, which makes Joe nervous and banal. But let us put Joe and Fred together a night later, for they are old friends, although they are uncomfortable with each other because of Joe's wife and even his career, which has never been promising.

They select a fact: neither Joe nor Fred have made new friends since college. Why not? Let us slip into the general: After some thirty plus years of living, there is too much people would have to know about each other. It is, however, not clear why this should inhibit friendship. Furthermore, this is too far from the problem. Try again: The years between fifteen and twenty-five are the best. People are most buoyant, vibrant, and alive. By the time they are thirty plus, too many infinite potentials have fizzled into a ten buck raise, and we are all a little down. Still, if two people knew each other when, they can show a shadow of the old spark and have it recognized as a sign that under the tense silence of maturity "the kid" still "does his stuff." Clearly, friendship must be based on buoyancy. As we have seen, friends can relax and enjoy themselves with each other because each knows the other is independent, bouncy, buoyant. Friendships can be formed in the early years and they can be maintained in the later ones because hints and vestiges of the old self are sufficient to keep the illusion of independence alive. All one can see of previously unknown contemporaries, if one can get beneath the disguises, is their depression.

Furthermore: Adolescence is a time of states and emotions; adulthood is a time of traits. It is not worse to be an adult; it is merely different.

Furthermore: As Dostoyevsky's Underground Man knew, men of action know nothing and are and have been and will forever be on a rim of a circle with a small radius. Successful people are too blind to enjoy their success. Only the slobs know the joy of success, but they would forget the joy if they ever got the success. (The last sentence takes all the bitterness out of the first two.)

Select another fact: Women tend to get unhappy as they get older.

Mary has two fine children and has even returned to her career, but she is depressed. Fred at this point is kind enough to admit that Susie has bouts of bitterness despite a similarly "fulfilled" existence. Joe and Fred then suggest that their sometimes heavy drinking serves the same function. (The last sentence takes all the bewilderment and resentment out of the first three.)

Why are they discontented? Upon comparison with others of their acquaintance, they discover that the people who are discontented are those who (like Joe and Fred) have tried to "do something" with their lives; while those who never grow up and never try to get anywhere and never even see what their potentials are, no doubt out of fear of failure, are not discontented. "Wait until they have to take a steady job," say Joe and Fred. This doesn't quite do it; it is too bitter. Let us not yet escape to far off Bangladesh. Let's just say that the penalty for seeing is discontent and sadness. The penalty for success is blindness. The penalty for never growing up is never tasting the sweet sadness of resignation. What the hell, the stars are apathetic but still shine brightly. Joe and Fred give up trying to justify themselves and grab another fact. A theory of development from adolescence into adulthood is growing in the bar tonight. Soon Joe will be snatching any fact he needs from his own life to prove whatever point is at issue. His chronological life history with Mary is shattered by these rapes of the order of time. A piece goes here, to show the special problems of women (not of Mary). Another piece goes there, to show the results of failure (of men, not of Joe).

It is a process of affirmation. What appeared the night before to be an ugly, sordid, and sad little relationship is now an illustration of a wide variety of general propositions about humanity. These propositions, as a matter of incidental fact, happen to explain Joe and Mary's bad situation, and relate it to the rest of the world. The sad little relationship has been the occasion (but not the cause) of the erection of a theory, and the sad little relationship is explained by the theory but not so directly as to be embarrassing. This fact is explained by this wing of the galaxy of the theory. That fact, formerly temporally related to the first fact, is explained by the opposite wing of the galaxy. The relationship itself is not affirmed; it is still ugly, sordid, and sad. The affirmation is that something so ugly can be the occasion for the building of an aesthetically pleasing theory and can then be an example of the theory and explained by the theory, but not as it once was. The relationship is shattered, broken up, and scattered to various parts of the theory. It no longer exists as a congealed glob of sadness in

Joe's mind. It has been opened up. Fresh air is let in through the spaces filled by examples from other relationships.

More important, the theory is something like a god, who watches over all relationships. Mere comfort, in the form of "Well, A,B,C, and D all have lives and relationships at least as bad as yours," merely confirms Joe's belief his life is miserable. Now, however, it is as if the god, man-made like all gods but no slave, has said that all relationships have a purpose and that purpose is to serve their god and to conform to its dictates. In this respect, at least, Joe is without sin. His relationship fits the theory, but not too obviously. It might look to a casual outside observer that Joe's relationship was merely fuel for the fire.

If the particulars of the portion of Joe and Fred's aesthetic solution presented here are not pleasing to the reader, that is probably because Joe and Fred are hypothetical skeletons. Aesthetic solutions are devised for particular and therefore rich, dense problems (which does not stop them from having universal validity), and are furthermore subject to limitations of the abilities of the people who construct them. If the reader can do better, Joe and Fred would be happy.

The theory is Joe and Fred's edifice; however, they have only recently constructed it, and it is not completely built. In addition, what makes the parts of the edifice stick together is not merely that they fit, but, at least initially, that Joe and Fred function as glue. Enthusiasm will have to do until the logic arrives.

The aesthetic method puts the problem in a "proper perspective" by breaking up its usual form, combining the resultant bits and pieces with bits and pieces from other sources, and weaving it all together to produce a theory which is without value judgments. We have seen Joe and Fred make several moves to remove bitterness and create neutrality. The transformation of personal facts to impersonal pieces of evidence is the hardest part of theory construction. Without impersonality, however, any theory, no matter how elaborate, will seem like a rationalization. This is the tragic flaw of the aesthetic method: Joe must return to Mary, who has not made the relationship grist for the mill of a theory, and who would no doubt be angry and offended if she knew the uses she had served. The method may make Joe feel better when he is with Fred or even when he is alone, but when he is with Mary it does him no more good than the simple ability to withdraw. Mary has no desire to be cut up into pieces and fed to whatever arm of a theory needs a particular piece. Her objection to this will destroy the carefully cultivated attitude of neutrality, or her normal responses to Joe will bring back the relationship as it was in its entirety. By the time an aesthetic solution has attained sufficient psychological reality to directly combat the influence of the relationship as it initially was, there is no need for it, for the relationship is already dead.

Nor can Joe and Mary create their own aesthetic solution. If Joe and Fred erect an edifice, initially it will be weak, and will require the presence of both builders. Its very fragility requires that Mary not be allowed to contribute, and so she is left out. If Joe and Mary create their own aesthetic solution, initially it will also be weak and will also require the presence of both builders. Joe and Mary must constantly be present *as builders*. The minute one of them moves (back into his or her old self), the whole edifice collapses. If neither of them ever moves again, the solution has ended the relationship, although Joe and Mary will be stuck together for all time.

The aesthetic method has been presented as a way of dealing completely and finally with a problem. As a *post facto* rationalization, it has its uses. As an attempt to solve the problems of situations that are to go on, it is at best a waste of time or perhaps a temporary escape for Joe (if that is good for him). The aesthetic method does not change the situation, and as soon as Joe reenters the situation, the solution is of no value and may give him an illusion of superiority over the situation which will help make things worse. The aesthetic solution is a *distractor*. It is most commonly used half-heartedly as a ritual sop for the minor problems of everyday life, and it is in this usage that the dangers can be most clearly seen.

The most grotesque example of the aesthetic method I have seen was provided by a plumber. Working on my toilet, he sighed and delivered what was obviously a well-practiced line: "Toilets. They're just like women. You can't live with 'em and you can't live without 'em." I later learned he used the same line with women, except the simile then equated men with toilets.

Even so precious an amulet as this can be an albatross. No matter what the plumber's wife screams at him, he is protected. He does not even have to listen to her, for she is like a toilet running in the night. There is no point in trying to stop it; all one can do is listen with peaceful resignation and perhaps a wry grimace.

The plumber's wife won't stop screaming, for whatever she is screaming about will not stop. Mine was a passive plumber; the new breed of servicemen believe there are some things about toilets, stoves, cars, heating systems, and people that are just going to be wrong. That's the way they are.

The problems in the plumber's relationship will run on like the toilet in the night—and so will his wife. If he would even tell her to shut her trap or he will beat the hell out of her, he would have some quiet and her voice would have some rest. The aesthetic method is a distractor; it breeds passivity; it allows problems to continue and grow.

The pragmatic solution is best introduced by Dr. Benway of W. S. Burroughs's *Naked Lunch*. He is speaking of a Dr. Tetrazzini: "Tumors put him in a frenzy of rage. 'Fucking undisciplined cells!' he would snarl, advancing on the tumor like a knife-fighter" (p. 61).

I have had the following dialogue with quite a few students, but especially in the late 1960s, when identity crises were common. The student enters and reports being unable to concentrate, feeling very flipped out, that many things are going on in his or her life, and that he or she doesn't know what to do:

Me: It sounds like you'd be a lot better off if you dropped out of school for awhile. It looks like you have plenty to think about, and life experiences are an education in themselves as you well know, so I'd go over to the Dean's office and drop out right now.

St: Right now?

Me: Yes. Why wait? You're just making it harder on yourself if you stay around trying to go to classes and do your work any longer.

St: But shouldn't I at least finish the semester?

Me: Definitely not. If you're as flipped out as you say you are, trying to take a bunch of finals and write a bunch of papers would be dangerous and certainly you wouldn't do well, and furthermore you wouldn't be able to concentrate on all these other exciting things going on in your life. And it's much better to make a clean, honest break than to try to have your cake and cookies too; life wasn't set up so you could do both things at once, and what kind of cowardly identity crisis is it if you can simultaneously write fifteen papers and read twenty-five books? People are likely to call it a fake.

St: But I'd lose all that money.

Me: What is money measured against your immortal soul? This is a critical time in your life, and you don't want to do something now that could endanger the rest of your life just to save a few bucks.

St: Gosh, do you really think so? Just like that? What should I tell my parents?

Me: Don't tell them anything, just go away, get out of here, get away from school, forget it, you're old enough to do what you want, and if your parents don't understand, that's their hang-up.

St: Thanks a lot. I'll think about it.

Me: Don't just think about it; *do it*. Now. Do it while you got your guts up. It's not easy, I know that, but if you wait, it's going to be harder. Get thee to the Dean's office.

St: Thanks, good-bye.

That's the pragmatic solution: Do it. As I saw it then, trying to simultaneously do two contradictory involving things led to two poor and confused performances. Furthermore, it was cowardly. I rarely saw such students again, for the dialogue shamed them. In addition, I did not give them what they wanted. They wanted me to play Jack Kerouac and say "Wow!" over the incredible complex beauty of their lives. Instead, I merely told them what to do with those lives.

In retrospect, while I still respect my right to fight off the boredom of hearing about pseudoidentity crises by giving advice that I know won't be accepted by more than the 1 percent of the students who would drop out anyhow, I think I was entirely wrong in giving such advice; I should have given a Kerouacian benediction.

In the context of intimate relationships, the corresponding advice is "Get a divorce" or "Break it up." It is tempting to give this advice also. It is a waste of time to worry about whether to end a relationship or not. People who are "ambivalent" in this respect love to latch onto someone who will take them seriously. They have a counterargument for every reason that they should stay in the relationship. They have a counterargument for every argument that they should break up the relationship. They have a counterargument to the suggestion that they should wait and see for a few months.

Nevertheless, they are also unhappy, and deserve to be explained rather than simply disliked.

The most obvious and concrete failure of the pragmatic method has been illustrated already: it simply doesn't work. Like all advice, it can be used only by those who can use it.

Like the aesthetic method, it has more insidious dangers too. My flip advice is a symptom of the underground workings of the method.

The last time I quit smoking I was successful; I haven't smoked since. I did it. I don't know how. I tell people: I just did it. "Wow!" they say. But it changed my life. I have much more energy and many more ambitions and can tolerate longer dialectics. I am not sure I like myself or my new life. I used to be able to sit for a few minutes and look at something in silence while I smoked a cigarette. Now I don't waste time like that. If I have a drink in my hand, I can sit and look, but pretty soon I start thinking and talking incessantly. Sometimes I even bore myself.

To be sure, during the several months before I quit I was at least as revolting to myself—buying ten packs a day to smoke ten cigarettes a day is not my idea of dignified behavior.

Briefly, life is not a bowl of cherries; it is a vale of tears. Getting out of something bad is not necessarily getting into something good.

Should I have continued to smoke? I have used this example because almost everyone who smokes wants (or claims to want) to quit. Almost everyone knows that smoking is of no value at best, and a deadly killer at worst; so of course I should not have continued, and I won't go back. I am stuck with a longer but tenser life.

Joe and Mary are as they were in the discussion of the aesthetic method. Should they get divorced?

If they go about solving their problem in a brisk, crisp, business-like manner and get a sensible divorce, it may be a tonic for both of them, although one must wonder about the children. On the other hand, they may find themselves in a worse situation.

If they do, though, they know what to do: get out of it, and fast. "I wasted seven years of my life with Joe; I'm not going to waste more than one with you." The pragmatic solution encourages further pragmatic solutions. Mary will have less patience with a second bad relationship; furthermore, she will keep a close watch on the relationship to detect telltale signs of potential badness. John, her new husband, will not take kindly to this: "Just because Joe got drunk and beat you whenever he had a night out with the boys doesn't mean I'm going to do it too." "But darling, can't you see how I might worry after what I've been through?"

If John is "into" pragmatic solutions too, he will immediately file for divorce. Who can blame him? People who bring their old marriages into their new ones create a threesome that is a definite crowd. Out with the old and in with the new.

Am I actually suggesting Joe and Mary should live through their misery? One could hardly suggest it. On the other hand, we have seen the problems of refusing to live with misery. That is an evasion just as much as the aesthetic solution. Perhaps the reason Joe and Mary are miserable has more to do with their prerelational personalities than with their interaction. If so, divorce is no solution. They will have the same problems in a new relationship. Even if the problems arise from something specific to their interaction, divorce raises the specter of future divorces and begins to make it flesh. The decision not to tolerate discomfort lowers the level of acceptable discomfort and produces an unfortunate consciousness of the implications of the present for the future.

What should Joe and Mary do? There is no solution, of course.

They can either end the relationship or continue in their present state of misery. What is their present state of misery? In addition to whatever it was prior to their exposure to the principles of pragmatic problem solving, they now have to suffer the torments of ambivalence. Once the snake has entered the garden, temptation will always be present. It is as if each, internally, makes constant damage descriptions and threats to the relationship. That is why my advice would have been potentially dangerous were it not merely a symptom of the prevalence of the spirit of pragmatism alive in American society today.

In the "old days," Joe and Mary would not have been miserable. How can one be a failure as a farmer? How can a farmer's wife have time to be depressed? We do not, however, need to go back that far. Before divorce was easy and relatively respectable, many couples who would today look critically at their relationships did not then. When they did look, they did not have the expectations they would have today. "That's life"; but nobody believes that anymore.

Do I seriously expect or desire that the human race go back to the dark ages before the burden of understanding forced us to see how depressed Mary is and how much of a failure Joe is and how bratty the kids are? Do I want couples to suffer? No answer can be given. I have merely attempted to describe the state of affairs: When man was a sociological being, he did not question his relationships; if he did, he lacked the concepts to see them as bad. Now that we have personalities too, we suffer and blame our suffering on our relationships, among other things. This either makes our relationships worse or forces us into new ones which are likely to be worse due to our even higher sensitivities. Kierkegaard put it well:

> If you marry, you will regret it; if you do not marry, you will also regret it; if you marry or do not marry, you will regret both; whether you marry or do not marry, you will regret both. . . . This, gentlemen, is the sum and substance of all philosophy.
>
> (*Either/Or*, Vol. I: p. 37)

In summary, the pragmatic method of problem solving involves either fiddling while the relationship continues to burn, or leaving the fire to start another. It not only fails to solve, but makes relationships worse. If one is worrying about whether to break up the relationship, how much attention can one give to the relationship?

The cathartic method, like the aesthetic method, is very good for ridding oneself of the influence of relationships that are over, especially if one has had the good fortune to have been abandoned. Like

the aesthetic method, it does not solve problems. This deception in-
hibits actual problem solution when employed in situations that are to
continue.

Greek tragedy is cathartic. The audience knows what is going
to happen, and is therefore freed from suspense or hope. We endure
the sufferings of life without complaint, while motionless and facing
and feeling the torment directly. As the wolf cub of chapter two finds
that his mother's absence can be endured, so does Mary find that Joe's
leaving her or his adultery is not as painful as it seemed initially. We
all know that the fear of a tragedy is much worse than the actual
tragedy. All that is necessary is that we face the facts; soon, like
familiar words stared at, they begin to lose their previous significance.
It is a strange irony that when one falls in love, the loved one is
mysterious and opaque; while when one tries to fall out of love, one
attempts to make one's former emotion seem mysterious and opaque.

Soon Mary does not know how she could have been so upset by
Joe's leaving her and the divorce, and, bent but a little by life, she can
go on.

If, however, Mary applies the cathartic method to Joe's adultery,
Mary is digging her grave deeper and deeper. Joe has been found out,
has been properly penitent, and expects a good month or so of vicious-
ness. But it is worth it to him to endure it, for he doesn't want to leave
his comfortable home in Scarsdale; he is too old and bulging to start a
new life in Manhattan, much less Watts.

The cathartic method is often attempted with tears, but this is
somewhat inappropriate. Tears are grasping and do not display sufficient resignation. A look of mourning is more appropriate. Joe discovers this on Mary's face, and feels guilty—does she think he has done
other things wrong? Upon inquiry, he discovers that she has tried to
"come to terms" with his adultery, and has succeeded. To be sure, she
feels the kind of sadness that is often called infinite, but Joe knows he
has gotten off easy. However, infinite sadness is hard to live with, and
it is that as much as his light sentence that sends Joe into another
affair.

The major failure of the cathartic method is that in order to
purge sorrows, one must accept them; and to accept them one must
become a doormat, accepting the sorrows inflicted upon one with a
more and more mournful face. Joe cannot do anything that will evoke
a "human response" from Mary, for she has found the sanctuary of
sadness. She is unreachable, it is obviously his fault, and there is
nothing for him to do. If he swears off all sins, she is not obligated to

become unresigned. After all, what she has gone through. . . . It is no wonder he attempts to goad her into a response of some sort. She is lucky if he succeeds. People sometimes vanish into their depressions.

The cathartic method, like the aesthetic method, is best (and therefore worst) when used with another person. Tears are more appropriate under these circumstances. The logic seems to be as follows: Juxtapose the bad thing with tears. Remember, you are crying about event X. Cry as hard, as violently, and as loudly as you can for as long as you are able. Soon your crying will come to resemble the more beautiful, resigned, mournful weeping of tragedy. Why? Because tears and laughter, being physiological phenomena at least as much as they are psychological phenomena, do not go on forever. Satiation eventually results. Why this is the case is beyond the scope of this discussion, which is psychological.

Tears become ridiculous, silly, or disproportionate after a time. And so does event X. But only by association. People have been known to "get rid of" awful pieces of information about the person they were about to marry by this method, and then go ahead and get married. Crying about an awful piece of information, unfortunately, does not make it go away. If Joe finds out that Mary had an affair, cries out his misery and marries her the next morning, if he can continue to forget that Mary had an affair, or if her affair has the same nonsignificance it had the night before in the context of too many tears, then the problem is solved. But if Joe is the kind of person who would find such information upsetting, it is unlikely he will forget it for long. If what Joe finds out about Mary is something that is likely to continue, then Joe's goose is indeed cooked.

The better the partner, the better the cathartic method. We do not laugh as much when we are alone. A smile or chuckle serves as well. If we laugh in the company of others we know, they have the right to ask why we are laughing, for usually such laughter is a signal as well as a response. Similarly, we cannot tickle ourselves, and laughing alone is considered nearly as pathological as drinking alone. Again, explanations here are beyond the scope of the discussion, for laughter, tears, tickling, and even drinking are in the twilight zone between reflex and intentional action. In any event, in good company the cathartic method can be truly cathartic, and that is too bad, for like the aesthetic and pragmatic methods, the cathartic method is an evasion. Either the person suffers more for having learned to endure the problem or the person dismisses as unimportant what will eventually become major again.

The reader may have observed the major flaw of all three methods, and the preceding paragraph is placed at the end of the discussion of the cathartic method to emphasize it. All three methods are undertaken by one member of the relationship without the other; particularly the aesthetic and cathartic methods are better (and therefore worse) to the extent that they are undertaken with someone from outside the relationship who is "good at it." The methods are betrayals as well as evasions. Nevertheless, they are common, and they share a number of features: each gives a brief emotional sense of relief; each avoids any problems that could be faced; each therefore allows real problems to grow worse; each avoids the other member of the relationships and each may strengthen or create other relationships that may be harmful to the first.

Relationships go bad while these methods are being employed. The methods are not so much process models as they are facilitative of process models. They sap the energy of the person employing them; they distract his attention from the relationship itself. If, for example, a person is trying to avoid being backstage with his loved one; if, finding it difficult, he attempts the aesthetic or cathartic solution with someone else, he has effectively left the theater. If a person attempts to come to terms with his in-laws using the cathartic method, he will be further victimized by his in-laws. If the couple finds that the status and quality of the time they spend together has decreased radically since they got married, and one member of the relationship attempts to find comfort by consulting books on relationships, he will be spending less time with his partner, and in addition is betraying her. Do you want me meddling in your relationships?

As usual, it is not necessary that either member of a couple attempt any of these methods. Unfortunately, they are very common methods, and they are associated with friends. The aesthetic method is especially strongly associated with men in bars; the cathartic method is especially strongly associated with women; the pragmatic solution, strangely, seems to me to be characteristic of cross-sex friendships. This may explain the fear and dislike of old friends that husbands and wives have. It is not that friends try to undermine relationships; but relationships, when exposed to the view of an "objective, neutral observer," have a way of looking bad. This is because people do not know how to describe their relationships except from their own point of view. Since people in such relationships must give up their normal rights ("You mean she called you an idiot? How dare she?") in order to gain their own abnormal rights ("You mean just because you called him an idiot he called you a slut? How dare he?"), they often appear picked on. Typically, friends know only one member of the relationship well—friendships between couples are not really friendships. Without intentionally meaning to play favorites, it is much easier to see our own friend's point of view that that of someone whose existence is largely hypothetical. When one knows and likes both members of a relationship as individuals (separately and one-on-one), one is no good as a partner with one of the members in any of these modes of problem solution.

This concludes the discussion of why relationships go bad. In the final section of this chapter, we shall examine some forms of bad relationships. In chapter four, we shall see why bad relationships continue to exist. It should be clear that chapters three and four are attempts at an aesthetic and cathartic solution, and are therefore of no practical value; even if they were, we have seen the value of discussions with practical value.

VARIETIES OF BAD RELATIONSHIPS

Thus far, no attempt has been made to define or describe bad relationships. A list and description of some *possibilities* is offered here. The list is neither exhaustive nor mutually exclusive. It is a list of kinds of pseudoends relationships can come to.

Deep in the pit

The couple is aware of each other but is unable to communicate or interact spontaneously. What interaction there is, is painful and stilted. People in such relationships can be witty and charming with people outside the relationship, and then return home and turn back into vegetables—the contrast is quite poignant. Sometimes the couple manages to get a divorce, although typically it takes a good many years, for it is hard to rise from one's lethargy to see a divorce lawyer. Furthermore, even jaded divorce lawyers demand more than "I have nothing to say about the marriage and haven't had for years. It is a dead weight on my soul, which is probably already squashed." It is of such couples that people say, "I would never have suspected." But if you know them well, you can feel how ill at ease and hesitant they are with each other. It is not that they are shy, nor that they hate each other or want to kill each other; nor even that they fear or disgust each other. They are simply unable to meet on the rim. One might think they were dead or neurotic people, but they can be very pleasant and enjoyable outside of the relationship, even if their spouse is in the room.

Conflict-habituated

J. F. Cuber and P. B. Haroff's (*Sex and the Significant Americans*) phrase describes couples who have deadened on the rim of the circle. Cuber and Haroff describe couples who enjoy or need constant conflict, but I don't believe it. I employ their phrase to describe couples for whom conflict is a habit, of no significance, with no intention, for no needs or pleasures, with no outcome. Such couples can be heard screaming at each other night after night; in the morning they are unmarked by shame, exhaustion, misery, or satisfaction. No doubt they are moribund, but if I recall high school biology, one can obtain full-fledged reflexes from dead and dying frogs. Conflict is of no more significance to such couples than that reflex. Such couples sometimes get a divorce, but it takes time too, for it is hard to get them to shut up. Furthermore, they don't hate each other; they just feel contempt.

Some members of couples of this type that I have met are not pleasant as individuals, for they talk of nothing but what a creep their spouse is. They are not individually neurotic; they are just deeply involved in a very dead but very active relationship.

Peaceful coexistence

This pseudoend could also be called a collective monologue. The couple gets along perfectly, without friction, each doing their assigned roles, but there is no live interaction. It would be difficult to give objective criteria for determining if live interaction takes place, and if so, how much; but most of us can recognize relationships that are habitual patterns of action with no further significance, without intention, without accommodatory or assimilatory activity, and without the real presence of the participants.

Such relationships may also end in divorce after a good many years. One member of the couple "wakes up," as it is often put. That is, one member becomes conscious of the role he has been playing in such a pedestrian manner for so many years. As the stereotypic story goes, the other member is surprised and often wonders what else the rebellious member could possibly want. Often the rebellious member doesn't know either. When I told a boss of mine I was going to quit work to go to college, he couldn't understand. He pointed out that the business was all under one roof: The office on one side of the front, the I.B.M. operation on the other, and the warehouse in back. What else could I want? I didn't know either, and almost didn't quit; but I did know that the office, the I.B.M. operation, and the warehouse were not quite enough.

One could well wonder what it is that *I* want out of relationships. After all, can't a married couple eventually take each other for granted? Or shouldn't we be suspicious of couples who have been married for years who still haven't settled into a rut? It is difficult to talk about peaceful coexistence in neutral terms; I seem to slip into such derogatory clichés as "for granted" and "into a rut." Do we have less negative ways of describing such relationships? Does one treat one's two-year-old daughter as one treats one's twenty-year-old daughter? If not, why should one treat one's fifty-year-old wife as one treated one's thirty-year-old wife? If, however, she hasn't changed, perhaps it is appropriate. But I don't think so.

A child will develop along the lines suggested by Piaget's theory if only he has novel objects. Perhaps most of us run out of novel objects by the time we are thirty. It isn't our fault; except, Piaget's theory suggests it *is* our fault. The child comes to know his ring as something to suck on and grasp; but rings have other uses, which the infant is not ready to master. What are the uses of a person? No general answer can be given but we can add here that there is no reason to think that knowing (having adapted to) a person at thirty will guarantee knowing the person at fifty. Perhaps it is this that causes people in peaceful coexistence to wake up: they come to know that they do not know their spouses (and perhaps that their spouses do not know them).

Am I not asking too much? Development results when an object is seen in a variety of contexts. "But what do you expect? She has to be home all the time because of the kids. I can't see her in Mozambique." The complaint manifests the common lack of differentiation between spatial and mental location and the common preference for the concrete. There are lots of different ways of seeing people, most of them nonvisual.

For this reason, I do consider peaceful coexistence "bad." It may be very pleasant; but someday one member may look at the other from a slightly different angle and the illusion of familiarity will vanish, for an object known only in one context is a complete stranger in all others.

Studied absence

This kind of relationship is often described in novels (John O'Hara is a master here) and in gossip column accounts of the "jet set." He's at their summer house in Maine, but she's in California entering tennis tournaments; he's out bowling on Wednesdays and her bridge club meets on Thursdays; or they carry on separate affairs and talk casually with each other about them. In such relationships, the participants may hate each other or be indifferent. The relationship is maintained for convenience or because it's too much trouble to break it up. In fact, the couple may be "genuinely fond" of each other and simply have no time for, or interest in, relationships.

I will not attempt to explain why this kind of relationship is "bad." It isn't. It is merely stupid, clumsy, inefficient, wasteful, or senseless. If I had a third arm which dangled, useless, from my chest, I would have it surgically removed. Even if it didn't get in the way and wasn't unsightly, I would get rid of it on the grounds that it could someday become a problem.

One often cannot tell whether the relationship has suffered due to outside interests or whether the outside interests have developed out of dissatisfaction with the relationship. Since the latter is a possibility, the relationship should be formally ended, at least out of respect for the outside activity. If one bowls to get away from one's wife, one will not be as good as if one bowls because one likes to; in the latter case, attention is more completely focused on bowling and it matters more how well one does. Given that one is a failure in relationships, one might as well do well at bowling.

Neurotic relationships

This is a vague and broad category since neurosis can take many forms and is a term that is used loosely and easily. It includes relationships which are not relationships so much as arenas for fantasies of the people involved. The male who stays married to help insure that he will not become a drunken bum (but is still as much of a drunken bum as his wife will allow him to be without leaving him) is a pre-relationship neurotic. As we have seen, relationships may make neurotics of us all, but many of us enter relationships already neurotic. Such relationships require two neurotics. If there is a sucker born every minute, for each man afraid of becoming a drunken bum there is a woman who wants to feel constant self-pity.

Such relationships usually do not need to go through the phase of romantic love; consequently, they do not need to go bad. The ones I know of seem to have been sidled into. In general, the members of these relationships have not searched far and wide for the person who fits their neurosis perfectly. I suspect, therefore, that the particular pattern is not of much importance, and that there is a common denominator. This is, I believe, a love of self-pity and a desire for punishment.

I should emphasize that these relationships are not properly called relationships. They are not really part of the subject matter of this book. They are, however, the limiting case of the general tendency of people in relationships to be unwilling or unable to adapt to another. In other words, relationships in "peaceful coexistence" try to verify the sociological view of social reality. Neurotic relationships try to verify the psychoanalytic view of social reality.

The preceding list of categories of bad relationships has, of necessity, been written from the point of view of an outside observer (hence my extreme use of the first person personal pronoun). Anyone who has been in a relationship with outlines similar to one of the above knows it is not that simple. It feels different, and it feels bad. In the next chapter, we will examine what happens when people try to get out of their bad relationships, as, it will appear, they constantly do. As we return to a more internal frame of reference, we will become more sympathetic.

4
Conceptions of Why Relationships Stay Bad

IT IS A commonplace observation that marriages tend to last indefinitely when the relationship is bad. This is true (though to a lesser extent) of relationships with less formal institutionalizations. Some people claim to know no happy couples. In this chapter some explanations of this phenomenon are offered. As we shall see, one ironic aspect of the phenomenon is that it is often the badness of the relationship that makes its formal dissolution difficult.

In the context of this chapter, divorce and other breakups will tend to look like "lucky" (random) events rather than like intentional decisions based on mature consideration. This in fact seems to be often the case. An extreme example is reported divorce contagion: one couple goes, and then another, and pretty soon everyone on the block has moved to Reno. Joe and Mary's divorce is not the straw that breaks the back of Fred and Susie's marriage. A straw exerts direct pressure on the back, but Joe and Mary's divorce functions more as a reminder. Clearly Fred and Susie were not happy prior to Joe and Mary's divorce.

As with the process models of chapter three, none of these processes are inevitable.

A STIMULUS-RESPONSE CONCEPTION

The stimulus-response concept of the structure of arguments generates an explanation of why arguments continue despite the wishes of the participants. The same conception generates an explanation of why relationships, having become bankrupt of resources, do not formally dissolve.

Let us suppose that Joe completes a message to the effect that the relationship must end, and let us suppose that this message contains derogatory comments about Mary. As we shall see in the next section, this is not much of a supposition. Instead of waiting for Mary's response (he has learned something about arguments over the years), Joe immediately walks out.

Mary experiences Joe's last message as a stimulus, but she cannot deliver her response. She can, however, try to track Joe down to make sure she has the last word. Complete escape is difficult. Telephone calls and letters are hard to avoid. Joe will probably have to return to "get his things." Mary will catch him.

When she does, she will deliver *her* message, which may sum up why *she* thinks the relationship must come to an end, and will at any rate have countering derogatory comments about Joe. Then she can walk out, but Joe will now be after her to deliver his new summary statement.

Probably, Mary will not have to come after Joe. People get very involved in their arguments; it makes sense to say that arguments take place on the rim of the circle. They tend to wander from subject to subject—there are no guiding schemata to keep Joe and Mary on a track. In the course of their wandering, arguments bring up a multitude of topics, most of which are not fully explored in the argument. The seeds of many possible arguments, then, will have been sown during the real time argument, but only a few sprouts will have been explored. When Joe and Mary part company in the heat of the moment, they are not aware of this, for being on the rim, they exist only in the present, and are aware only of their recent interaction.

After Joe leaves, confident that he has gotten Mary good, he realizes that he neglected to respond to several of her sallies, having been occupied with responding to others at the time. In addition, perhaps, he realizes how many good ones she got in on him that he did not even hear, being so preoccupied with getting in good ones on her.

Thus, Joe and Mary separately and internally grow new arguments. But it is of no value to Joe to say something nasty about Mary unless Mary is present.

Relationships have been defined as interactions. They may in addition be considered a set of chains of stimuli and responses. Each stimulus leads to a variety of responses, and each response may be reached by a variety of stimuli. Under a given set of circumstances, the responses to a given stimulus will have different probabilities of occurring. Both Joe and Mary have cognitive maps of their relationship, and the relationship has the status of a complex network of habits. An interaction is one stimulus-response chain engaged in, in real time. At any given time, much of the relationship is "submerged," somewhat like the unconscious.

Unfortunately for the unhappy Joe and Mary, Joe's responses are to Mary's stimuli, and vice versa, and Joe's stimuli are not responded to except by Mary. Joe's initiation of sexual behavior does not take place in a vacuum, but is *attached* to Mary, since Mary is the primary respondent to Joe's sexual behavior. Moreover, most of Joe's behaviors are not so general; theoretically, most women *could* respond to Joe's initiation of sexual behavior, but almost nobody could respond to Joe's pet name for Mary.

Joe and Mary are caught in a spiderweb of their interactions with each other. Thus, if Mary has called Joe a pig, Joe's preferred response is to call Mary a whore. *She* called him a pig, so *she* should receive his appellation. To call Mary a whore to himself when he is alone in the hotel room he got when he left Mary, or to tell the bartender in the hotel, is not the same as calling Mary a whore to her face. It is not a behavior that takes place in the web of the relationship, and therefore it will not elicit a response from Mary. Joe may be trying to leave the relationship, but he can do so only by making comments that have no meaning to him unless they are directed at Mary, and unless they receive a response from Mary. His attempted departure reaffirms the existence of the relationship. Just as Joe's sexual behavior with Mary is not merely sexual behavior (Mary is an important part of it), so is Joe's hurling the derogatory epithet *whore* not merely hurling a derogatory epithet.

After all, the value of the epithet is only in the response it evokes from Mary. Joe has a cognitive map of the relationship, but the relationship exists in real time. He knows how Mary hates being called a whore, but just as a joke isn't funny until someone laughs, a comment isn't cruel until someone cringes. Furthermore, his map contains several possible responses to his stimulus of the epithet. If Mary is in a particularly bitter mood, calling her a whore only makes her sneer all the more infuriatingly. He must make sure she is in a sad mood, when the word will make her cry.

There is pressure for Joe and Mary to get together again. But suppose they don't. Suppose they both desire fervently to end the relationship. They separate. Each in isolation talks to the other—relationships, like arguments, have lives of their own. Their relationship is in the process of extinction, however. Mary, for example, says again and again, "Why didn't I listen to my mother?", a comment that has no meaning separate from the relationship because it has always been used to get at Joe. That particular stimulus-response will eventually drop from her repertoire as long as Joe's habitual response ("You should have, she told you to kill yourself once too.") is not elicited. Still, there is always spontaneous remission; teach a dog to salivate at a bell because food follows, and take away the food. Eventually he will no longer salivate at the bell. Try him the next morning, however; the habit is still there, almost at full strength. Eventually, spontaneous remission will cease. But pair the bell and food again, and the dog will learn to salivate at the bell more easily than the first time. The sight of Joe, even ten years later, may be enough to make Mary moan about her mother. Joe brings up everything she thought was dead.

If Joe and Mary never see each other again, the separation may work, although they will be tempted to test it to see if they really have extinguished the relationship. If they never test it, the relationship lies dormant, an unknown power; but cold turkey withdrawal is difficult in this society.

If Joe and Mary do meet again, there is little or nothing they can say that will not remind them of the relationship. Either Joe's greeting will be familiar to Mary—a stimulus to which she has several familiar responses—or it will be brand new, in which case it could be that Joe is trying to resist a relationship that still has a strong pull on him.

If, in romantic love, it is difficult to disentangle self and other, in (or after) a relationship it is difficult to disentangle self and relationship. If Joe has developed a brand new repertoire, it may be that it is *his* and it may be that it is his attempt to pretend the relationship doesn't exist. Rebelling adolescents have a similar problem. It is not clear to them or anyone else whether their new "life styles" have been selected out of respect to their quintessential selves or merely to differentiate themselves from their parents. Since children are to some extent a product of their parents, they *cannot* develop quintessential selves without being different from their parents. Thus, the ambiguity is unavoidable at first. The same is true of relational breakup.

Relationships of the sort discussed in this book tend to incorporate most of the response repertoires of the members. That is, there is very little Mary can do that cannot be interpreted as being a response in the network of the relationship. If Mary tries, Joe will probably be infuriated at how indifferent she seems (even if he is also putting on a good show) and will prod, perhaps with an insult. If Mary ignores the insult, she is trying to resist the still strong relationship, for ordinary people respond to insults. If she responds to the insult, the relationship is still alive and ill.

Thus, if a relationship is to end, both members must resist contact of any sort with each other. If a couple *can* decide that they must end the relationship and that the only way to do so is to avoid each other's company for a long time, the relationship is probably already dead (extinguished), for if Joe says maturely to Mary, "I think we should end it," Mary will probably have a strong tendency to think that Joe is just trying to put her down by being mature. Just as a joke isn't funny until someone laughs, Joe won't be mature until Mary replies in an equally mature way. Even then he may be infuriated that Mary is pretending to be so mature at a time like this, even if he wasn't *simply* trying to put Mary down by being so mature himself.

It looks as if the separation must be accidental or the result of some random event. Even then, of course, both members must want the relationship to end. As the next section will show, this is highly unlikely.

WHO DID IT?

It is well known that a divorce or similar breakup is not the fault of just one person. People say "It's just something that happened," or "We couldn't get along," or "It's both our faults." Some people insist it is all their former partner's fault, but we know they are deluding themselves. It is bad form to say it, although it is acceptable to secretly believe it.

Except when speaking in vague formulae or mouthing ritual chants, we don't know how to do anything except blame one person at a time. Let us then see why in fact it never is one person's fault.

The breakup of a relationship is simply not the kind of thing one of the participants can have nothing to do with. Consider an extreme case: Joe and Mary are happily married. One day out of what appears to be nowhere, Joe goes screaming out of the house and is never heard from again, although by proxy he divorces Mary.

Mary will most certainly be asked what happened. If she claims she has no idea, it is unlikely she will be fully believed. If Joe were "simply" crazy, why did he go to the trouble of divorcing Mary? Why did his insanity manifest itself exactly as it did—by leaving Mary? How could Mary have lived with Joe and not seen signs that something was wrong? Furthermore, she has been in continual interaction with Joe, and it seems unlikely that that interaction had nothing to do with Joe's going crazy, if that is what happened.

Perhaps she does know what happened. Joe had beaten her severely the night before. The next morning, when she regained consciousness, she told him she would leave him if he ever beat her again. This bothered him so much he went screaming out of the house.

Mary doesn't really deserve blame, does she? Perhaps not, but she had *something* to do with it. She told Joe not to hit her again. If only she hadn't done that, she and Joe would still be married. "But doesn't she have the right not to be hit?" Yes, but that doesn't mean she wasn't to blame *for the ending of the relationship*. She was part of a stimulus-response sequence which resulted in Joe running, screaming, out of the house. Furthermore, she put her own personal well-being over the continued existence of the relationship. "But what good is a relationship if one is constantly beaten?" Not very good, but that is irrelevant. In fact, it begins to look as if it were all *Mary's* fault that the relationship ended. Joe was happy beating her up now and then; and we can imagine that if Joe ran out of the house and killed himself, Mary would feel guilty. She would say, "If only I hadn't worried about a few little beatings, a human life would have been saved."

In any interaction it is difficult to separate the effects of self from the effects of the other; what the other has done has all been in response to what the self has done. There *are* cases where one person *drops in* on an interaction and interrupts it with something new. If, for example, Joe comes home from a bad day at the office and is very nasty to Mary, Mary is not to blame—for Joe's initial nastiness. Whatever happens next is her fault. She could have done things differently, she participated (even if by withdrawing), so the interaction is their joint product. There is no escaping it. A relationship is the product of two people and anything that happens in the context of the relationship belongs to both of them. It is only when someone drops something from outside the ongoing interaction into the relationship that blame can be assigned to one person. It is hard to do this. If Joe has an affair, Mary may blame him, but Joe will point out that if only Mary hadn't had so many headaches, he wouldn't have had to do it. That is, Mary will attempt to define Joe's affair as something that occurred outside the context of the relationship, but Joe will deny that and counter with the proposition that it was Mary's headaches that were introduced from outside. She will have another counter of her own.

If both parties are always at fault, why not say that neither is at fault; that it was the relationship, the peculiar things that happened between them, that is at fault? This is a legitimate point of view. As we have seen, a tragedy in drama is often defined as a sequence of events leading inexorably to the tragic end. The tragic hero often has a "tragic flaw." This flaw, which can be a personality trait, leads to the hero's downfall. Given the initial situation and the nature of the characters, the tragic end *is* inevitable; nobody had a choice. Greek Tragedy, however, was intended to be cathartic. It is nice to believe we are actors in a drama whose plot has been written for many years; but it doesn't feel that way, mainly because we believe we do have a choice. The above point of view, while legitimate, is not much comfort, especially if your former partner is trying to blame you. One person writes a tragedy. Two people construct a relationship.

The fault that both parties have is a watered down version of the kind of fault usually assigned. It is content free. It is guilt by association. It explains nothing. A tragedy doesn't explain why we had to start out as we did. Similarly, a theoretical position explaining why both people are at fault doesn't explain why we had to do what we did. It is of no value to blame a relationship, for relationships cannot exist without people. Joe and Mary have no choice but to try to blame each other or themselves.

Why not just accept the fact that one is a worthless human being, incapable of maintaining a relationship? *Probably because it isn't true.* If Joe blames himself, he can't be satisfied, because he is wrong —it was also Mary's fault, and it was also nobody's fault. Nor can Joe be satisfied if he blames Mary entirely, not only because that is not in accord with the facts, but because if it were, then he took it; he let Mary put one over on him.

This is a good place to begin discussing the dialectic between the need to escape without blame and the impossibility of such escape.

Suppose that Mary is a good cook, but also has a career. She neglects the quality of the meals, but Joe is understanding, and makes no fuss. In fact, he does not think of himself as not making a fuss. He does not think of making one—or of not making one. In the context of an existing relationship, Joe's behavior is normal and requires no special explanation. But when the relationship no longer exists (or when Joe imagines the relationship no longer existing), Mary becomes a stranger, and the relationship comes to be judged on a behavior exchange basis. From this point of view, Joe has been a passive loser, for he has put up with lousy meals.

Joe comes home from the office and sometimes snaps at Mary. She feels sorry for him; she knows it isn't his fault things at the office are going poorly; she believes he isn't properly appreciated. When Joe's behavior is seen from a strictly business point of view, however, Joe has used Mary as a scapegoat. Behavior exchange terminology is not, as we have seen, appropriate when a love relationship exists. To misuse this terminology one might say that Joe's gaining release from tension is Mary's reward and exceeded her cost of taking abuse. After the relationship is over, Joe's release is no longer rewarding to Mary—what did it get *her*?

Consequently, to leave a relationship with the other to blame is unsatisfactory, for two different reasons: (1) one has been taken advantage of; (2) one is the kind of person who can be taken advantage of—one is impotent, weak, stupid, dependent.

On the other hand, it is equally unsatisfactory to leave the relationship with the blame, again for two different reasons: (1) one has ruined the relationship; (2) one is the kind of person who ruins relationships—one is cruel, selfish, childish, incapable of love.

The problem is further compounded by the fact that the establishment of blame must take place in the context of the relationship. This is not simply because Joe gets no satisfaction from telling the bartender Mary is a whore. It is mainly because for every description that blames Mary, there is a description on the other side of the same coin which blames Joe. If Mary was too weak to stand the pace of Joe's fight to get to the top, Joe was too frenzied about getting to the top. If Mary had a right to see her parents once in a while, Joe had a right to an autonomous relationship.

Such arguments are real. They are not moot points debated for the sake of venting anger, gaining revenge, or establishing superiority. There really are people who cannot take the pace of modern life, and there really are people who take modern life too seriously. If Mary is too weak for Joe, then Joe is too pushy for Mary. These are the opposite sides of the same coin. Joe can say, "Mary was too weak." Friends and lawyers can agree, and this can solace Joe somewhat. But if Mary says, "Joe, you were too frantic," her position has far more psychological reality to Joe than anybody else's; and not merely because Mary was closest to the scene of the crime, or because the relationship demands that Joe respond to Mary's opinion.

Regardless of the opinion of outside observers as to how frantic Joe was in relationship to other American males, relational behaviors are measured idiographically rather than nomothetically. In other words, Joe's behavior is not compared to other American males but to himself, and his relationship.

Mary cannot *merely* say, "Joe, you were too frantic"; Joe 'and Mary have (or had) a relationship. Regardless of Joe's standing relative to people outside the relationship, he has been too frantic for Mary, and in the context of the relationship that is something more than being frantic. It is more significantly described as "being selfish with his frantic behavior, since he knew it would make Mary miserable." A personality description cannot be given in this context without an implied damage description. If Joe leaves the relationship without having *Mary* admit that it wasn't because he was too frantic, he is stuck—not with being frantic—but with being selfish, inconsiderate, cruel, and incapable of love.

Similarly, Mary would not like to leave the relationship with Joe's side of the coin up—with the reigning description of Mary as unable to take the pace of modern life. In the context of a relationship, that is not merely a weakness; it is "not trying hard enough to help one's husband's career"—it is being selfish, inconsiderate, cruel, and incapable of love.

Thus, it is not always the case that people raise their voices when they have nothing to say; they often raise their voices when they do not want to hear the other person's point of view, for they know it is correct in that it is the opposite side of their own coin.

In summary, because the relationship is an interaction, the end of a relationship must be the fault of both members (except in rare cases so deviant they cannot be handled by a general discussion). It is not the fault of the relationship, for relationships require people; blaming a relationship is scapegoating an empty vessel. Joe, however, neither wants to leave the relationship with the blame, nor does he want Mary to leave the relationship with the blame. Furthermore, there are two sides to most of the coins in the relationship, and unless Joe can get Mary to put most of the coins with Joe's sides up (unlikely, of course, since Mary usually can see only her side), Joe cannot leave without most of the blame. If he does, Mary will be after him with apologies, for she *knows* it isn't all his fault.

Nor can both Joe and Mary accept or split the blame. Once the relationship is over, or threatens to be over, Joe is stuck with his blame; it is no longer satisfactory to him that Mary has half. In fact, her half is an insult to him just as it is if she has all of it.

Consequently, while Joe and Mary try hard to banish their own blame, the relationship must continue until the blame has been settled. There is even reason for Joe and Mary to try to make sure all attempts at blame are kept within the relationship. If Joe is seen around town muttering that Mary is frigid, he is likely to be believed, at least to the extent that where there's smoke, there's fire. Everyone knows Joe is trying to get the relationship out of his system by blaming Mary; but he wouldn't be talking about frigidity if there hadn't been something wrong with their sex life. Furthermore, if he hadn't believed that in this area Mary, relative to the rest of womankind, wasn't pretty low, he wouldn't have mentioned it. Of course, in the context of the relationship, Mary's position relative to the rest of the women in the human race is irrelevant. Joe either is not as much of a man as he thinks he is, or he has not tried hard enough in this area to help Mary. Even if Mary were proven to be frigid with every male on earth, as long as Joe and Mary have a relationship it is not *Mary's frigidity*, but *Joe and Mary's problem*. If Joe says Mary is frigid (to himself, to Mary, to anyone else) he is trying to talk himself out of a relationship.

It is unlikely that Joe *will* be found around town muttering in the bars, for spilling the beans about one's spouse is another cruelty, one that Joe would rather not be accused of.

Thus, the couple is stuck with a rather difficult problem. Each needs to emerge from the relationship without blame, but each must receive absolution from the other, who would then by the same process (turning over the coin) be accepting the blame. Furthermore, that solution is not acceptable; for if each wants to leave the relationship without blame, each wants the other to leave blameless as well. This convoluted state of affairs produces bizarre maneuvers, which we will now discuss.[1]

People often accept blame, usually as a means of attaining another state of affairs. Joe may accept blame merely to gain peace; his acceptance may be similar to the ritual throat-baring of the wolf. It is incumbent upon Mary not to attack the bare throat.

Unfortunately, often the acceptance of blame, even for praiseworthy reasons, results in the growth of resentment. It was not after all, entirely Joe's fault. In fact, Joe often admits blame in order to get Mary to admit that it was her fault, which is what Joe believes. Mary may accept all or part of the blame. If Joe counters by insisting that she had nothing to do with it because he was to blame, and if Mary counters similarly, the amplitude of the oscillations of the blame curve may approach zero. If Joe fails to respond to Mary's counteracceptance, however, the score is not even, since Mary is left holding the blame bag. Joe has pulled a dirty trick.

On the other hand, Joe may offer to accept the blame; Mary may then counter with an acceptance Joe has not yet heard. That is, Mary may shed new light on the relationship and the sources of its problems. As we have seen, this may disturb Joe: "No, darling, it is all my fault. You see, I have been keeping secret lovers on the side for several years, and that *has* led me to be somewhat less attentive than usual." While this is extreme, almost anything will do. The simple fact that Mary admits she has been at fault may send Joe into a rage. It is one thing to admit hurting someone. As long as the hurt party stays around so you can lick the wounds you have caused, it is "ego-enhancing." It is another thing to know that the other has hurt you. We like to be in control; accepting fault is also accepting control. If Mary is at fault, Joe is out of control and impotent.

A maneuver with a more specific intent is the acceptance of a specific kind of blame in order to demonstrate reform. If Joe loses his temper too often, he can admit it and blame all the problems of the relationship on his temper and only on his temper.

Mary is stupid to accept this devious maneuver. Here is a legitimate and safe countermove: "Joe, the problem isn't so much your temper; it's the childishness that leads to the temper. I know you like to think of yourself as a big ugly bear like Marlon Brando, Dick Butkus, and Nikita Kruschchev, but you're just a little boy who throws temper tantrums when things don't go your way."

This example illustrates negotiation on the level of personality description, and suggests a way out. Many males do not mind being known to have lightning tempers; almost all mind being known as little boys. If Joe and Mary can agree that Joe is not a little boy but the proud possessor of a lightning temper, Joe will be satisfied; but Mary can still be wounded by a temper. Thus, Joe and Mary will have to come up with an equally satisfactory description of why Mary withdraws for days when Joe loses his temper. Mary must come out of it with as much dignity as Joe, but she must be granted a personality description that is not harmful to Joe. For example, they cannot describe Mary as "becoming so upset that she must withdraw for days to pull herself together," for then she is weak and Joe is strong. Nor can we attribute to Mary an iron determination to settle things by reason (she therefore withdraws until things have calmed down enough that reason can prevail) ; for then Joe must have been being unreasonable.

The recipient determines whether a display of temper is a manifestation of lightning temper or a juvenile tantrum. If Joe rises up in anger against oppression, he has a lightning quick temper. If Joe rises up in anger against Mary's bad coffee, he is a spoiled little boy. The recipient of Joe's temper is always Mary, and it is also always Mary who has to legitimate Joe's personality descriptions of himself. The virtue of withdrawal is similarly determined by its provocation. When Mary refuses to negotiate with the forces of evil, she is standing up for reason. When she refuses to talk to Joe because he threw a little tantrum, she is being just as childish as he is. As Mary's fortunes go, so go Joe's. If he is to make her look small, he must make himself look small; he must change his lightning temper into a little explosion of no significance. It looks as if an acceptable personality description must either make Joe look bad or be directed against Joe, neither of which is acceptable. The way out through personality descriptions does not seem promising.

Let us then assume Joe has to admit to a childish temper. Mary should not accept this either. Let us assume Joe will be able to keep his temper under control. Let us assume that at first he decided to accept the blame for peace and harmony's sake, and because it is more comfortable to know where the blame is—free-floating fault being as unpleasant as free-floating anxiety. It still can't be all Joe's fault; even if he does have a childish temper, it is childish of Mary to get upset about it. Problems therefore will arise, and for two reasons: It *is* childish of Mary to get so upset about a childish temper; furthermore, Joe will eventually look for trouble, for he will not enjoy being stuck with the blame bag.

A good reason for Joe to accept such blame is that if he can establish that his childish temper was the sole cause of the problems with the relationship, any further problems must be Mary's fault. Joe doesn't even really have to keep his temper. Once a flaw is out in the open and confessed, it is hard to attack. It is almost like double jeopardy: once one has suffered the pain of accepting blame and a negative self-description, it is considered bad form to blame the confessor for specific manifestations of his sin. This is especially true if he has been giving demonstrations of how hard he has tried to keep it under control: "I think I'd better take a walk, darling; that awful childish temper of mine is acting up again." If Mary has accepted Joe's confession that he has a childish temper, she has also implicitly accepted his temper's right to an autonomous existence, although Joe must struggle mightily against it.

Furthermore, if Joe accepts the blame, Mary feels guilty, for she knows it is not entirely Joe's fault. Joe can bring this home very nicely by waiting until he catches Mary at something he would have a legitimate right to object to, and then act as if she has done nothing by very sweetly saying he'd better take that walk. For example, if Mary bangs up the car and one of the children is hurt and Joe takes the walk, Mary can be understandably close to suicide or murder.

Fortunately, she will probably have perceived Joe's drift before then. Her response? Naturally, she begins heaping blame on herself. Soon Joe and Mary are involved in a contest to see who has the most sins.

This is ruinous. All confession ruins people. Because the confessions are political, people are likely to overdo it, to become histrionic, to reveal flaws that had nothing to do with the relationship's problems, and to codify. ("Yes, and when I was ten I threw my sister's doll out of the car at high speed and when my father went back to look for it, it was destroyed, and she cried all the way from Salt Lake City to New York.") Codified personality traits are gravitational fields, assimilatory schemata. Negative descriptions are particularly powerful (D. E. Kanouse & L. R. Hanson, *Negativity in Evaluations*). They should be brought forth with all the care of a newborn baby, who can be counted on to assimilate a good deal in the next twenty years or so.

Let us, however, assume that Joe does indeed have an extremely childish temper, and that Mary does have a legitimate objection. Let us assume that Joe sincerely tries to lick his problem, and succeeds. He has shown great strength. He has become a new and better person, and the world loves a person who has reformed better than a person who never had to reform. Joe has done it on his own; it is *his* success. He can rub this in: "You didn't help me control my temper, dear; you behaved as you always have, which is of course perfectly blamelessly; I did it on my own—and why not? Why should you have to help me control a vile little habit?"

Why shouldn't Mary simply be happy with her new Joe? She may be—if the relationship was one of those rare ones which would be very satisfactory if it were not for one little problem—but in most cases, Mary will still be dissatisfied (after all, tempers are not *that* serious). She can't blame Joe, for he has been a model of deportment; so she must blame herself or develop a neurotic symptom or feel impotent and helpless. Joe has done his part; now she must do hers, but she doesn't know what it is.

Blaming persons is a dead end, no matter how sincere we are. Relationships have problems. Only in rare cases is it legitimate to blame one person. Dissatisfaction in relationships often comes from inadequate translations of romantic love. It appears that we are in a primitive state with respect to our ability to deal with each other as individual human beings with personalities. Dissatisfaction in relationships is, therefore, to be expected. This dissatisfaction is not the fault of either person. We don't know how to blame a person-relationship complex, but our behavior demonstrates that we know (although as yet not verbally) that relationships are not the kind of thing that *can* be improved by changing one member.

I will demonstrate this by deriving the classic case of the alcoholic and his wife from a relatively normal relationship. It is said that behind every alcoholic is a good woman. A classic syndrome is the alcoholic with the loving, understanding wife who takes good care of him and weeps for him. The explanation may be found in almost any textbook on abnormal psychology: "It sometimes happens, however, that a woman originally selects her husband because his drinking satisfies her own neurotic needs. After marriage her need to dominate, control, and punish him or to be a long-suffering martyr may push him deeper into alcoholism" (Page, *Psychopathology,* 2nd ed. p. 323). Typically, such women get very disturbed when the husband makes a successful recovery. The game between the prerelational alcoholic and the prerelational neurotic is then over. Let us explain this in relational terms rather than in terms of the prerelational personalities of the participants.

Drinking may or may not be the real cause of difficulties. If it causes financial hardship or if Joe beats up Mary, it is a problem. But if Joe merely gets somewhat sloppy, or overly tender or touchy, depending on Mary's mood, it is not *necessarily* a problem. Drinking, however, like sex and money, is concrete, visible, and quantifiable. It is a good scapegoat. Let us assume that Joe, who drinks more than Ann Landers thinks he should, decides he is an alcoholic for the good of the relationship, and swears off the stuff.

Now problems creep in on little cat feet. Joe and Mary are tense with each other (for drinking was not the real problem). Perfect! Joe is obviously tense because "whatever causes his alcoholism" is still in there causing away. Thus, one night he goes out and ties one on, telling Mary he has tried, but he couldn't take it, and he will try again, but he knows he messed up good. She is grateful that the tension has been broken, and is helping, kind, and therapeutic. The next time problems blow in like the fog off the bay, Joe clears the air with a good clean visible drunk, and Mary mops up.

Someday Joe may get tired of the endless climbing on and off the wagon. He may decide to stay off it—he abandons Mary, who is of course miserable ("I thought we almost had it licked")—or just as bad, if not worse, he decides to stay on the wagon and succeeds. As the description of the classic syndrome goes, Mary no longer has anyone to comfort and punish. She goes nuts.

Let's look at it this way: Relationships are attempts to translate emotions into behavior. When we enter a love relationship, we have projects in mind, projects that can only be satisfied in a relationship with another person. Being rather primitive in this area, we do not have specific projects in mind. We tend, therefore, to over-accommodate. In other words, we think what we have is what we wanted—in terms of chapter two, we invent theories to fit the facts of the moment. Thus, we need the relationship to carry out any of our projects. When Joe abandons Mary or stops getting drunk, he is destroying the relationship. *Mary has nothing left to accommodate to.*

It was a lousy translation, but it was a translation. To a certain extent, "Joe had no right to ruin it"; but we are more than just members of relationships. Having prerelational and extrarelational personalities, we at times reach our limits, and must sacrifice the relationship to survive. Joe *has* tried—he has turned himself into a broken-down bum whose existence is defined and circumscribed by the fact that he is off the sauce. Look what he has done for Mary!

It is important to realize that Joe's drinking was caused by Joe and Mary together. Edward Albee's play, *Who's Afraid of Virginia Woolf*, provides a nice analogy. George and Martha have an imaginary child because Martha can't have children. After a night during which George and Martha reveal the terrible strength of their terrible relationship, George decides to have their son killed in an automobile accident. Martha is quite upset. She cannot, of course, call the police. Nor does she try to tell George he had no right to do it. He was *their* son, so of course he had the right to do it (people do not have the right to destroy others' property, but they can destroy jointly owned property). Martha merely says it wasn't necessary. Similarly, it was Joe and Mary's drunkenness; Joe has the right, therefore, to kill it, but Mary's unhappiness is understandable—Joe has ruined the focus of their relationship, and may even have left the relationship entirely.

He will not leave, however. Let us not forget whom the show is for and who the characters are. Joe has changed either to get one up on Mary or to keep the relationship going. If the latter, he will be happy to stay with Mary, for he will find nobody else. If the former, he will of course stay with her—his reform means nothing to anyone else.

In general, the acceptance of blame and the defeat of the problem further embeds the relationship in the bottom of the East River. Whatever little triumphs Joe or Mary may have are only triumphs in the context of the relationship. Consider the problem of a temper. What would it profit Joe to be mild-mannered in a new relationship? To be sure, Susie may like mild-mannered men, but the contrast effect is missing—mild-mannered men who have the demonstrated capacity for rage are different from mild-mannered men who are merely passive and weak. If Joe tells Susie he used to be an ugly old bear, she will recognize this as an attempt to show he is really a man. Similarly, reformed alcoholics are not socially in great demand. They tend to look run down, can always go wildly back to drinking, and, worst of all, remind us of what we could turn out to be.

In summary, the acceptance of blame is a move in an interpersonal relationship that almost always has negative consequences, but which tends to bring the couple closer together. George and Martha are not on the verge of breaking up; in fact, they are much closer than they were when the play began. Similarly, if Joe does stop drinking, Mary will obligingly go nuts, giving Joe and Mary's relationship a new focus. ("I can't leave her now, old chap, not after what she did for me when I was down and out.")

That acceptance of blame leads to further closeness demonstrates that we (act as if we) know that relationships cannot be changed by an autonomous change on the part of one member. Given the general level of unpleasantness in marital relationships, people are suspiciously tolerant of the weaknesses of their partners. To accept blame is to accept the role of a child in a parent-child relationship. Lacking a good translation, the parent-child relationship is at least temporarily valuable, for everyone knows the lines; we are grateful to the person who is willing to have the illness and we are grateful to the person who plays the parent. Everyone behaves for the benefit of the relationship, their individual selves be damned.

But people do try to extricate themselves from these self-destructive relationships. Let us return to an examination of the search for the way out.

Acceptance of blame at least leaves the door open. If Joe admits he has a childish temper, Mary *could* say, "Yes, I've known that for years, and I've had it up to here with you, good-by forever"; but, initially, she won't. Too much involved in the process of apportioning blame, she will grasp at the thread of spider's web Joe throws her. Only later, when the relationship has been through thousands of arguments, will Mary be ready to finally shoulder the burden and leave, not giving a damn that Joe is really implying that it is all her fault.

The closer the relationship is to reaching this stage, however, the stronger will be the desire to avoid blame, and Joe will not make such admissions. The more time and room one has to work with, the more blame one may accept. Nothing ventured, nothing gained, and the more blame one accepts, the more blame one may hope to eventually stick the other with. Thus, couples may bask in romantic love and confess sins in the hope of getting them accepted and loved; but as there is less time and room, there is less leisure for accepting blame and promising modification. It is time to start blaming the other. It is easier to walk away from an implication than from a direct statement; and so Joe may begin to heap increasingly serious charges on Mary *to make sure she will not walk out.* He doesn't want that because he doesn't feel blameless (nor, of course, does he want her to accept it all and walk out, for that would not only make him feel guilty; it would leave him abandoned).

Statements assigning total blame to Mary are likely to sound ridiculous: "It's all your fault, you've always been out to get me, you've thought of nothing but how to make me as unhappy as you can." Thus, one would think that eventually Mary would no longer feel bound, and would say, "Oh, to hell with you, you're just an ass." Unfortunately, there is something very pathetically vulnerable about a person who hysterically whines that another is a monster. Furthermore, it makes one feel powerful, certainly powerful enough to forgive or laugh. Furthermore, Joe is making himself into such a baby that Mary can count on being one up for months. Why quit when so far ahead?

The preceding has been a description of a maze with no exit, yet people can avoid blaming each other. Moreover, they do. I don't know how to explain it, but I call it *acceptance,* define it as the refusal to codify wrongs done to oneself, and discuss it in chapter six as a strength and resource of relationships.

MOOD SWINGS AND OTHER EVASIONS OF ZERO

People have mood swings. When the mood swings down, so does the self-concept and the view of the world. Everything looks bad. Some people leave it at that: The world looks bad. Others attempt to adapt to this vague, undifferentiated schema by developing a self-contained and logically consistent, specific, detailed account of the world from that point of view. Such people can tell you why the world is a lousy place to live in with excellent logic.

Some people take up residence in the downswing of a mood fluctuation; they are called "depressed." Depression often appears to be a defense mechanism—to put in proper perspective the revolting fact that one masturbates, one sees the rest of the world as disgusting too.

It is possible, however, to distinguish honest accounts of the underground from defensive blackenings. The "perceptions" of the former kind of account cannot always be rejected on logical or empirical grounds. They can, however, be forgotten by a mood swing in the upward direction.

When the mood swings up, so does the self-concept and the view of the world. Everything looks good. Some people leave it at that: The world looks good. Others attempt to adapt to this vague, undifferentiated schema by developing a self-contained and logically consistent, specific, detailed account of the world from that point of view. Do you know of any such accounts that cannot be rejected on logical and empirical grounds? If so, please call me collect or hold a press conference.

Novelists who paint pretty pictures of the world are considered "sentimental." People who always look on the bright side are called "Pollyannas." Psychologists who claim that man has a natural tendency to grow are called "humanistic psychologists," and are sneered at by many of their colleagues. Young adults who believe they can change the world are called "idealists," and adults who think things are really pretty good are called "naive."

Most people know that if the world is *really* anything, it is bad. As we have seen, empirical work in attribution theory has shown that the negative has a good deal of power. Still, most of us, after a certain age, usually sometime in the twenties, live a relatively habitual existence which is occasionally disturbed by states of joy or despair, but which for the most part is—*ok.* Everybody leaves is at that and nobody attempts to adapt to any vague, undifferentiated schemata in this case, for there aren't any. To be in a habitual existence is by definition to see nothing new that needs analysis. It is not necessarily a "shallow, superficial existence"; it is merely the nonmood traitlike state in which most of the work of the world is carried out (unless one listens to the prophets of doom, who may be right, and who believe that most people lead lives of quiet desperation, frenzied despair, or incapacitating anxiety) .

While it is generally recognized that the world is *really* awful and therefore best left unexamined, there is a panacea accepted by lots of very different kinds of people (who mean lots of different things by it). It is, of course, love. Some people try to love the world. Freud didn't think much of this idea—he felt that we only have so much to give, and so there's little point in spreading it so thin it will do nobody in particular any good. On the other hand, to the extent that his account of development has any basis in reality, the investment of too much love in any one person, as that of the child in a parent, is not a very good idea either. So "love" as solution can and does mean anything from a universal love for everything to one intense love relationship. Often, the word is simply paraded, as in the song which claims that sweet love is the only thing in the world in short supply. Nasty pessimists have no trouble with such nonsense. These days, there's very little there's enough of—except people.

The love that poets and song writers claim will cure the world is best considered a form of romantic love. But it is not clear how love cures. Perhaps the emotion can be translated to the good mood, which is nonaccommodatory, not particularly contagious, and evanescent—when it is not, we describe the person as being mentally ill with "mania."

When couples fight, they often swing down to an underground view of each other and the relationship. Usually this view is not completely elaborated into concrete details. It is an incomplete translation, leaving free-floating negative emotion, which makes things seem worse than warranted and masks the translation's inadequacy. But therefore the emotion is the rope we can jerk to signal we want out. As long as we have the emotion, we are not stuck in the hole, for it reminds us that the things we say, feel, and believe in the heat of a nasty fight are not *real*—they are too much the creations of ourselves. Consequently, negative views of the relationship usually do not have sufficient psychological reality to force the couple to break up.

Nor should perceptions from the hole be grounds for divorce, for they are usually of the defensive kind. They are formed with the guidance of self-pity, paranoia, and low self-esteem rather than with concern for an accurate rendering.

It is also the consequent inaccuracy of such perceptions that forces the couple out of the black hole. As many people have noted, too much sadness leads to joy; similarly, too much joy leads to sadness. In the present context, this is because the sadness is silly and ridiculous. In arguments, Joe and Mary, ordinarily rather decent people, become transformed into monsters with singleminded malevolence. This is simply too much of a transformation.

Nevertheless, something *is* wrong. It is as if the couple descends into the black hole in order to get out by bouncing off the excesses to be found at the bottom. On the way down and again on the way up they pass something more like the truth, with which they do not know how to deal.

The couple bounces back either to a mood of joy—this is common enough, especially in the beginnings of relationships—or to their stolid solid habitual existence. It is remarkable that a couple can one minute scream at each other and conduct business as usual the next, but it happens; and, when it does, the purely cathartic nature of the black hole is revealed. It is as if the depth of the hole and the zero of habitual existence must average out to the depth of the real problem.

Thus the couple never has a reason to break up. The descents into the hole are ignored as not real, and when the couple returns to habitual existence, there is nothing to talk about (although sometimes couples will promise to "talk about it" to facilitate a return from the hole). Consequently, when a breakup does occur, it is the result of a chance occurrence.

Falling Out of Love

Matt Helm has been a member of a highly specialized group of killers during World War II. He is leaving the leader of that group, a man known as Mac, to return to civilian life after the war. Mac tells him he must never reveal the nature of his activities. Matt says,

> "No disrespect intended, sir, but how are you going to enforce all that, now?" I thought I saw him smile faintly, but that wasn't likely. He wasn't a smiling man. He said, "You've been discharged from the Army, Captain Helm. You've not been discharged from us. How can we give you a discharge, when we don't exist?"
> (D. Hamilton, *Death of a Citizen*, p. 16)

Love is like that too.

People do not fall in love with each other because of valued personality traits. Mary falls in love with *Joe,* and will resist translating *Joe* into an ordinary language sentence with a predicate full of descriptive adjectives. We do not fall in love with lists of traits; we fall in love with *people*. Even if Mary does not actively resist translation, she does not meet Joe and immediately draw up a list of his traits to compare with her ideal list. (People can do this, but they are not in love.)

In addition, as we have seen, love is the kind of thing that transcends faults and problems. If Joe says, "I love Mary, but I worry about whether we can be happy together," he simply does not love Mary in the normal sense—his feeling is (taken to be) too weak or he is (taken to be) the kind of neurotic worrywart who fears love.

Because love avoids particulars, if Joe and Mary's relationship goes bad, they will have difficulty thinking that they no longer love each other. Since love is sufficient for the continuation of a relationship, they cannot break up.

If Joe becomes a mean and habitual drunk and Mary threatens to leave him, Joe can ask her, "Don't you love me anymore?" This scene is common in the movies and on television. The heroine thinks about it, bursts into tears, and embraces the worthless scum. She did not love him for his sobriety, and love makes matters such as mean and habitual drunkenness minor. Mary can say, "I love you, but I don't love you when you're drunk," or, "I love you, but you will have to stop drinking so much," and this kind of move is a threat that could lead to formal dissolution of the relationship. In the meantime, if Joe doesn't stop drinking, whenever he is sober he can force Mary to admit she loves him (after her initial anger is over), and the process starts all over again. Eventually, perhaps, Mary will file for divorce or walk out, but she will have to avoid Joe, for she still loves him and he knows it.

This is an extreme example, and lucky is the unhappy woman whose husband has an obvious vice. How can Mary cease to love Joe just because he's gone to fat? She didn't fall in love with him for his slender body (although she wouldn't have fallen in love with him if he had been fat). How can Joe cease to love Mary because the sparkle has gone out of their relationship? He didn't marry her for that (although he wouldn't have married her if it hadn't been there).

Romantic love is an emotion, and people in romantic love want to express it. Getting married and having children is one thing people can do with love, but *whatever* a couple does after they decide they are in (romantic) love is an expression of that love. When we say, "I love you," we are not *merely* reporting an emotion, although that may be all that is present at the time. We are reporting an intention to express that love. We are indicating that future behavior will be an expression of that love.

Future behavior is then taken to be an expression and translation of that love. Minor events are blessed and given additional significance by the love they express and translate. Does Joe go to the store for Mary to pick up her medicine? Yes, and why does he do it? "She needed it and wasn't feeling well." But is that all? "Well, I love her, of course. I'm happy to do things for her." Joe does not merely help Mary on with her coat. He expresses his love for her by helping her on with her coat. He helps her on with her coat lovingly. In the early stages of a relationship, the love will be visible—he will place the coat on her gently, caressingly, with a few soft words in her ear. If the transition from romantic love to love is the translation of emotion into behavior, then eventually merely putting the coat on should be a complete expression of Joe's love. As we have seen, when the daily existence does not quite embody the fantasy, often emotion remains, surrounding the mundane acts to simultaneously enliven them and disguise their inadequacy. When Joe begins to put the coat on "without thinking about it," Mary may begin to suspect that he has ceased to love her; but she cannot determine whether the love has ceased or whether it has merely been well translated.

Helping someone on with a coat does not seem like the kind of thing that in and of itself, without the prop of emotion, can embody love. There are, however, things that do: "What do you mean, do I love you? I work my fingers to the bone at the office, trying to get ahead, spend two hours a day riding the train so we can have this house in the suburbs, and I even take you out to dinner after a hard day at the office, and when I don't put your coat on in a certain way, you start complaining that I don't love you."

Thus, it is easy to make a moderately successful translation. Little gestures, especially if accompanied by little expressions of emotions, and the things we all must do—making a living—count as expressions of love. Until they stop, the couple still loves each other, no matter how bad the relationship has become. A couple may never talk and never have sex because they are too tired from showing their love for each other by working. This is not altogether ridiculous. If a family is on the edge of hunger and both the husband and wife have to work two jobs, what more could one ask? Communication, sex, tenderness, good times—the things that seem most like concrete embodiments of love—are luxury items under some conditions; therefore, claims that they are luxury items under somewhat less severe conditions cannot be totally disregarded.

Therefore, when the couple examines their relationship to see if the love has gone, they find themselves surrounded by translations. They may claim the translations are now empty gestures, that the spirit (love) has left them; but it is hard to tell if this is the case or whether the emotion has merely been adequately translated.

Translations do not merely exist; they are *lived*. Joe still helps Mary on with her coat after they have had a quiet but vicious argument at the restaurant where he took her when they first met. They have had nothing to say to each other for years, but Joe still takes care of problems with the house and children with total skill and composure, and so is very decent to her.

Friendships are more easily made during youth because everyone is simultaneously full of infinite potential (and therefore approximately equal) and nothing in particular (and therefore similar or at least not different). As friends grow older, of necessity most of them must become something in particular, and therefore differences in success emerge. Perhaps more important, friends develop different life styles. One is ambitious; the other lives for the moment. One is married with three children; the other is single. Friends come to feel contemptuous of each other's existence. Ambition is stupid—why kill yourself selling toothpaste? A series of unrelated unimportant jobs wastes one's life even if one has fun when not working. It is sad to see how tied down one is with a wife and three children. It must be very sad to always go home alone to one's apartment, and to have to find girls in singles bars.

Friends made during youth endure anyway, while friendships made later are less lasting. Another explanation of this phenomenon has been offered elsewhere, but here let me suggest it is because the enduring friendship was made when the two people were "in love with life"—on the rim in general. Consequently, the quality of interaction between the friends has a drawing power, and even if each friend can be heard to say, "I don't want to see that pig anymore," when they get together they have a good time, and even like each other for a short time after having been together.

Similarly, it is difficult to deny the drawing power of the translations, for they were conceived out of love. If Joe helps Mary on with her coat in that special way, it is hard for either of them to avoid *feeling* love. The next time Joe and Mary are about to break up, one of them may experience a moment of love (Joe remembers to change the empty toilet paper roll), which proves it is still there, perhaps hidden by the various messes they have gotten themselves into, but there, the eternal flame, and one simply does not throw love away. Again, the irrelevance of details is shown: if a spark of emotion can be elicited, the messes Joe and Mary have made of each other are as nonessential as all of Joe's virtues and faults were when Mary first fell in love with him.

Love has no official residence. If it is in behaviors, it is invisible, and we can't tell if it's there or not. It is not in the specific personalities of the members of the relationship so its loss cannot be found in changes of personality. Sometimes we experience the emotion of love, but that is not love's official residence, for the emotion is pressing for expression, even by such a literal translation as saying, "I love you," which momentarily dissipates the emotion. Suppose the emotion does not return for some time. Where has it gone? Given that love is so hard to locate, it is no wonder it is hard to tell if it has gone for good. To some extent, love is considered a state and an emotion, and it can always return. States are the kinds of things that come back; so even if it looks as if love has gone, it is not wise to throw the relationship away, for love may be just about to pop up again somewhere. Furthermore, to the extent that love has been deposited in interactions, people can suddenly find themselves caught up in a loving interaction, no matter how much they may have hated their partner a few moments ago.

Relationships that have gone bad are plagued by the couple's inability to locate love with sufficient precision to get rid of it or to know that it has gone for good. When relationships are completely bad, love's haunting is not a major force against formal dissolution; but when the relationship is not completely bad, love is at once an indication that it isn't and a deterrent to breakup.

THROWING LOVE AWAY

Even if a relationship has gone bad and even if love seems to have vanished forever, people are often unwilling to "give up on" the relationship.

When Joe tells Mary he loves her, he is at least defining his feeling as a serious one. Furthermore, "I love you" is an active statement, although it is not specific. It is a statement of intention rather than a passive report of a feeling. If our definition of romantic love is adopted for the moment, Joe is expressing the intent to discover the essence of Mary and of himself through interaction with her. In addition, he is announcing that he has projects he wishes to carry out with her.

Love, being serious, is not the kind of thing one throws away. We have seen the relationship between love and the experience of works of art. A love relationship and a work of art have certain similarities. Each proceeds from a vague concept of the whole; each must be translated into details; and each is best perceived as a whole. This comparison is not romantic—most works of art are as bad as most love relationships, and they suffer from the same kinds of defects—too sociological (in art, too much an imitation of an old and overworked genre; in relationships, too much like the stereotypic marriage) ; or too psychoanalytic (in art, with obscure, autistic symbols and juxtapositions; in relationships, with each treating the other merely as a symbol).

We put ourselves into our works of art just as we put ourselves into our relationships. To throw away either is to throw away part of ourselves. This notion is even a cliché; it is another force operating against the formal dissolution of relationships that "should" dissolve.

Unfortunately, a translation is a translation, and once the emotion is expended into a translation, even a horrible one, the loved one is no longer a mysterious vague schema full of infinite potential. It is not possible to "start over." The details of the first translation would interfere with the second translation, even assuming there was something left to translate. Usually there isn't. It is true that people fall in love with the same person more than once, but at different periods in their lives or after changes, when the former loved one now can be seen in a new light. The charge of love, once expended, is gone. That is why "working on a relationship" is impossible. The process of translation is guided by the vague, global schema; when that schema is expended, it cannot guide. The various combinations the couple may try out will therefore be randomly selected. Nor are they likely to be very good if the original translation wasn't very good. It is like trying to reconstruct Cicero from an eighth grader's translation.

Variable Forces

I shall conclude this list of forces operating against formal dissolution with three which are variable and do not really belong in a general discussion. They are accidental to the pure course of love and relationships. They are brought in from outside. While they do not have to operate, they do so with such sad, monotonous regularity that they must be included.

Inertia and the weight of possessions

Once a couple has been married or has lived together for any period of time, they have established a relatively habitual existence. No matter how bad the relationship is, Saturday night Joe and Mary must go to Fred's son's wedding; Monday morning Joe must arise at six A.M. and drive to work over the same route he has driven these twenty years. To break up the routine would be a good deal of trouble, and in the absence of compelling reasons, the couple won't.

In addition, if they do decide to break up, the various possessions will have to be divided, including the children. This problem can be almost prohibitive in some cases, but even a couple who have lived together for half a year will have some things to which they both lay claim.

It seems incredible that such minor considerations could be operative forces "at a time like this," but let us recall the way we felt about "home" when we were children. That was where we *belonged*. Even if we didn't have that emotional sense of belonging that children are supposed to have, we did have the cognition that we belonged—where else would we go? Since most of us had no alternatives, we belonged at home, just as love and marriage go together like a horse and carriage.

Given the strength of this feeling of belonging, the inertia is understandable. I know of college students who could and should leave home, but don't, on the grounds that that is where they live; so why should anyone be surprised that a couple is reluctant to leave what has become their home? It is Joe's home, and it is Mary's home. It does not have to be *their* home for the force to operate: children who live in houses that are not homes still consider them their homes.

The social stigma of divorce

Divorce is still not as accepted as the common cold. Employers, especially large corporations, don't like it, and employees know it. Children don't like it much either, especially when their Mom and Dad fight all night and during the day give them this song and dance about how adults sometimes can't get along even though they love each other. Not only does a divorce destroy the psychological reality of the concept of home, but children have to witness their parents lying through their clenched teeth. Friends don't like it sometimes because it is threatening—"There but for the grace of my cowardice go I." Other friends like it too well and arrive bearing pity and sympathy when it is most needed and most unwelcome. Friends will even try to help by cursing the partner, an action which of course revives feelings of solidarity with the partner. The landlord and the mailman and the garbage man will know, will know you know they know, and yet will look at you as if you didn't know they knew.

Parents will make the divorcing couple feel guilty by feeling guilty: "How did I raise you wrong that you can't even stay with a marriage for more than seven years?" In an informal poll of relatively happily married couples, it was their parents' reaction that was most feared. There is an amusing but probably apocryphal story about a modern poet who was said to have delayed publication of one of his poems until after his mother had died. His answer is an apothegm: "How would you like *your* mother to know you were being fucked in the ass by saintly motorcyclists?"

Divorce is not much of a sin anymore, but it is embarrassing. If in the past it was like venereal disease, now it is more like a bad case of acne; but nobody will be elected president who has a bad case of acne, not if Nixon lost the 1960 election because his upper lip perspired. The garbage man stares as if there is nothing to stare at; friends tell you it doesn't look so bad; and, just as the world is full of books, articles, and authorities telling everyone how to handle or prevent divorce, you can check with the appropriate media to find the latest medicine for pimples.

Parents' reactions may similarly be the most painful—"Oh, no, now I'll never get you married."

If a couple is merely living together or going together, this force is much less powerful, but friends and acquaintances will be sure to make the most of it.

I have juxtaposed a collection of reactions that do not really seem to belong together. The leer of the mailman when he hands you the alimony check surely does not belong with your children's tears—but it does. It again seems incredible that such minor considerations as the mailman's leer or even the parent's hysteria could be operative forces "at a time like this." We understand and accept that the children must be taken into consideration, and this is a common reason for staying together. But the rest of the objections seem of minor importance.

But the view that they are of minor importance stems from a very narrow focus. It assumes that we have only one relationship in life of much importance, our relationship with the member of the opposite sex with whom we have set up housekeeping. This is simply not true. Through the first part of life, parents' reactions are very important; later, the opinions of friends are very important. We cannot be expected to become suddenly indifferent to these when we get married. Mary is allowed to have a say about Joe's other relationships. That is, while we might prefer that Mary not object to Joe's friends and parents, we recognize that within limits she has a right to. Why shouldn't

Joe's parents and friends have a say about Joe's relationship with Mary? When they do, it is called meddling. When Mary has her say, at worst she is overly possessive, and if Joe visits his parents or friends "too much," or if they hang around Joe and Mary's house "too much," she is sympathetically described.

This narrow focus can be explained by a now familiar theme— our tendency to be able to deal with concrete, visible reality more easily than with other forms of reality. Joe and Mary live together. Joe does not live with his parents anymore. Therefore, Joe's parents should have nothing to say about Joe. Joe's parents, however, do not feel that Joe has stopped being their son because he has moved out.

The ravages of time

Particularly to the extent that Joe and Mary have gone into a very backstage region with each other, they will have forgotten the modes of self-presentation required by the hunt. That women don't find Joe attractive when he hasn't shaved in a day will surprise him. That he is suddenly aware of his paunch will frighten him—Mary hasn't looked at it in years. That his life is boring to himself and others will strike him hard when he attempts to describe it to someone he is trying to hustle. That people will wander off if he becomes ill tempered will bemuse him.

In addition, the world is changing, and has been for some time. One must learn a good deal to stay current.

The hell with it; have a fantasy instead.

Many people want to have another fling at life. One hopes that they sample symbolically first, for when they slink home defeated, it will not be with a perception of the desperation, loneliness, and vacuousness of the world of the single and free, but with an unpleasant perception of their own impotence. They will not have learned how good they have it at home, but that they won't have it any better elsewhere. It is better if their spouses don't even know they've gone; that way they can spare themselves the possibility their spouses might want to terminate the relationship or, worse, might take it out in ridicule.

In short, time spent in a long-term relationship tends to disqualify people for new relationships. It is not merely that people tend to let themselves go in long-term relationships, but that they become accustomed to a different mode of existence, basically horizontal rather than vertical, relaxed rather than ready, and flat rather than up and down. To the extent that people are aware of this, it keeps them from giving up relationships that are not perfect. People who aren't aware of it and leave their relationships are in for something of a shock.

A LITTLE PERSPECTIVE

Romantic love was described in chapter two in rather glowing terms. It was described as the beginning of an attempt to adapt to the complexities of another human being's personality. In addition, it was placed in good company—with the direct experience of works of art. Chapters three and four have been pessimistic about the quality of adult intimate sexual relationships in the United States, and much of the blame must be given to romantic love. Much of the problem stems from the fact that romantic love changes into love or into something else. The last two chapters have described how romantic love changes into something else, and in chapter three a brief list of some end states of the processes was given. Love, the translation of romantic love into behavior, has been largely ignored on two grounds: (1) it is not possible to give a description of a highly individualized matter in a general account; (2) (perhaps the only grounds for optimism in the account) we may currently be in a primitive state with respect to our ability to deal with other human beings. After all, historically speaking, the involvement of personality in marriage is relatively new and still largely confined to the West, and particularly the United States. Marriages used to be (and still are in most parts of the world) between sociological entities. Only in the last few years has the notion that a woman's place was in the home been threatened on a society-wide basis.

Marriage East & West, by David and Vera Mace, is an interesting comparison of marriage as it used to be (and still is, to a great extent) in the East with marriage as it is coming to be in the West. It is a highly liberal book in the following senses: the authors are open to all varieties of experience; they attempt to see the good (and bad) in all forms of family structure; they believe in the importance and worth of the individual (what I would call the personality), and refer to "our tremendous venture in seeking to create a society of men and women free to find themselves and to be themselves" (p. 53). And yet even though the book is less than twenty years old, portions sound like heresy, and would not pass the censor:

> *A man and a woman may be equal as persons in society. But as husband and wife, acting out their masculine and feminine roles in marriage, they are different and complementary; the concept of equality is meaningless here. A parent and a child simply cannot be equal, because the child needs the protective authority of his parents to give him the security without which he cannot grow healthily into an adult.* (p. 328)

The nonsequitur is not entirely explained by the context. Also:

> In Western marriage many troubles are arising because the reciprocal
> husband-wife interaction pattern is out of kilter. If the husband can
> no longer play his part as leader and initiator, the wife is paralyzed
> in her responsive function. She may retaliate by developing resentful,
> hostile attitudes and trying to tear him down. She then becomes the
> so-called demasculinizing female. The more she succeeds in destroy-
> ing her husband's masculinity, the more she deprives herself of the
> potential source of her own feminine fulfillment. (p. 329)

It is true that romantic love, which can exist only between equals,
has caused troubles in our society and in others; we have seen how tor-
turous it is to people in love. It is also true that the woman's movement, which Mace and Mace obviously would have believed has gone
too far, has been blamed for the decay of the family and morality. We
can see here that the woman's movement is the inevitable concomitant
of the high value placed on romantic love, and that both are the inevitable concomitants of the existence of individuals.

Let us take a brief look at Eastern marriages with respect to the
role of love. We shall see that most of our process models of relationships going bad would not operate. We must keep in mind, however,
that the well-structured family, with firm hierarchical order-
ings, does indeed suppress the individual:

> The security that the patriarchal family offers is therefore purchased
> at a price. That price is the severe limitation of individual aspira-
> tion. Ambitious and rebellious persons are doomed, unless they have
> the good fortune to inherit positions of power and prestige, to suffer
> acute frustration. Fortunately the age-old philosophy of the East,
> embodied in its religions, does not encourage ambition or rebellion,
> but inculcates resignation and acceptance. (p. 36)

Several of the process models are set in motion by the fact of
formalization. Formalization occurs in the East also, but often the man
and women have not met. As an Asian described it, " 'In the West you
fall in love, then marry. In the East we marry, then fall in love' "
(p. 132). The status of time spent together cannot decline; they have
spent no time together. The couple cannot move to backstage; they
have never been onstage.

We have seen the problems that result when people desire love.
People desire love and marriage in the East also, but it does not cause
the same kind of problems: "The Indian girl, as she grows up, is en-

couraged to look forward to love in her marriage, but not to allow this desire to be focused in advance on a particular man" (p. 133). In addition,

> *The Indian girl never experiences uncertainty because she does not have to choose. She has only to give the love of her full heart, unhesitatingly and completely, to the one chosen for her. She is brought up to believe that she will inevitably develop love for any man who is kind to her, and that the way to make him kind is to give him unstinted devotion and adoration.* (p. 133)

There can be no letdown when marriage occurs, for that is the beginning of love. Love is entirely appropriate, for the couple is married. One *can* achieve domestic bliss with a stranger if he happens to be your husband. And if one wants marriage too much before marriage, the excessive desire can do no harm to the relationship, for the relationship does not yet exist.

Furthermore, the problems encountered in translating romantic love into individual behaviors are avoided; the Indian girl knows what to do, as does her husband. But more important, there is no individual one must accommodate to. Tagore is quoted: " 'When at length they get this husband, he is to them not a person but a principle' " (p. 133). So the Indian girl merely gives love to her principle. There is no rim to be on, since she knows what to do; and no pit to be pushed into, since she can suffer no uncertainty.

The problems of territory and family are simply nonexistent. The woman's place is in the home. Sometimes it is in the "purdah," rooms with little or no ventilation and shuttered windows.

> *The number of Indian women who, as a result of this system, never saw the outside world, from their marriage day throughout the rest of their lives, was estimated as recently as thirty years ago to be somewhere between eleven and seventeen million.* (p. 75)

The family, particularly in the Orient, cannot *interfere*—the couple never leaves the family. The husband dominates the wife, but the husband's father dominates the husband. Everyone has his proper place and does not expect to go forward or backward, up or down.

What about Joe and Mary, miserable because Joe's career is bad, Mary is depressed, the children are bratty, and the relationship has gone to hell? In the East, as we have seen, resignation is taught; but in addition, married couples don't expect too much:

Fortunately, in the East ideas about love are not distorted by roman-tic illusions. . . . So the young couple do not ask too much, but are content with the simplest tokens of affection. (p. 228)

In addition,

In the East, men and women are more realistic. They do not marry primarily for happiness, but to fulfill their family and social obliga-tions. Any happiness that marriage brings is, therefore, accepted as a gift and not as a right. This being so, the probability is that far more couples are satisfied with their marriages in the East than in the West. (p. 241)

Joe and Mary would have nothing to be unhappy about.

Arguments and incongruent messages are our only remaining process models. Incongruence is a product of uncertainty and ambiva-lence, and we have seen how this is not allowed in the East. Everything is well-programmed; but surely a husband and wife could get in a self-perpetuating argument. No, that too has been taken care of:

Eastern marriage is weak in the development of interpersonal rela-tionships between husband and wife. The difficulty is that the un-questioning obedience of the wife, and the rigid separation of their spheres of action, prevent any dynamic interplay between the two per-sonalities. (p. 231)

One of the Maces' Indian seminars was asked what happened when an Indian husband and wife got into a "serious quarrel." The reply was that they didn't—because " 'the Indian wife has been trained from childhood to look up to her husband as a god. So in her eyes he can say no wrong and do no wrong' " (p. 232) .

The Eastern and the Western ways involve suffering. The Eastern way, as described by Mace and Mace, involves the suffering of many women and the few individualists of either sex. The Western involves the suffering of nearly everyone. In fact, we should not be as surprised and horrified as we seem to be that Western marriage is the disaster it appears to be. The suffering is just spread about more evenly between the sexes. Furthermore, Western suffering is more self-inflicted than Eastern suffering.

The real question however, is whether romantic love is a good thing. Romantic love has been criticized by many respectable thinkers. In the East,

Romantic love was outlawed. When we seek the concrete reasons for which this was done, we find three of them. Romance, it was believed, led to sexual license; it encouraged unwise choices of marriage partners; and it undermined the stability of family life. (p. 127)

The question is similar to the question, whether individuals are good things. Obviously, no answer can be given: but the evidence is that the individual, the personality, and romantic love are inevitable, and that they are developmentally later than man as a predominantly sociological animal. The United States is the California of the world, and here romantic love has become the reason for getting married (or living together, or whatever). Yet even in well-programmed societies, and even in the distant past, romantic love has appeared: "The attempt to suppress romantic love has not been easy. And it has not been successful" (p. 137). As Mace and Mace point out, the East is becoming more and more like the West.

Mace and Mace seem somewhat worried about the effect that the importation of romantic love will have on the East. They wonder if the East can handle it. Certainly the East can handle it—at least as well as the West has. Things are bad all over, and getting worse. Still, there is nothing to be pessimistic about, although there are no specific grounds for optimism. If personality is a relatively recent phenomenon, Piaget's theory suggests a period of confusion and maladaptation is inevitable before accommodation and assimilation get coordinated and equilibrium is approached. Things will settle down. In the meantime, things are bad all over, and in the next chapter I present some arguments that they are getting worse.

5

The Future
of Sex
and the Individual

THIS CHAPTER PRESENTS a few brief essays describing trends in society
that seem to be repressive of the individual and his personality. In
previous chapters I have held open the possibility that the human race
was in a period of natural preadaptational confusion about personality, particularly in intimate, sexual relationships. In the past in
this area (and many others), the sociological view of man has been a
very good one; that is, it explained much of the variance in human behavior. The sociological view is becoming increasingly insufficient as
an explanatory tool, particularly in countries like the United States.

Some of the more recent developments in sociological theory have
had to do with the analysis of rules and strategies we follow in the conduct of our daily lives. H. Garfinkel's "ethnomethodology" and the
voluminous work of E. Goffman are prime examples; but Goffman
admits in his most recent work (*Frame Analysis*) that there has not
been

> *much success in describing constitutive rules of everyday activity.*
> *One is faced with the embarrassing methodological fact that the an-*
> *nouncement of constitutive rules seems an open-ended game that any*
> *number can play forever. Players usually come up with five or ten*
> *rules (as I will), but there are no grounds for thinking that a thou-*
> *sand additional assumptions might not be listed by others.* (p. 6)

I shudder at the thought of endless lists of rules. There are so
many and they contradict and nullify each other to such an extent that

I often feel paralyzed and overly self-conscious. Unlike simpler societies of the past, United States society has many contradictory and
vague rules, and sociologists who make us conscious of them are doing
us no favors. A review of *Frame Analysis* promised me I would learn
why the stools in cafés are usually faced by mirrors. I missed this on
my first cursory reading of the book, and *I don't want to know*. Having read most of Goffman, I imagine it is something like this: We need
to know what kind of creep is beside us but it is very much against the
rules to turn one's head ninety degrees to scan a stranger. Now I'm
afraid to look in the mirror. Actually, I always was, for I thought
people would think I was vain. Such complexity is very tiring.

I have claimed that personalities are emerging from behind the
masks of sociological roles. Perhaps the breakdown of a massive, well-
coordinated social structure resembles the smashing of a pane of glass:
the results are small fragments, pointing in every direction, dangerous,
and best avoided. Perhaps, the proliferation of confusing rules and
strategies will merely insure the survival of the fittest personalities.
Only strong people will stroll heedlessly along the glass path. Weak-
lings like myself will refuse to meet people because of uncertainty as to
what to call them, while strong people will call everyone whatever they
feel like calling them.

It may be, however, that the mindless rather than the strong will
survive. Many people resent being called by their first name by people
they don't know; any reasonably sensitive person, it seems to me,
would inquire, although not necessarily directly, how another would
prefer to be addressed. Well, if the man of direct, thoughtless action is
the man of the future, I am glad I only have a few more decades to go.

In addition, it is an irony that personality and the population explosion are arising simultaneously.

The preceding has been an attempt to put into some perspective
my rather vague claims scattered throughout the first four chapters
that we were "just going through a phase" in our interactions with
human beings, particularly in our intimate sexual relationships. While
in the past there were rugged individualists and personalities, they
usually existed in science, the arts, exploration, and—accepting Seidenberg's claim that romantic love was primarily a homosexual phenomenon—in homosexual relationships. Now, I have suggested, the
human being as an individual is emerging in ordinary interpersonal
relationships. Now, everyone can be an individual—not everyone can
be a scientist, painter, or explorer.

While the arguments presented so far tend to support this position, I have others to present that are equally legitimate, but in opposition to the claim that personalities are emerging in interpersonal relationships. The presentation will take the form of three brief essays.

WHY THE SEXUAL REVOLUTION IS ANTISEXUAL

In 1971, Viktor Frankl, in a lecture cited by Cartwright, reported on a survey of 8,000 American college students.[1] While making "a lot of money" was the primary concern of only 16%, the primary concern of 78% was to " 'find a meaning and purpose in my life.' " Since the categories Frankl employed appear to have been mutually exclusive, this leaves only 6% of the sample free to have other "primary concerns." This sounds unlikely, and suggests either that Frankl offered only a few other possibilities, all at least as declassé as "making a lot of money"; or, that he used content analysis of open-ended responses and showed extreme favoritism to his favorite category. "Finding meaning and purpose" is a sufficiently broad goal to include almost anything. After all, even making a lot of money is a purpose. It is only that if that is your purpose, your primary concern cannot be to find a meaning and purpose in your life, for you have already found it—it is to make a lot of money. So perhaps Frankl's results merely reflect a normal lack of total certainty in college students as to what they plan to do with their lives.

The true significance of this "survey" is that Frankl got results and that they can be reported seriously.

Let us ask a factory worker at the beginning of the industrial revolution what his primary concern is. If he has the time to answer the question, he will tell you he wants to get some sleep, hopes sometime his family will have enough to eat, and wishes he could get Sundays off. His college-age son would have been working since he was eight years old; if he had taken time off to wonder about the meaning and purpose in life, his father would have given him five good purposes to avoid, and sent him back to the sweatshop. By eighteen or nineteen, he would have had his horizons narrowed or been dead of starvation.

We do not even need to go back in time. There are hundreds of millions of people semialive today who do not have a time perspective or a purpose even as exalted as that of our factory worker. When on the brink of starvation, one does not hope for Sundays off, but for a job. One does not hope for enough to eat, but for a crust of bread.

The factory worker in the industrial revolution may be at just about the historical mean for this planet. For every person close to death by starvation, there may be one who doesn't know what to do with himself (has as a primary concern the discovery of a meaning and purpose in life). If the factory worker is about average, then it would appear that the variance around the mean is increasing, for there are more people starving and more people without purpose than at any other time in history. We in the United States are on the latter wing of the curve, so let us explore it a little further.

Some years later, our factory worker will have attained a thirty-five hour, four and one half day work week. He is drinking beer and watching a baseball game on his color television set. Ask him his primary concern. I hope he says it is getting you the hell out of the room so he can watch the game. Unfortunately, he probably has become "sensitive." He does not wish to be associated with Archie Bunker, who is not so much a lovable bigot as a man who insists on maintaining completely insular concerns. Our factory worker probably agrees with Creon in Anouilh's *Antigone* that life is more than beer and skittles. Perhaps he has taken up a hobby and now works twelve hours a day seven days a week collecting coins.

Many years ago in our society (and now in many societies), people had plenty to do to stay alive. That, therefore, was their primary concern. It was also the meaning and purpose of their lives. When they had "free" time, they saw no need to take up another concern *as primary*. They already had their primary concern, and were free to play during whatever free time they had. That is, they were not required to engage in what they considered serious, important activities when they weren't trying to survive. But now keeping alive is not as hard nor nearly as time-consuming. Even when jobs are scarce, survival pure and simple has been too easy for too many people for it to be a legitimate primary concern. Man no longer lives by bread alone.

As many observers have pointed out, today very few occupations are considered inherently worthwhile. Garbage men become sanitation engineers. Still, all they do is pick up the refuse of others and deposit it elsewhere. Obviously an important job, it is equally obviously considered demeaning. Who would say, "My primary concern in life is to make sure the people of this city have their garbage collected efficiently?" Perhaps the top man in the garbage administration would say it because he is paid $50,000 to be top man in the garbage administration.

All of these familiar trends in modern society are particularly strong in college students, who do not read the works of Kerouac,

Shakespeare, Kierkegaard, Proust, and Swift in preparation for a life of picking up garbage.

Let me ask myself what my primary concern was circa ten years before Frankl's survey, when I graduated from high school and entered college, and let me be something of a caricature of a stereotype of a male of sixteen to twenty in the period of 1959–1963. It is necessary to be relatively specific if one takes the following quick and dirty, off-the-cuff, armchair amateur historical sociology seriously: In the 50s, the college generation's primary concern was security, a reaction to growing up during the war; in the later 60s, it was getting the government, a game similar to Albee's getting the guest and humping the hostess. This game was played in reaction to growing up in the shadow of big gaseous mushrooms and under the influence of little psychoactive ones. In the early 70s, if we take Frankl's results seriously, it had mellowed into a search for meaning and purpose. For a short period of time life was soft, there was nothing to do, and there wasn't even anything to rebel against. Fortunately, before the college generation died of boredom, high status jobs became scarce—partially, because many high status jobs had become low status. By the middle 70s the primary concern of the college generation has become getting into professional school and to hell with meaning and purpose. But between 1959 and 1963 for males of sixteen to twenty it was different.

My primary concern in 1961 was getting it. I can only speak for my brothers; my sisters must have been up to something somewhat different, or getting it wouldn't have been our primary concern. They couldn't have been completely unresponsive, however, for complete lack of satisfaction breeds apathy and somnolence, and my brothers were frenetic in their pursuit of it. The burning questions of the day were "What'd you get?" or "D'ja get any?" We talked of girls from dawn till midnight, planned strategies, dreamed of sex, got some sometimes but never enough—only enough to make us want more. We made the criterion for success in life not academic success, not athletic prowess, not achievements in the arts, not wealth or possessions, not notoriety. None of this profited us anything unless we got It, and he who got It could not be faulted, for the rags to riches story of the day was about a guy who was ugly with pimples, not bright, skinny and clumsy, with a stammer. Everyone sneered at him; he was the high-school scapegoat. Then it came out: he was getting it with Susie the Cheerleader, who had been quoted as saying, "Well, girls, he ain't much except in one way but that's enough."

What did we do that was not subordinate to our desire to get it with the fair sex? Did Joe care that he had gotten into Harvard? You bet. It increased the probability Mary would give him some. Was Fred glad he threw four touchdown passes? Of course. Susie liked football heroes.

Slipping safely back into jargon, sex pervaded our life spaces.

We were indeed uncool, and I have known the contempt of the current college generation. It is often a kindly and curious contempt, for they simply don't understand how it could be that boys and girls would not do it when they wanted to. They do not even have residual "hang-ups" and so they do not have to sneer. They are so much more, well, *mature* about such things, and the excitement of older people about the sexual revolution seems odd to them. Their maturity makes us feel simultaneously ashamed of ourselves and (of course, what else?) lecherous. They too are ashamed—of us. Do we have to, they ask, make such a big deal about it (sex and its revolution)? "I mean, it's no big deal. If you like it, fuck it."

Precisely. Today's slogan. If you like it, fuck it. Why not? In *Naked Lunch:* " 'Let it be! And no holes barred!!!' " (W. S. Burroughs, p. 79).

Let us introduce an analogy. In the old days, people spent much time in the preparation and eating of meals. For example, the American Indians first had to hunt; then they would have a feast. Some tribes had elaborate ceremonies about the harvest. The whole process of obtaining and consuming food took up much of the time and energy of the Indians, and so it is understandable that they would not gulp down their meals on the run.

In those days, the process of obtaining and consuming food was *part of life* (just as in some societies today it is all of life). Thus, for example, one could show that one was a man or a woman by being successful in an aspect of the process. When the process was going well, that was a reason to be happy. When the process was going badly, that was a reason to be sad.

Fine, but why should *we* spend time on eating? It is something that has to be done. It is *just* a natural bodily need. Why make a big deal about it? If you like it, eat it, but don't make a production number of it. Don't show signs of enjoyment—that is considered disgusting in our society. Just do it.

After all, we have more important things to do.

And yet, despite our businesslike attitude about the consumption of food, the United States is constantly reminded that it is a nation of fatties.

When something is a part of the mainstream of life, it is constrained by the other parts. If we spend hours in the preparation of a meal, those are hours during which we can't eat. If we are on a three-day hunting trip, we cannot eat until we find the bison. Probably good manners will dictate that we wait until we return home for the feast before we rip into the meat. Eating is not part of the mainstream of life in our society; therefore, perhaps, we overeat because eating is not constrained by the other activities of life. We can grab a bite here and another bite there. In fact, we are irritated if we have to wait. City dwellers often ask suburbanites how they can stand having to drive to the store, which may be as much as two miles away; suburbanites on vacation in the country are horrified by the fact that stores may be ten or more miles away from their cabin or campsite.

So there is nothing to prevent us from having something to eat at any time. In addition, people justify their fat with the argument that food is so bland and tasteless today that it is necessary to eat more in order to get a hint of true satisfaction.

But perhaps true satisfaction cannot be obtained by food alone. The food the Indians ate symbolized victory over the elements, another year in harmony with nature, a skillful hunt. We are trying to taste that in our food, and we eat more and more in an inappropriate attempt to taste what is not and never was in the food itself.

We don't have time for elaborate preparation. We must get to work; we must get to our night classes. We must finish so we can go to the opera, the ballet, the theater. We want to get into bed with our sexual partner of the night. *These* are significant activities. We have it better than those Indians. They didn't have night classes, opera, ballet, the theater. They had only food, and they made what they could of it, but we have more important things to do, and thank heavens food is so much easier to obtain and prepare than in those days.

The Indian ceremonies, however, were opera, dance, theater, religion, education, and no doubt other things, all in one. Perhaps we run off to the opera, dance, or theater because they have been taken out of our own lives.

The gustatory revolution has led to more eating. Similarly, the sexual revolution has led to more sex. And therefore we are robbing the bodily aspect of sexual behavior of mind. Who needs the dance of courtship? Who needs cultivated conversation to seduce? Just as we do not have to hunt the bison, skin it, cook it, and finally, three days later, feast on it, we do not have to engage in pointless conversation, insincere compliments and "sweet talk," flowers and other symbolic gestures, a kiss and then two, and finally, a week later, satisfaction. Just as we can step right up and calmly say, "One Big Daddy Burger please," we can step right up and say, "Let's fuck in the broom closet, please." Nor will we tolerate delay. Just as urbanites want a slice of pizza *now*, the modern member of the sexual revolution wants orgasm *now*.

But just as we are eating more and enjoying it less, we will eventually have sex more and enjoy it less. In fact, we will eventually frantically pursue sex in an attempt to recapture the taste in the sex itself. But it isn't there. It is in the won fooball game or the week long hunt. The excitement of the other parts of life "rubbed off" on sex and sex "rubbed off" on the other parts of life, and both were richer for it. Furthermore, we needed less sex, for what we had was a summary of the entire process of obtaining it. Therefore, not so much was expected of the "act itself." Nor could we have as much sex, for if we need to win a football game in order to procure sex, we must often play football instead of having sex. Using "sex" in the broad sense, however, the football would be sexual at least by virtue of its attachment to sex in the narrow sense; and the sex (narrow) would be sex (broad) —sex as life, sex as a climax to a thrilling day of victory.

Sex will become bland and tasteless, and so we should consume more in order to feel full. Alternatively, we can add spices, which take the form of increasingly popular group sex, bisexuality, swinging, swapping, or what you will.

The analogy seems to break down at one point, however: While there are good reasons not to eat too much, there are no good reasons not to engage in as much sex as one wants to. I mean, that stuff about precious bodily fluids went out years ago. In fact, speaking of kinky sex, a person recently suggested that *sex is a good substitute for food*. When you get hungry, have sex instead. It expends calories.

In fact, the analogy does not break down. There is no reason not to be fat. In some areas of life fat people are ridiculed and discriminated against. For example, large corporations do not like their top executives to be obese. Since most of us can't expect to be top executives, we might as well eat. Sure, we'll probably die sooner, but what is life without the joy of eating? It may be that fat people cannot get as much sex as thin people, but when the revolution is complete we will realize that sex is sex and it is always beautiful. Showing a preference for thin people is like showing horror at the thought of a homosexual encounter. It is drawing lines. It is square.

The gustatory revolution, however, freed us from food. It follows that the sexual revolution should free us from sex; and it does. The more available sex is, the less necessary a particular act of sex is, and the more sex can be subjugated to the more important activities of life. Marriage provides an analogy here:

People used to get married so they could get sex regularly; but it is well known—at least in folklore—that after marriage sexual behavior decreases in frequency and passion. A common explanation for this and for extramarital intercourse is that it gets boring with the same old person. This is absurd. Imagine a young male of 1959–1963, whose major outlet was masturbation, saying, "It gets boring with the same old penis." Why should two people get bored with each other sexually? It takes as much time to properly develop the sexual aspects of a relationship as it takes to properly develop other kinds of intimacy. If marital sex has become boring, it is probably because it has lost its surplus significance. It no longer means (or is part of) winning a football game, proving one's virility, or even "succeeding in getting 'It.' " It is too available and it has been disconnected from some of its sources of motivation.

Furthermore, sex is of necessity put in a time slot once a couple is married or settled into adult life. Sex is therefore no longer free to follow its own dialectic. It is subjugated to the couple's schedule and therefore by definition of decreased importance. Since it makes no sense to walk off a job to have sex with one's wife when one can have it when one gets home, sex makes less sense and has less value than work. Marriage—and the sexual revolution—free us for the more important things.

The current college generation's primary concern is grades. Perhaps more important than the "practical reasons" is the fact that they don't have to be concerned with sex. Nor, of course, do they have interpersonal relationships to be concerned with, because from our present perspective much of the interaction between males and females in 1959–1963 was presexual. In a word, personality is unnecessary, for who needs anything to talk about? Who needs to know how to get along with—or even hustle—another person? All one needs are the magic words, "Let's do it."

Being "hung-up" on grades is hardly a step forward. I torment my students these days by bragging about the fourteen C's, D, and an F I received in college and about my low grade point average (slightly over a *B*, which was good in those days because a *B* meant—and nominally still does mean—good). My students do not enjoy my kindly and curious contempt for their neurotic preoccupation, but they do not try to counter with their liberated sexuality—would I have thought of trying to put down a guy who was getting it by mentioning my academic and athletic success?

The availability of sex decreases its value. In addition, availability should eventually lead to loss of interest. A stimulus is a change from one state of affairs to another. To live a life of sex would be like stimulus deprivation, like living in a tank of water with all senses experiencing a totally homogeneous stimulus field—experiencing nothing. If an organism is constantly exposed to a stimulus, the stimulus will cease to function as a stimulus; that is, the organism will cease to respond. Sex must either be a respite from, or immanent in, other activities. Sex must receive meaning from other activities; the receipt must be reciprocal. If so, the ideal state described in chapter two is approximated: Everything is sexual. Even sex. If not, sex is meaningless, and eventually will become less popular. Today, sex means something more than just sex—it also is "taking part in the sexual revolution"; but when the revolution is over, sex will be totally bereft.

What about guilt? Many people have had their lives ruined and twisted by guilt about sex. Isn't it better to do away with guilt? Relief from guilt is often cited as one of the positive results of the sexual revolution, and it does seem to be the case that liberated individuals feel less guilty.

But people *should* feel guilty about sex (sometimes). It is absurd to spend so much time and energy on an activity as pointless as sex. When sex is not pointless, who feels guilty? Similarly, people *should* feel guilty about coveting an *A*. It is absurd to put so much time and energy into something as pointless as receiving an *A*. When it isn't pointless, when the *A* is immanent in hard work that comes from love or interest in the subject matter, who feels guilt? Similarly, even in the old days, when sex came from love of the sexual object guilt was less common.

In the case of sex, people feel guilty. In the case of grades, many people *should*. I don't think many people do, even about cheating to get an *A*: but neither do many people get much satisfaction from *A*'s anymore. I'm sorry, but it's true: What you don't work for, you don't enjoy; and absence of enjoyment suggests the operation of guilt.

Guilt is "nature's reminder" that what we are doing is pointless, just as pain reminds us that what we are doing is dangerous. If our parents teach us that sex is pointless, we will have to learn—not that it isn't, but *when* it isn't. It is not, however, to be expected that everyone will triumph over his upbringing. Nor is it necessary that our parents teach us that sex is always pointless.

To remove the possibility of guilt concerning an activity, it seems to be necessary to define the activity as pointless but necessary—an activity which must be removed from the mainstream of human existence. To the extent that it stays in the mainstream, it *can be* unnecessary. Guilt can keep us in line. If the activity is removed from the mainstream, doing it too much has no effect on the rest of life, and guilt is unnecessary.

Eating is in the process of being removed from the mainstream of existence. The elimination of waste products *has* been removed. Elimination is a model case of a pointless but necessary bodily function completely outside the mainstream of life. Most people consider urination and defecation necessary inconveniences. Most of us cannot imagine taking pleasure in or giving time to elimination, and most of us cannot imagine sex taking on the nonsignificance of elimination. How could elimination be a part of the mainstream of life? It would appear that whatever is being done to sex and eating has been done so well to elimination that we can't even imagine it being anything but bodily and necessary.

The attempt at isolation has not been totally successful. As Freud said, the repressed always returns. I once read a report of a study which showed that women had more urinary disorders than men because they "went to the bathroom" less; presumably they are more ashamed of their natural bodily functions than men are. It seems that when you want to put something in the closet, it wants to stay there. Guilt gives way to shame. In addition, toilet humor remains popular, which hardly seems congruent with our officially businesslike attitude towards the toilet. Freud's insistence on the importance of the anus seems ludicrous. Nobody denies they have to go to the bathroom; they just don't make a big deal about it. "If you gotta go, you gotta go" is very similar in implication to "If you like it, fuck it." But the former line is often delivered as if it were witty, and people often laugh at it. If the anus is so unimportant, why are those women ashamed, and why are those people laughing?

Sex is repressed, and that's why we laugh at sex, says Freud. Elimination is *isolated*. Isolation is a kind of defense mechanism; all defense mechanisms involve repression. To protect oneself from a painful or threatening situation, one isolates it from the rest of life and removes all affect from it. One represses the affect. The repressed returns. If eating is being repressed or isolated, the return of the repressed takes the form of overweight. What about elimination? The repressed escapes and returns in the disguised form of overt eliminatory behavior in culture—pollution is the major example—and in the individual—constipation and diarrhea. A major locus of psychosomatic disorders is the anus.

We take eating out of life and get a nation of fatties. We take elimination out of life and get pollution and psychosomatic disorders of the anus. When we take sex (narrow) out of life, we take sex (broad) out of life. Other activities are not enlivened by sex, nor is sex enlivened by other activities. We also destroy personalities, much of the development of which is in the service of sex.

Won't sex itself be more enjoyable after the revolution is complete? In 1961 sex may have been our primary concern but, perhaps for that reason, it could not be fully enjoyed. For example, it was necessary to get off the rim sufficiently to be able to remember all the details, to savor and to tell. Sex was for ego, in Mailer's phrase.

When sex was embedded as a significant part of a larger plot, it was quick and dirty. Matt Helm, the Donald Hamilton hero, often has sex in the line of duty, either as a respite from the difficult business of being a secret agent, or for a reason related to the plot. And Matt Helm would no more linger over an orgasm than the stereotypic American family would linger over the dessert in their T.V. dinners.

When sex is more than *just* sex, undivided attention cannot be given to the physical experience itself. While concentration on one's own physical sensations seems onanistic to prudish sensibilities, still the pleasure is greater as long as there is no guilt about the onanism. After all, why should there be?

In that case, one is logically compelled to ask, why bother with a partner? Animals find electrical stimulation of the pleasure centers of the brain more rewarding than anything else. They will press bars with greater insistence for this reward than for sex, food, or water. Letters to the editor of magazines dealing with sex indicate that some people find more pleasure in masturbation (by themselves or with partners) than in ordinary genital intercourse. If the aim is pleasure, why mess with people? Not only are they clumsy; *they have needs of their own* one must satisfy; in addition, they have personalities which mess things up in ways too specific for a general account. Someone with too much self-esteem changes and complicates sex in one way, while someone with too little self-esteem changes and complicates sex in another. We have seen how personalities make romantic love more difficult; they also make sex more difficult. They are extraneous distractors.

It has also been found that rats who learn to press bars for electrical brain stimulation unlearn (extinguish) bar-pressing faster than they unlearn for rewards like food and water. Brain stimulation is not addictive in the same way food is. It's nice, but unnecessary. If sex is merely pleasurable, people will work hard for it, but if it isn't immediately forthcoming they will lose interest. If sex is not attached to war and conflict and the mainstream of life (which is being reduced to a trickle by all these removals), why should it be attached to·people? Who needs them? Masturbation or a portable brain stimulator are more practical and free more time. Why go to the trouble of having to find a person, say "Let's fuck," find a place, take the clothes off, engage in intercourse, put the clothes back on, and perhaps even say thanks? Just press the button on the portable unit with the electrodes already attached.

A consequence, if not the purpose, of the sexual revolution is the dementalization of sex. This makes the possibility of enjoyment greater; but the evidence of the rapidity of extinction of "merely" or "purely" enjoyable activities suggests that rats and humans are not merely hedonists. In the recent past, sex was too hard to get, a task of impossible difficulty. This meant it could not pervade the life space but could cause a great deal of frustration and guilt. Sex passed to and through a phase during which it was a task of moderate difficulty. Psychological studies have shown such tasks are preferred to overly difficult or overly easy tasks *by normal people*. During this phase, interest in sex was at what appears, from the points of view of other phases, to be at a pathological height. In the current phase, sex is too easy to get (from the point of view of the previous stage) and thus has little value. There is no reason for sex to occupy so much of the life space.

I don't know why, nor can I speculate on the future of sex any more than I can speculate on the future of romantic love (although the extrapolations seem contradictory). It does appear, however, that self-indulgence is depriving us of sex as we once knew it. Meanwhile, suffering from unnecessary guilt is less. To relieve guilt we have desexualized sex. The trade is no doubt fair, but entropy has increased, and life is duller. Furthermore, relationships between people are being dismantled, for one of the major reasons for people to get together is being undermined.

Some textbooks employ the gimmick of the hypothetical party. The writer, a representative of his field, arrives and tells us what kinds of things he is able to tell us. To our party everyone is invited. But you need bring only your body. If you bring yourself, please be unobtrusive. We don't want the evening ruined by exhibitionists. We don't need personalities or individuals.

In summary, the sexual revolution appears to be leading to the desexualization of sex. Sex is becoming detached from life, a natural bodily function and not much more. Sex will no longer be sexual in the broad sense of the term. The individual will become superfluous in relationships between the sexes.

WHAT GAY LIBERATION HAS DONE FOR ME

To the best of my knowledge, I am and always have been exclusively heterosexual; but I would not have said so until recently, for you would have asked, "I wonder why he is telling us that?"[2] Perhaps even now you are asking that. Your answer is, "Because he is trying to deny his latent homosexuality." You could be right, but I don't think so. If I had any homosexuality in me, I would come right out and admit it. It's nothing to be ashamed of. Parents are coming to understand, some employers are coming to be tolerant, and some laws are being changed. It wouldn't hurt me to admit it, and it might even help sell this book: "The author, a practicing homosexual . . ." But once the revolution is complete, it would draw no more attention than the revelation that I am a practicing heterosexual would now.

So what? What is good about the fact that I am no longer afraid to admit I am heterosexual? Let me become again the stereotypic young man that I was in the last section. I (the real me) went to a co-educational boarding school for grades nine through twelve. The school was not a breeding ground for homosexuality as nonintegrated schools are said to be, but it did have rather restrictive rules about the kind of contact boys and girls could have, and the authorities sincerely attempted to enforce these rules. The boys lived in boys' dormitories, and the girls in girls', so that feature of the traditional English public school was preserved. Furthermore, there was a great deal more interaction between people than in the ordinary high school, and life was in a goldfish bowl. Even so, the rules were helpful to the timid. We could chomp at the bit without giving off the suspicion that we relished it.

Nevertheless, latent homosexuality was always the monkey on the back, the incubus of the night, the cause of much hysterical giggling and averting of eyes in shower rooms, and a nasty and potentially dangerous insult to throw at someone. Who might not, in a moment of doubt, believe it were true, give in, and hang himself (as did the woman in *The Children's Hour*)?

The result? Fear of friendship in some. Fear of females in those who feared the myth of latency and dared not expose themselves to a moment when they should be aroused but wouldn't be. Fear of impotence. The perpetuation of the notion that the absence of heterosexual desire equals the presence of homosexuality. Finally, the slight feeling that to engage in sexual relationships was not merely to do what one wanted to do, but to deny the homosexuality latent within one.

Now we are all free to be whatever we want. Remember, if you like it, fuck it. Male, female, whatever. There is no need to be exclusively heterosexual or homosexual. People are beautiful. Why draw all these lines?

Now, however, if P and O are of the same sex and are good friends, why aren't they also lovers? Friendship between members of the same sex which does not involve sex will begin to take on the connotations of the term "platonic." To turn down a friend's request for physical sexuality *will* be a rejection. As argued in chapter two, even now we do not feel comfortable *denying* that we have sexual feelings for friends of the same sex. Friendship will disappear by the process described in the preceding chapter; it will be swallowed by sexuality, which in turn will be desexualized.

What about the bad effects of belief in latency? (Not to mention the well-documented sufferings of homosexuals?) They will be alleviated, just as guilt about sexuality is being alleviated by the sexual revolution. We receive freedom from guilt. We pay by having sex denied the surplus significance that made it equivalent to life. The homosexual revolution is a deal. We receive freedom from doubt, uncertainty, and fear. We pay by losing friendship as a sexual, that is, alive, kind of relationship.

The homosexual is making a trade too. He receives freedom from persecution and from guilt; but he pays too. The "Gay Life" will not be so gay when it becomes normal. Who has heard of an impotent homosexual? Previously, it was an impossibility. If one was not aroused in a homosexual encounter, one was merely not homosexual, at least not at that time. Heterosexuals fear not being aroused, for even when the specter of latent homosexuality has been banished by the years, one's manhood or womanhood is often defined by one's ability

to become aroused. Homosexuals have been free of that dreary definition because if one was fool enough to be a homosexual, against all the
prejudices of society, one obviously *was* a homosexual. Now we will all
have our worth defined by how well we can become aroused and what
we can do with this arousal. Life will continue to equal sex, but sex
will be defined more narrowly.

In summary, if sex removes individuals from their relationships
with their sexual partners, they have more free time. Friendship and
similar relationships are still ways of spending this time that require
personalities (individuals), but the homosexual movement threatens
that too. If P and O are friends, why not be lovers? And if they are
lovers, there is no need to be friends. And if they are sexual lovers,
there is no need for individual personalities.

THE DESEXUALIZATION OF THE MIND

If sex as life is being taken out of sex, with the consequent erosion
of the need for individuals, it is also being taken out of the life of the
mind, as an examination of the publish or perish philosophy in col-
leges and universities illustrates.

In an increasingly large number of institutions of higher learning,
one must publish to receive promotion and tenure. On the face of it,
this is suicide. Simultaneously, an increasingly large number of institutions of higher learning are going broke because of higher costs and a
decreasing interest in college educations, which are not worth as much
as they used to be. Therefore, it would seem to be important to pro-
mote and give tenure on the basis of "teaching ability." At least teaching should be receiving increasing instead of decreasing attention.

Some people argue that the best scholars and scientists are the best
teachers. It is often said that those who can't do, teach. To this I have
added—and those who can't teach, teach teaching. I am joking, but I
am also reflecting the priorities in the world of higher education. First
come those who push back the famous frontiers of knowledge. Then
come those who merely report back from the front. Finally come those
who teach people how to report back from the front.

Who would you rather have lecture to you on the moon: an astronaut, someone who had very carefully looked at all the pictures the
astronauts took, or someone who knows how to organize a presentation
about the moon? Ideally, someone who had been to the moon, studied
the pictures, and knew how to organize a presentation; but astronauts
don't have time to study pictures or learn how to organize presenta-

tions. They have, however, been to the moon, and are therefore preferable. In fact, you might even choose a college because an astronaut was on the faculty. This is another argument for promoting and tenuring people who have pushed back the frontiers of knowledge: they are more glamorous. A famous scholar is said to have said that it is more valuable to be within 500 feet of a great man than within fifty feet of a good man. This is supposed to debunk another argument—that small classes with discussion are better than large lectures with note-taking and gasps of admiration. One cannot expect a former astronaut to deprive the hundreds of students who want to sit at his feet, and so he must lecture to hundreds rather than discuss with thirty. This is better than talking with a reporter, a mere teacher, a second-rate mind. Some of the glow emanating from the great man reaches the student and warms him. The mere teacher has no glow. *Like the student of the great teacher,* he is a moon, not a sun; he is warm only because of his contact with the works of great men.

In both cases the student remains a moon, so what's the difference? None.

This argument is too metaphorical to be of real power, so let us examine another example. Most scholars are not former astronauts, but we have seen that astronauts are limited to some extent by their lack of time to do anything except explore the moon. They cannot study their own pictures, nor can they try to develop effective modes of presentation. Specialization is a fact of life for those pushing on the frontiers.

Dr. Smith has published forty-five articles on the sexual behavior of the titmouse. This is not an especially narrow specialization. It is unlikely that he will attract many students to the institution at which he teaches, despite the popularity of courses on sex. Interest in the sexual behavior of the titmouse is not high. Besides, Dr. Smith cannot really teach a course on sex. So much is being "done" in the area of sex that he is really qualified to talk only about the sexual behavior of the titmouse.

Here is the deadly joy of specialization. Having published, Dr. Smith is allowed to perish. If Dr. Smith's major activity in life is the investigation of the sexual behavior of the titmouse, he has the right to rest on other occasions. And so if a student were to ask, "So, what's new on the sexual behavior of the mouse?" Dr. Smith can smile happily and say, "I'm so sorry, I'm so busy with my field and so many scientists are so busy with *their* fields that I can't keep up with the sexual behavior of other birds, much less mammals." Dr.

Smith is relieved of responsibility for knowing about anything else. In fact, he *should* refuse to know anything else. It is considered unprofessional to talk about things outside one's specialty. Thus, Dr. Smith cannot be much of a teacher except within his specialty. It is said that the teacher who publishes remains alive and active. Perhaps; but not necessarily in the classroom. Who but other specialists can understand Dr. Smith's understanding of the sexual behavior of the titmouse? Perhaps he remains active, but not in any areas outside the specialty; for if Dr. Smith puts all his energy into the titmouse, he cannot be expected to have any left over for anything else. In fact, he shouldn't. The truly dedicated scholar puts all his energy into his specialty. Other expenditures are wastes.

Consider another example: I teach statistics to college students. It is considered difficult subject matter. I'm pretty good, if I say so myself, and I will have to, for it is not a popular course and it is required. One of the reasons I am good is that I am stupid.

The standardized tests of mathematical ability I have taken over the years indicate I have a great deal of ability. But I am no mathematical genius; I know, because I have been in classes with mathematical geniuses, and they see things quickly it takes me some time to see. Furthermore, and more important, they see these things *directly*. Complicated topics in mathematics are difficult for me to grasp; they are mysterious and frightening, like Odette is to Swann. I try to crack them by the use of initially inappropriate assimilations. Even after having taught statistics seven times and having used it and read about it for almost ten years, it still has tinges of mystery in various places. These things are like emotion in untranslated love, simultaneously attracting me and masking my lack of understanding.

I know the problems students have because I have been through them myself; furthermore, since I have not completely grasped the essence of statistics, I am motivated to try new approaches, and I care if I am understood because sometimes only if I am understood do I know that I understand. Mathematical geniuses find nothing mysterious in the kind of statistics I teach. Professional mathematical statisticians are beyond that, pushing back the frontiers of knowledge, rolling the ring while I am still trying to grasp it. It is not that they are such clods that they have missed the nuances, the major integrating themes, and the intricacies of conceptual arguments; they simply don't need them to understand elementary statistics to go on to the frontier. They see statistics directly, and have no need of approaches.

Paradoxically, of course, the better I understand statistics, the worse a teacher I will be. It is already happening. Things that a few years ago I did not understand clearly are now so obvious to me that I cannot understand how anyone cannot understand them. Therefore, I simply dismiss those who cannot understand these things as "stupid." I should soon give up teaching statistics.

Thus, it does not appear that those who push back the frontiers of knowledge are best qualified to teach. Then why the emphasis upon publishing? It is a plot against joy in the use of the mind:

The more people who *must* publish, the more material will be produced and the more specialization will become a necessity. It is impossible to keep up with the new developments in any but a narrow field. Scholars and scientists must know more and more about less and less.

Furthermore, if I am honest, you are blunt, and he is tactless, I am a Renaissance Man, you are a dilettante, and he is living proof of the dictum that a little knowledge is a dangerous thing. There is less and less about which one can feel free to make comments. The world is cut up into smaller and smaller fields, each well-fenced in. Specialization insures that nobody will be watching you. After all, it is not sufficient merely to publish. One must go where nobody has gone before; otherwise, one is a mere disciple, a second-rate mind, a research assistant, certainly not worthy of promotion and tenure.

Dr. Smith is one of the world's leading authorities on the sexual behavior of the titmouse, but that is partially because he is one of the three people working in that area. Dr. Jones's research has focused mainly on the cues titmice employ to signal they have a territory and are ready to breed; Dr. Brown's research deals mainly with the courtship phase; Dr. Smith has studied the act of mating itself. These three scientists all received their doctorates from Dr. Black, now considered something of a generalist, being the only specialist of his day in the sexual behavior of titmice.

Surely Doctors Smith, Brown, and Jones get together at professional meetings and excitedly compare findings on the titmouse. What have they to say to each other? If sexual intercourse is taken out of the mainstream of life, it becomes meaningless. There is nothing to say or think about it. It just is. It is only through relationships with other segments of life that it has any significance. We have nothing of interest to tell each other about our bowel movements, for bowel movements are isolated and unrelated to anything else. When things are related, one thing leads to another, analogies and juxtapositions are suggested, and the whole world is implied by a droplet of water. When

Freud, Swift, Norman O. Brown, Norman Mailer, and others attempt to relate elimination to the rest of life, they are sneered at and hated for trying to bring elimination out of the closet into the open air, for trying to destroy the splendid isolation we have created for this nasty fact of life. We don't want it related.

Similarly, Dr. Brown's work is not really related to Dr. Smith's work. The relationship is in name only unless Dr. Brown and Dr. Smith attempt to integrate or relate their work. But each is in a *different* area. Similarly, on the way to work Joe stopped off to go to the bathroom and to engage in sexual intercourse with Mary, but going to the bathroom, engaging in sexual intercourse, and being at work have no real relationship to each other. They happen to have occurred in the same two hour period, but that is not much of a relationship. Similarly, people in huge apartment complexes happen to live close together, but they do not necessarily have relationships.

Norman O. Brown equated division of labor with death, and the preceding discussion has demonstrated that specialization is compartmentalization and desexualizes the life of the mind by removing mental activities from the mainstream of life. It is considered bad form to ask a psychologist what relevance his work has for everyday existence, and not merely because it usually has none. Science is supposed to be pure, and in the context of this discussion the use of the word to mean uncontaminated and antiseptic is valid.

The mind is a pleasure to use if it is free to wander the fields of knowledge; but a little knowledge is a dangerous thing. It could disturb and threaten us. The nonspecialist threatens to put the specialist's work in *some* framework or structure. It is not that this threatens to reduce the work's significance. It is bound to increase it. It is that the specialist's splendid isolation vanishes; and so, therefore, his peace (death). If a specialty has two practitioners, there is the possibility of disagreement and conflict. This is hard. And, as we have seen, recent trends tend to the easy way out. Guilt about sex? Remove it at all costs. Can't tell if you like your friend "in that way?" Remove the uncertainty at all costs. Of course you like him that way.

Scholars are killing themselves by cutting themselves off from the mainstream of existence, which by now is not even a trickle, but a dry bed. In addition, they are trying to kill students, and they are not doing a bad job.

For example, I did not know until my third year in graduate school that I had to publish in order to get a job after I got my doctorate. Therefore, the courses I took in graduate school encouraged exploratory research, new theories, and attempts at integration. There was something of a spirit of play involved. Today, even undergraduates are encouraged to try to publish to get into graduate school. Naturally, these publications will have to be of the accepted type. Play stops earlier.

For another example, let us consider the teaching of literature on the undergraduate level and see the possible effects of some approaches to teaching.[3]

No doubt artists have always resented critics. They feel that critics do not translate them correctly. Can one understand the Romantic Poets by knowing the life histories of Keats, Shelley, and Byron? The question is identical to one asked earlier: Can Swann capture the essence of Odette by knowing the little bits and pieces of gossip he collects? Much of the scholarly work that deals with novels, poems, drama, and essays has the status of gossip. Gossip is something most of us know how to do—but only about other people. This "schema" has been applied to literature.

Great works of literature are difficult to adapt to; children confronting them for the first time, especially if they are not quite ready, find them boring. It is analogous to the infant who cannot even think of rolling his ring. Shouldn't we give him a start?

It is unlikely that introducing a person to great works of literature by giving him things he *can* assimilate will assist him in eventually being able to have a direct experience of the work. This would involve the development of a global, undifferentiated schema which could be analyzed and would guide its own analysis. The student can deal with the fact that Keats died in 1821 of tuberculosis, but if he gets the idea that this fact has anything to do with Keats' poetry, he will be less likely to try to confront it directly. It is boring and insignificant that Keats died in 1821 of tuberculosis. Furthermore, this fact comes between the student and the poetry. Joe's details are unimportant and often resisted by the assimilatory schema of his lover. While I have given other explanations of this phenomenon, here it may be suggested that words, labels, and categories *come between* Joe and Mary, and that is why they are resisted. Similarly, the dull knowledge that Keats died in 1821 of tuberculosis hangs around his poetry trying to make it mundane. As I have said, to me it now is. I no longer appreciate the Romantic Poets, perhaps because the course I had in them dealt in such details.

Another danger: Byron died in 1824; but Byron had a pretty good sex life, even by today's standards (he may have had incestuous relationships with his half-sister). Knowing that Keats died in 1821 of tuberculosis does not tell us much about Keats, but we have lots of old habitual schemata about sex. Byron can be assimilated into these schemata and his essence missed entirely. The student may think of Byron as he thinks of modern movie stars, and may read him voyeuristically, to find out what kind of a man could do that kind of thing.

In conclusion, many of the jobs performed by academic scholars in this area actually mitigate against the probability that the writer will be understood; either by boring the prospective reader, or by providing him with inappropriate, premature assimilatory schemata.

I have no doubt that other academic disciplines do similar things to their students, but that is another subject in itself. I will conclude this section with a discussion of how some common approaches to education are antiindividual and antirelationship. The discussion is brief because it is beyond the scope of this book; only a few samples are offered.

Some teachers (usually those with big names and big classes with assistants) lecture and leave everything to the assistants, who, because of their age and similar status, have a pseudopeer relationship with the students. Anything bad they must do to the students is not their responsibility. The Great Professor has decreed that the cutoff point is here. If the student can find the Great Professor, he will pass the buck to the law of large numbers, which states that one can't give 500 people individual attention, or to the law that if one can't be just, one has no choice but to be arbitrary.

In any case, few students will attempt to approach the Great Professor with their complaints, because large lecture courses (or small lecture courses, for that matter) do not involve interaction with the teacher and consequent evaluation of the student. The student in a lecture course has no relationship to the teacher and therefore does not need to feel shame at failure.

A very large number of college and university courses require not much more than the memorization of facts, followed by their regurgitation. Particularly if testing is by multiple choice or short answer question, there is no doubt about what is true and what isn't. Evaluation, interaction, debate, and thinking are then not required. After all, facts *are* facts.

For example, it is a fact that there is a study by T. J. Johnson, R. Feigenbaum, and M. Weiby ("Some determinants and consequences of the teacher's perception of causality"). It is a fact that this study is discussed in a textbook called *Attribution* (E. E. Jones, D. E. Kanouse, H. H. Kelley, R. E. Nisbett, S. Valins, and B. Weiner). There were two experimental conditions. In both, teachers explained to two boys (A and B) how to multiply by ten. A did well and B did poorly. The teachers then taught A and B to multiply by twenty. In one experimental condition, A did well and B continued to do poorly. In the other, A did well and B did as well. It is a fact that the textbook reports that the "teachers tended to attribute B's improved performance to themselves but to blame his continued low performance on B himself" (p. 19).

If I make up an exam on this book, I can either ask whether teachers tend to give themselves the credit if students improve but the students the blame if students don't improve, or I can ask whether Johnson, Feigenbaum, and Weiby found in an experiment that this was the case. The former is an empirical and conceptual question of considerable complexity. If no other studies in this area have been conducted, the student must decide if there was something special about the experimental situation that led to the results; if there is an alternative plausible interpretation; if this is an "error" in attribution or a case of people operating on the basis of the information they have; if this phenomenon is best explained in motivational or cognitive terms; or if some other artifice is at work. The latter question is a question of fact requiring merely memory, and can be answered correctly; the former cannot be answered correctly, and so students and teachers might disagree. One can see that disagreement about this particular study might be worth avoiding.

It is clear why asking the question of fact is antirelationship and antiinteraction; but in what sense is it antiindividual?

There is only one right answer. Students cannot "express their personality" through their answer. They need only bring a very small portion of themselves to the exams—their memory. On this question, they will be divided into two groups, right and wrong, and there will be no within-group variance. Everyone who is right is right and everyone who is wrong is wrong. An illusion of variance and individual differences is produced by summing all the students' right answers. Some will have more right answers than others. Personality seems to have entered the picture; but this is like making gold out of lead and silk purses out of sows' ears.

In summary, much of higher education seems designed to deprive students of pleasure in the use of their minds. This is a serious charge, and I have given only a few examples, none of them in their proper depth. Furthermore, I have confined the discussion to higher education. I believe the same "plot" operates on all levels of education.

SUMMARY

The essays in this chapter have discussed tendencies in modern society toward the elimination of individuals, relationships, and sex in the broad sense of the term. I have said that I do not know why these trends are to be found, and I do not. I *can* make one suggestion. The first four chapters are a detailed account of the pain and suffering entailed by romantic love and its associate, the individual with a personality. I have suggested that much of this pain and suffering is the natural result of the fact that we are in a preadaptive state with respect to interacting with individual personalities; we are in a preadaptive state because a psychological picture of man has only recently become valuable; in many parts of the world today, a sociological picture accounts for a vast proportion of the variance in behavior.

Perhaps our experiment has been a failure. Perhaps the trend against sex, individuality, and relationship (which can be only between individuals—if not, relationships are collective monologues) is a retreat to a sociological reality. Perhaps the trends indicate that we couldn't stand the heat and are now getting out of the kitchen—that is, perhaps the trends reflect our cowardice.

There is still no need for total pessimism however. The infant at first has no thought of rolling his ring. Then he conceives the project of rolling it. He fails. Perhaps he gives up. But two months later, he tries again. He has more cognitive-motor capacity, and although he fails, he can see the possibility of success. He keeps trying and eventually he succeeds.

If the United States has been an experiment in romantic love and individualism, it has also been an experiment in technology and population growth. If, somehow, these are the same experiment, then there is no hope. I do not see why technology and population growth are the inevitable concomitants of the growth of personality and romantic love, but they may be.

6
Measurement
and Research

IT IS NOT quite all very well to be theoretical, construct process models, and engage in speculation. Psychology and other social sciences prefer empirical investigations of a less subjective kind. They, too, have value. This final chapter presents a report of an experimental field study of arguments I conducted. I present it not because of the finality or respectability of its answers, but because it contains some evidence relevant to some of the conceptions advanced in earlier chapters.[1]

Social scientists often use an analogy (sometimes called a paradigm) to study something. Rather than studying conflict between nations, they invent games and have college students play them; they hope that college students playing games are similar to nations in conflict. I doubt if they are, so I selected a paradigm that resembles as closely as possible the real life phenomenon I wanted to study.

In addition, I wanted to measure relationships adequately. The vast majority of experiments in the area of interpersonal relationships have employed operational definitions that reflected extremely simplistic conceptions of relationships. Most imply that one person's relationship with another can satisfactorily be quantified by asking, "How much do you like O?" I was sure this was outrageous.

Therefore, I developed a seventy-five item Relational Strength Questionnaire (RSQ), composed of fourteen sub-scales, each representing a "sub-relationship," and measured by several questions each. After some moderately complex analysis, I was forced to conclude that if a psychometric approach to relationships is to be taken, that is, if we wish to measure them, one person's relationship with another can indeed satisfactorily be quantified by asking, "How much do you like O?"

Does this mean that relationships are simple? Not at all. It may mean that measuring relationships is not the only way of gaining understanding of them. The preceding five chapters have presented another way of gaining understanding, and constitute something of an alternative to the usual approach in the behavioral sciences. In this chapter, I discuss some aspects of the measurement attempt and of the study that have relevance to preceding chapters; we shall see that this more typical approach augments what has gone before.

THE MEASUREMENT ATTEMPT

I developed the concept of "sub-relationships." Most have ordinary language names, such as trust, intimacy, and admiration. Each is a separate concept. Each is at once an area in which a relationship can be violated and a strength and resource of the relationship. For example, if Joe is untrustworthy, he violates the relationship by violating the sub-relationship of trust. Mary's trust in Joe is a strength and resource of the relationship. If she trusts Joe, she is less likely to consider Joe's behavior really untrustworthy because she will accept his explanation of why he behaved as he did.

I divided the sub-relationships into four groups on the basis of conceptual considerations developed by P. G. Ossorio (*Persons, Notes on Behavior Description, Meaning & Symbolism*). I then administered the RSQ to both members of thirty couples (young, married or living together) prior to the experimental procedure, which is described later. Using a mathematical procedure called factor analysis, I found a four factor solution with extremely "simple" structure. Each sub-relationship helped define one and only one factor, and each factor was defined by several sub-relationships. The factor analysis produced, then, four groups of presumably similar sub-relationships. This empirical grouping came very close to replicating the conceptual grouping (only one sub-relationship changed groups). Therefore, I will discuss the results of the conceptual and factor analyses together.

The first group is composed of four sub-relationships. They are named and given brief conceptual definitions.

Trust: P believes O will have P's interests in mind and will act with them in mind.

Respect: P believes O's feelings, emotions, behaviors, and attitudes can be justified.

Acceptance: P ignores, lets go, doesn't codify, or forgets O's behaviors, which could be cause for annoyance, mystification, anger, or disturbance.

Stability: The relationship will continue unless something happens to change it. It is not going downhill.

These sub-relationships represent P's cognitions of O that allow P to take O's behaviors to be non-violative. For example, if Mary dislikes expensive gifts but Joe gives her one, Mary may believe that there is a reasonable explanation for it (respect), or that it is not an important matter (acceptance).

These four sub-relationships defined the first and strongest factor, named *Stability*. Couples high on this factor have good, honest, solid relationships. It is precisely such qualities as acceptance, trust, and respect which should allow a relationship to remain stable during times of stress.

Here is the second group of sub-relationships.

Enjoyment: O's presence increases P's enjoyment of activities.

Behavioral Exclusiveness: P does things with O he wouldn't do with others; in addition, doing something with O is "different" from doing the same thing with someone else; finally, P directs intense and constant behavior at O.

Emotional Exclusiveness: P feels emotions about O that he doesn't feel about others; in addition, he feels intense and constant emotions about O.

Fascination: P directs intense and constant attention at O.

Admiration: P admires many of O's features.

To the extent that P is high on these sub-relationships, he will be motivated to approach and remain with O; he will in addition have good reason not to violate the relationship.

These sub-relationships, with the exception of Admiration, defined the second most important factor, called *Romantic Love*. Fascination and Enjoyment represent respectively the passionate and idyllic aspects of romantic love; another aspect, clinging and jealousy, is represented by Emotional and Behavioral Exclusiveness.

The third group of sub-relationships contained Understanding (P doesn't find O's behaviors mysterious) and Knowledge (P knows the facts about O). They defined the third factor, called *Pragmatic Knowledge*. These represent P's cognitions of O that allow P to treat O as O would like to be treated. For example, if Mary dislikes expensive gifts, Joe will know it and will buy her cheap gifts.

The final group of sub-relationships, which defined the factor, *Interactive Efficiency,* contained the following.

Intimacy: Communication about personal matters takes place.
Spontaneity: P is willing and able to behave with O without consider-
    ing the consequences; deliberation is not necessary.
Confiding: P is willing to tell O things he wouldn't tell others.

To the extent that P is high on these sub-relationships, he is able to communicate with O on matters of importance to their relationship. If a couple cannot interact freely and openly with each other, then they are likely to be unable to behave in ways that will please each other. If Mary doesn't like expensive gifts but doesn't feel free to let Joe know this, she will probably receive fancy cars and fur coats.

The four groups can be considered four kinds of resources rela-tionships can have, especially for dealing with problems. To be high on *Stability* is to perceive O as non-violative. To be high on *Pragmatic Knowledge* is to be (able to be) non-violative. To be high on *Romantic Love* is to want to be with O despite potential violations. That is, it is to want to solve problems. To be high on *Interactive Efficiency* is to be able to solve problems, often before they arise. These are four conceptually distinct kinds of resources, and it is valuable to be able to make the distinctions; the nature of a relational problem can be speci-fied and therefore more easily solved.

In addition to the pleasing correspondence between the con-ceptual and empirical clusterings, there was an interesting finding which sheds some light on the distinction between people and rela-tionships.

It would not be surprising to find that members of a couple have similar factor scores. If Joe is high on *Romantic Love,* we would ex-pect Mary to be also, as they have one and the same relationship. But this was not quite the case.

For two of the factors, the cross-couple correlations are statistically significant (*Stability,* $r = .56$; *Interactive Efficiency,* $r = .40$). These may best be described as relational factors. That a relationship is stable is a fact about the relationship rather than a fact about P or O. A *relationship* is or is not stable; P and O must agree. If P thinks it is stable but O doesn't, it isn't, for O can break it up. Mary can trust Joe, but he can be untrustworthy anyhow. Similarly, interactions are either spontaneous or they are not; they are either intimate or not. They involve two people. One person cannot be spontaneous with another who is tense and rigid—what initially might appear to be spontaneity soon appears to be non-accommodatory logorrhea. Nor can one be intimate with another who is nonreciprocal or nonreceptive. What appears to be intimacy soon is obviously foolish confession.

For the other two factors, the cross-couple correlations were positive but not statistically significant (*Romantic Love, r* = .20; *Pragmatic Knowledge, r* = .34). That P is in love with O is best described as a fact about P. O does not have to cooperate. In fact, in Proust, the loved one is loved most when he least reciprocates. Similarly, that P knows something about O is best described as a fact about P. O cannot stop P from knowing it.

Thus members of couples have significantly similar factor scores on those two factors which are best described as representing facts about relationships, but do not on the two factors which are best described as representing facts about individuals. This gives some empirical validation to the differentiation of individuals from relationships discussed in chapter two. That the correlations do not differ greatly in magnitude (and are not large) testifies that the distinction is not absolute.

Unfortunately for my belief in complexity, the factor scores are highly correlated within individuals. If Joe is high on one factor, he is likely to be equally high on the others. The mean correlation between factor scores is .81. Therefore, for this sample, there is really a general relationship factor. A human relationship can be summed up by its position on one rather vague dimension. A seventy-five item RSQ is not necessary.

However, there are reasons for retaining the sub-relationships and the rationale for their grouping, as the following propositions illustrate.

1. *Quantitative correlation may indicate conceptual overlap; it does not demand we reduce the number of concepts. Correlation does not equal equivalence.*

Knowledge and Understanding emerged as the factor, *Pragmatic Knowledge*. This requires that they correlated highly with each other. The correlation was in fact .70, which is approximately equal to their reliabilities. Thus, they are empirically undistinguishable. The sample uses only one concept; subjects answer the Knowledge questions just as they answer the Understanding questions. Do we need both concepts?

As defined and measured, understanding is something like uncodified knowledge. It is a feel for the whole of a person. Understanding *can be* codified into verbal behavior, but its home is the unassimilated *gestalt*. Knowledge, as defined and measured, is specific; it consists of a body of not necessarily related bits of information. Its home is ordinary language. Nevertheless, knowledge can contribute to understanding, and vice versa.

The distinction between the two concepts is not often made because it is not often needed. Under many circumstances, the words can be used interchangeably. A high correlation is to be expected. It is still worthwhile to maintain the distinction, however, particularly when talking about intimate relationships. Understanding is, in the terms of chapter two, the language of love, while knowledge is the language of everyday life. People can know others without understanding them; people can understand others without knowing them. The commonness and importance of these two states of affairs demonstrates the value of having two concepts. To claim you know but don't understand someone is to identify the way you feel when someone changes— not just the way Mary changes when Joe reaches puberty but the way Joe changes, which causes Mary to feel that their twenty year marriage is threatened by some mysterious malady. To claim you understand but don't know someone is to identify love at first sight, the kind of understanding television and movies show by an exchange of glances.

Thus the two concepts, while very similar, are both needed. They do overlap, which means, in this case, that many specific comprehensions of individuals are not easily classified as either understanding or knowledge, for example, "I know he's unhappy about the way his work is going." One can find out another is unhappy by sensing it (understanding) or by observing overt manifestations of unhappiness (wails and breast-beating). In this case, however, the distinction is really not worth making. How could one sense unhappiness without *some* overt "signs" of what we take to be an internal state? On the other hand, how could one know it was unhappiness without some sense of the whole? Sometimes people wail out of frustration rather than unhappiness.

In conclusion, related concepts should often be retained. Sometimes the distinction they codify will be needed.

2. *The sub-relationships are a language for the discovery of information about relationships rather than for other kinds of information. If you want information about relationships, avoid leaving the language of the sub-relationships.*

"Joe and Mary are not intimate because they don't trust each other"; but why don't they trust each other?

It is useful to have a system of sub-relationships when dealing with such questions, for the temptation is to *leave the system.* "Joe and Mary don't trust each other because we are all programmed from infancy to be suspicious of other people." This may be information about society, but it is not information about Joe and Mary's relationship. The only helpful way out of the language of the sub-relationships is into more specific detail about the relationship. If we can give only out-of-system answers, we should use the system to move us to a more promising point of departure. We could and often should move to another group of sub-relationships, but it is not necessary. "They aren't intimate because they aren't spontaneous." This is almost a meaningless conceptual tautology, but not quite—it focuses attention on the quality of their interaction. The next move is to ask, "But why aren't they spontaneous?"

1. "Because they are so much in love that they are shy and hesitant with each other."

2. "Because whenever Joe gets carried away by an interaction, he suddenly catches himself and becomes very quiet."

The answers are both satisfactory; they both move into details. The first gives a fact about the relationship; the second a fact about a person. As we have seen in chapter four, person answers to relationship questions are usually unsatisfactory. It is misleading to "blame" one person. Thus the second answer could lead us to another question. "What is it about Mary that makes Joe that way?" This is likely to be a dead end. We can go far into Mary's past; the farther we go, the farther we are from the relationship. We should return to the language of the sub-relationships: "Is it because they don't know each other—or that Joe won't let Mary know about him because she doesn't probe hard enough—that they aren't intimate?" "Or are they too dependent on each other (high on Exclusiveness) to dare talk for fear of finding problems?"

In summary, the language of the sub-relationships allows a search for information about relationships. Trying to stay within it will help us avoid premature exits to personality descriptions, philosophy, or statements about the nature of society.

3. *If certain parts of the brain are damaged, other parts take over the functions of the damaged portion. Similarly, one sub-relationship may take over the functions of another, either absent or destroyed.*

One could claim that interactive efficiency is necessary for relational behaviors to proceed. Some people are doomed, by virtue of reticence, shyness, or lack of verbal facility, to be unable to talk or

behave freely. It is not necessary that such people have bad relationships. Joe may not need to find out why Mary is acting strangely if he
trusts her.

Similarly, when romantic love is gone, the "traditional virtues"
represented by *Stability* can take over; on the other hand, couples with
an otherwise unstable relationship have good relationships because
they are still in love. A common example: "I know he beats me, is always drunk, never home, and always broke; but I love him." The
opposite state of affairs: "Lord knows he's boring, quiet, and not
very bright; we haven't had sex in years; but he's always there in his
own plodding way."

This suggests that a sample of older couples might have differentiated more between groupings of sub-relationships. Older couples
may "specialize" on one factor.

4. *The sub-relationships are meaningless in isolation. They acquire
meaning only in the context of the relationship as a whole.*

Spontaneity is not necessarily a good thing. It is often confused
with invasion of privacy or lack of considerateness. This confusion is
understandable. When one feels free, one feels free. Joe feels free; so
he starts asking Mary about her divorce, she gets mad, and that's the
end of the relationship. One can be perfectly free with Mary without
bringing up her divorce. One is tempted to claim that this is not true
freedom, however; that it is like telling a guest to make himself at
home but not to go into the Purple Room. One can still be at home. If
the guest is not allowed into the bathroom, that is another story; but
who would want to know what is in the Purple Room? Someone more
interested in the house than in the person. Someone more interested in
some irrelevant aspect of the person than in a relationship with the
person. If Joe refuses to enter a relationship with Mary until he knows
the details of her toilet training, he is more interested in toilet training
than he is in Mary.

Can Mary be perfectly free with Joe without telling him about
her divorce? Why not? Perhaps the subject merely bores her. All that is
important is that she feels no need or desire to discuss it; then she can
talk freely and never mention it.

If Joe thinks his knowing about Mary's divorce is sufficiently important that he is willing to make her uncomfortable in order to try to
find out about it, then he values the relationship with Mary less than
he values knowledge about her divorce. Of course, we could have said
that Mary valued her desire not to talk about her divorce more than

she valued her relationship with Joe. Nobody is to blame. Couples must negotiate such matters—or be lucky.

We are now in a position to make the distinction between spontaneity and invasion of privacy. Joe's behavior is spontaneous only if it takes the relationship into account. If it doesn't, it is invasion of privacy—if it didn't turn out to be invasion of privacy, it was just dumb luck. Spontaneity is interacting freely. Invasion of privacy is acting with only oneself in mind. Sometimes the object of the invasion doesn't happen to mind, but it is still an invasion.

Similarly, intimacy outside the context of a relationship is not intimacy but selfish, cathartic, egocentric, nonaccommodatory logorrhea. Intimacy is the exchange of personal information for purposes of enhancing or maintaining a relationship. The exchange of personal information is not intimacy unless it occurs in a relationship.

Knowledge changes with the values of other sub-relationships. For example, consider the fact that "Joe takes tranquillizers." This is perhaps a simple fact to Joe, who has taken them for years. But in most segments of society, people do not *simply* take tranquillizers. The fact means something, for example, neurosis. If Mary respects Joe, Joe's pill-popping may mean that "the pace of modern living is impossible, especially when you are trying to accomplish as much as Joe is." If Mary doesn't respect Joe, his behavior may mean that "Joe is neurotic and scared of life."

In summary, the sub-relationships provide a vocabulary for talking about relationships. They let us talk about the complexity of relationships, a complexity that was not to be found by my ordinary empirical methods.

Let us now turn to the experiment on arguing; it used the RSQ. The RSQ is an adequate *measure* of relationships. It is no worse than one or two questions about how much one person likes another. It is longer, but my subjects did not complain. They believed, as I did, that a measurement instrument that long was required to assess the complexity of their relationships.

The Experiment

My subjects were obtained through an advertisement in a student newspaper. It did not specify the exact nature of the research, requesting couples "married, living together, or involved" to participate in an experiment lasting 2½ hours for $5.00 per couple. When couples called, I told them the nature of the research. Of all who called, only three couples did not eventually engage in the research procedure. All were married or living together.

Upon arriving, the couples took the RSQ in separate rooms. They then engaged in the experimental procedure. Each couple engaged in five arguments, three initiated by one member of the couple, two by the other.

The provoker (P) was instructed to start an argument by making a complaint, statement of intention, threat, or report of deed or feeling. A general content area was specified, but P was asked to bring up a real subject he felt like arguing about, or had in the past.

P's message to the violated member of the relationship (V) was tape-recorded and played to V, in another room, who then gave a free response. Meanwhile, in his room, P filled out a questionnaire (called the TIQ for its ten items) which assessed his current emotional state. V's free response was recorded; while V filled out the TIQ, P responded to V's response with a situation, personality, or damage description (weighted respectively 1, 2, and 3 for violation potential) according to instructions he had in front of him and had studied and discussed prior to the experiment. The instructions did not name the kinds of descriptions, but said they were three different ways to respond in an argument.

After P had given the description requested, he filled out the TIQ; V then responded according to instructions, and the argument continued until its programmed end, with each person filling out the TIQ after delivering a message. At the end of each argument, each person filled out a brief version of the RSQ.

There were five different "argument structures." They differed in length and level reached. All started with a situation description; some moved up to personality descriptions; others moved through personality descriptions to damage descriptions. The severity, or violation potential, of a structure was the sum of the weights of the descriptions. The least severe consisted of four situation descriptions, two from each participant, and had a weight of four. In this argument structure, each delivered three messages (counting the initial message or the free response). The most severe structure went 1...2...2...3...3...3 and had a weight of fourteen.

All messages were tape-recorded and later transcribed. Three judges rated them as to what kind of description they were. Under the circumstances—that the couples were arguing, and that I tried not to intervene unless the message was clearly of the wrong sort—couples were judged able to usually give the kind of description requested.

All couples but one found the procedure interesting and realistic; all claimed that it nevertheless had not been harmful. Many spontaneously said it was good for them. In fact, if one analyzes the structure of the experimental situation from the point of view of the literature on small group problem solving, it is a situation that in many ways maximizes the ability of the couple to solve their problems. Interruption was impossible, for example.

One can, of course, question the extent to which the experimental procedure resembles real life arguments. The couples themselves found it naturalistic, and the arguments sounded realistic to me. I think it is fair to say that the procedure produced arguments of *average* intensity. Many real life arguments are more violent. People often employ paralinguistic distractors, such as interruptions and facial expressions, impossible here, but often a source of rage. On the other hand, many real life arguments are not as substantive and verbal as the ones induced by this procedure. Throwing plates and expletives is violent in one sense, but a laconic vicious comment can do much more damage. In addition, real life arguments are often constrained by children and neighbors. Finally, of course, there is no such thing as the typical real life argument. From that point of view, the procedure induced arguments as typical as is possible.

Hypotheses

Hypothesis I: *The stronger a relationship, the less damage it will incur as the result of an argument. Operationally, the RSQ will drop less.*

A strong relationship has by definition stronger resources for dealing with problems. If Joe trusts Mary, he will accept her explanations of behavior that could have been considered a violation. Therefore, the argument can end. If it continues, it will be less damaging than it would be if Mary's explanation were greeted with distrust. If Joe doesn't respect Mary, he is more likely to give her a negative personality description. If Joe and Mary have interactive efficiency, they can communicate about problems. If they are in love, they have a reason to try to solve their problems. If Joe knows Mary, he knows what kinds of explanations will satisfy her.

The definition of the sub-relationships makes this hypothesis a conceptual tautology rather than a causal-theoretic statement. Not giving negative personality descriptions is *an instance of* respect; accepting a description is an instance of trust.

Hypothesis II: *The relationship will be damaged (operationally, the RSQ will decline) as a function of severity of argument structure.*

The rationale for this hypothesis is provided by the logical structure of arguments (chapter three), and is a conceptual tautology. Personality descriptions are more damaging than situation descriptions because they indict more of the person. Damage descriptions are more damaging than personality descriptions because they not only indict P's personality but implicate his intentions. Thus injury is added to insult. As we have seen, damage descriptions lessen interactive efficiency, since giving a damage description involves a retreat from the relationship into oneself. Finally, threats to the relationship (not manipulated in this experiment for ethical reasons) are more damaging than damage descriptions because they imply that the damage done is irreparable.

Hypothesis III: *Damage of the relationship is a function of the number of arguments the couple has engaged in. Operationally, the RSQ will be lower the further through the procedure the couple is.*

Two arguments should be more damaging than one. New content will be introduced. Old content will continue to operate. While each argument was a separate event in the experiment, no attempt was made to induce subjects to forget what had happened during previous arguments. It does not go that way in real life. In addition, each argument should weaken the relationship. The next argument should then be attacking a weaker relationship. If Hypothesis I is correct, not only should further damage be done, but proportionately more should be done as the relationship weakens.

Hypothesis IV: *During the course of arguments, the values of the variables measured by the TIQ should change.*

Specifically, the following should increase: anger, feelings of distance, feelings of being ill-at-ease, hurt feelings, and assessment of the seriousness of the situation. The following should decrease: favorability towards the other, trust, respect, understanding of the other's behavior during the argument, and willingness to stop the argument.

These are provisional hypotheses, advanced on the basis of the assumption that arguments are bad. There is no evidence they are not. These hypotheses have no more complex theoretical status.

Results

Let us first consider Hypothesis III. Each of the sixty individuals who took part in the experiment took a version of the RSQ six times, once prior to the experiment, and after each argument. The means of the RSQ at each of these administrations were examined. They differ at a high level of statistical significance and there is a strong linear tendency for the means to decrease during the course of the experiment. Because the subjects may have been sensitized to problems in their relationships after the experiment began due to the fact but not the content of arguing, a similar analysis was performed on the five post-argument means. Again, there was a strong progressive drop in means.

This hypothesis appears to have been confirmed. One could generalize to real life and conclude that relationships lose strength as a function of the number of arguments a couple engages in. But in this experiment the arguments followed each other immediately. Given time, relationships may rebound. Only further research could answer this question. One value of research is that it suggests further questions of this sort, questions that are best attacked empirically rather than theoretically.

Hypothesis II, that arguments with higher severity ratings will cause more damage, was confirmed except for one not very small anomaly. The most severe argument structure produced a mean RSQ almost exactly equal to the mean produced by the least severe structure. It is not at all clear why this happened, but some brief *post facto* rationalization may be entertained.

Damage descriptions can contain the remedy for the problem. Attention is focused on "where it hurts," while personality descriptions focus on the nature of the person who caused the pain. Attitude change research has demonstrated that people are more likely to cease self-destructive behavior if they are given an immediately available means for doing so. Damage descriptions may do so. Perhaps the worst aspect of damage descriptions is that withdrawal is involved. But the experimental situation did not allow this. Thus it is possible that the experimental situation brought out the best but inhibited the worst aspects of damage descriptions.

Unfortunately, an argument with two damage descriptions had the second lowest mean RSQ; the most severe structure had only one more. It is unlikely that one more would make that much difference.

It is also possible that this structure was simply too severe for the couples. It was a long argument, conducted almost entirely in personality and damage descriptions. Perhaps it required couples to become harsher than they would ordinarily have been given the gravity of the subject matter. If they recognized a disjunction between what they would have said and what they were required to say, they would have partially discounted the truth or intensity of the messages. In fact, one way out of arguments is to explode into hyperbole. If Joe grouses about burnt toast and Mary bristles, Joe can try and pretend he wasn't really grousing by becoming humorously histrionic about the importance of toast. Mary may accept this maneuver. It is possible that this structure forced subjects to say ludicrously untrue or unkind things. We have seen in chapter four that this is a way out of the pit.

There are other possibilities, some of them technical. Only future research and thinking can deal with them.

Hypothesis I, that strong relationships would be more resistant to arguing, received no confirmation. The correlation between initial relational strength and mean loss on the RSQ was .16, indicating a (weak and statistically insignificant) tendency for stronger relationships to suffer more damage than weaker ones.

There are a variety of technical rationalizations of this failure. They are beyond the scope of this discussion and not entirely persuasive anyhow. Let us consider the possibility that strength of relationships manifests itself largely in stopping arguments before they get out of hand. That is, if Joe offers Mary an explanation, she accepts it, and that's it. In the experimental situation, the couples were not allowed to end the argument when they wanted to. Perhaps arguments are the great levelers. This is the implication of the stimulus-response model of arguments. Perhaps once a couple has gone through an argument of a certain severity, they suffer a certain amount of damage. Again, another experiment, which allowed couples to end arguments when they wanted to, would allow a test of this speculation.

Hypothesis IV dealt with changes in emotions during the course of arguments as measured by the TIQ, administered immediately after the delivery of each message. While a legitimate time to assess subjects' reactions, it is a particular time, and the results may be applicable only to that time. They might, for example, be different if the TIQ were administered immediately after receipt of a message.

The results reported here are often based on only the two longer argument structures. The three shorter ones showed fewer trends. It may take time for escalation of emotions to take place. Again, only future research can answer that. Because this study is exploratory and there is little other data of this sort, however, I shall act as if this were true and shall be somewhat more free with the data than I perhaps should be.

Members of couples tended to feel increasingly less favorable about their partners during the course of arguments. Anger tended to increase, as did hurt feelings. Assessment of the seriousness of the situation remained at a constant level, as did respect. Trust declined. Couples felt more distant and ill at ease.

Finally, for both longer and shorter arguments, there was a very strong linear trend for increased willingness to stop the argument. It is not easy to interpret this finding. Perhaps the participants feel the issue has been settled; perhaps they feel there never was a real issue and that therefore the argument is increasingly worthless. Perhaps they feel the argument is increasingly worthless because they are saying more and it is helping less. The tenor of the results make this latter interpretation seem more likely. The data suggest that it is the increasingly unpleasant arousal and damage to the relationship and to the self that leads to the desire to stop the argument. And while it might be objected that in real life people can stop arguments if they want to, and that therefore my subjects' willingness to stop merely reflects the fact that I was forcing them to behave unnaturally, the stimulus-response conception of the argument discussed in chapters three and four is operative in real life also. The experimental evidence gives some tentative corroboration to theory. Arguments have a "life of their own," and continue despite the wishes of the participants.

But not once did a subject ask to stop an argument. It is as if they were sucked into the vortex of the argument, hated it, but didn't complain, knowing it was inevitable.

The composite picture, based largely on the longer arguments, is as follows: People understand each other better as arguments progress and therefore do not take the situation progressively seriously. The familiar is not frightening. But damage is being done and negative emotions aroused nevertheless. The familiar can be unpleasant. There does not appear to be a desire to discharge the negative affect in further argument. Quite the contrary. It appears that people become increasingly willing to end arguments. Arguments appear to be aversive and people wish to escape arguments more than they wish to punish people.

It is somewhat paradoxical that emotions are being aroused that we ordinarily think press for expression—anger for example—while at the same time the desire to express them is progressively decreasing. The experiment provides evidence suggesting that arguments simultaneously pull people apart and bring them together. An examination of this evidence will help explain the somewhat paradoxical progression of arguments.

Before the experiment, couples filled out the RSQ. The cross-couple correlation was .40. This is not an extremely high correlation, but it is uninflated by response sets. Furthermore, while Joe is being asked to what extent he trusts Mary, she is being asked to what extent she trusts *Joe*; in that sense they are not even filling out the same questionnaire. Thus the correlation may be considered moderately substantial.

Even higher is the cross-couple correlation of ratings of success of the relationship ($r = .65$). This was a scale included in the RSQ but not a sub-relationship. The questions on this scale were quite content-free and may be taken to refer to the present ("To what extent are you happy in your relationship with O?" "To what extent do you wish your relationship with O was better?") This scale, then, would seem to measure the quality of recent interaction. It is not surprising that couples can agree on this even more than they can agree on the RSQ; recent interaction has not yet been committed to the quite active process of memory.

The cross-couple correlation between mean levels of post-argument strength, as measured by the RSQ, has fallen to .23. It appears that couples agree somewhat less about the strength of their relationships after arguments than they do before. This suggests that couples often experience different outcomes from arguments. This would weaken the relationship by reducing the extent to which the couple has experienced what is called a "common fate." (Many studies have shown that groups which have experienced a common fate are more cohesive than groups without a common fate.)

The cross-couple correlations of amount of affect aroused during arguments can also be examined. The amount aroused by the female during an argument is statistically independent of the amount aroused in the male (what numerical tendencies there are, are negative). Thus the emotional responses of members of a couple during an argument are not similar. This provides further evidence that arguments are not experienced as a common fate but that they pull participants apart.

The pulling apart would seem to be more of an emotional separation than a disagreement about the nature of the the relationship. The sub-relationships are defined as being more like traits of the relationship than states, and as representing facts rather than feelings. Agreement on relational strength, which is the sum of the sub-relationships, fell only from .40 to .23. On the other hand, couples strongly agreed, to the tune of a .65 correlation, on pre-argument success of relationship. During the arguments, however, the couple "agrees" to the tune of a zero-order but slightly negative correlation as to how much emotion they are experiencing. The .65 cannot directly be compared to the zero-order correlation, but the evidence suggests a process of emotional separation.

Let us consider another source of evidence. I attempted to manipulate content areas of arguments, with various hypotheses, none of which were supported. However, the sub-scales of the RSQ were differentially affected by arguments.[2]

Ratings of success of relationship showed by far the greatest loss of the fifteen sub-scales. This provides evidence that subjects did use this scale to reflect their feelings about the current state of the relationship.

Intimacy, Spontaneity, and Confiding drop a good deal. These are three of the four sub-relationships defining *Interactive Efficiency*. Thus, the couples have lost some of their ability to communicate effectively, and in that sense also have been pulled apart.

Behavioral and Emotional Exclusiveness and Stability increased somewhat. Combined with the fact that understanding increases during arguments (and, as a sub-relationship, lost very little), it would appear that the couples have been pulled together. It is as if arguments encapsulate couples or tie them together. It is as if couples are held together by bonds of negative affect. They lack the communication resources to resolve their problems. It is as if they have been isolated not only from each other but from the outside world. Argumentation may be described as a process that separates couples from the rest of the world, isolating them, and bringing them together, but without the resources to deal effectively with each other.

This empirically suggested picture makes sense. An argument may be considered similar to a crime committed by two people. The crime having been committed, the couple is walled off from easy intercourse with the outside world. How well can one think of oneself after a violent argument? Can one forget the argument occurred and have a relaxed conversation with a friend? Does one not feel different from one's friends, as if one has gone through a hell they haven't experienced? For this reason alone, the couple is thrown together. Presumably because of the content of the argument, the couple also loses trust for each other (as two criminals fear what the other can do). In such an atmosphere, any understanding gained is likely to be the kind of familiarity that breeds contempt.

In short, many of the webs described in chapter four have received some empirical confirmation in this investigation, admittedly with the aid of some slightly impressionistic data interpretation.

A Brief Summary and Conclusion

The research tends to demonstrate that arguments are bad. We did not even find that stronger relationships can better resist the negative effects of arguments. While one might have hoped that if a couple argues it will at least lead to the relationship's eventual death, the research provides evidence that arguments also produce a kind of self-perpetuating spider's web of ever increasing complexity. There was clear evidence that arguments produce progressive damage to relationships. In the limited temporal context of this experiment, subjects did not start over again fresh with each new argument.

I do not suggest that arguing is less healthy than other approaches to problems. An argument has been operationally defined here as a direct verbal attack on the problem. The procedure and instructions attempted to induce precisely such interactions. The tone of the various lines of reasoning presented throughout the book suggests that such arguments are less damaging and, particularly, less entangling, nightmarish, and destructive of individual dignity than indirect approaches to problems.

One can hope that people do not have the memory of elephants. Much of the reasoning presented in this book is based on the assumption that what happens makes a mark. Many of us know that it seems to be possible to forget an argument entirely. In addition, I have said that arguments often take place on the rim, where memory is not good. But many of us also know that what has seemed to have been forgotten for many months can resurface as if it had never been gone.

Personally, furthermore, I would hate to think that what I do has no significance and can be dismissed by myself and others as a momentary aberration when seen in the guilty context of the morning after. I personally do not find it possible to treat acts of people I like as tics, whims, random fluctuations in mood, or manifestations of moronic insect-eyed mindlessness.

Finally, of course, the question must be asked: What shall we do about the problem of conflict between people? I don't know. I don't even know what I'll do about my problems. I'm not sure problems are bad; they are often silly. It would be boring to be without them, and they may be manifestations of better things to come. On the other hand, they may not.

Notes

Preface

1. H. Harré and P. F. Secord, *The Explanation of Social Behaviour*, p. 231.

2. T. S. Szasz, *Ideology and Insanity*, pp. 20–22. Szasz's italics.

3. Most of my discussion of Piaget throughout the book is based on John H. Flavell's excellent *The Developmental Psychology of Jean Piaget*. I have read a good deal of Piaget, but depend upon Flavell for much of the understanding I have of Piaget's work.

Chapter 1 Blind Mazes

1. Adaptation, or intelligent behavior, proceeds by assimilation and accommodation, two conceptually different functions that are usually impossible to separate in a given act. To assimilate an object (to an existing *schema*, in Piagetian terms) is to behave toward it in a given way. An infant assimilates a pen to the schema of grasping by grasping it. Adaptive behavior must involve accommodation. The infant cannot assimilate a baseball to the schema of grasping by grasping it as if it were a pen. Adaptation must take the nature of the object into account. When a novel object is encountered, assimilation and accommodation, usually in equilibrium, go awry. Romantic love will be described as a novel object encountering another novel object and attempting to adapt to it.

Chapter 2 Love

1. Part of the reason for the reluctance to call this behavior altruistic is that it is not sufficiently quixotic or self-sacrificing. If, however, a person became a bird watcher at the behest of his parents, we would tend to think him crazy rather than altruistic.

2. The blindness extends to the future. Potential problems are typically given vague dismissal. The couple does not give detailed proposals for solving these problems, nor are we told why the problems don't apply to them. This follows directly from the definition. If Joe can't accommodate or assimilate to Mary, there is nothing familiar about her that would allow him to use previous experience as a basis for predicting a problem—or the lack of one. That lovers' denials are curiously vague and unassertive follows from their inability to even see that a problem is possible.

3. The male child is said in Freudian theory to want to kill his father and sleep with his mother. This is the Oedipus complex. It could be attributed to the child's unwillingness or inability to see that his mother does exist in more than one context, in this case in a relationship to his father. One of the child's major attributes in Piaget's description of development is his egocentrism, his inability to take over other people's points of view. The child would understandably find it difficult to see that his mother was also a wife to his father (and vice versa). The Oedipal solution is a solution, although Piaget's theory suggests it is not likely that a child of five could concoct it.

4. I have taken some liberties in my usage of generative-transformational grammar. Recent research does not tend to confirm the proposition that the negative and positive forms of a sentence come from the same deep structure (R. W. Brown and R. J. Herrnstein, *Psychology*). However, the closeness of opposites has been noted for ages. In any case, generative-transformational grammar is offered only as an analogy.

5. An interesting demonstration of the validity of this description of driving as compared to the more normal description of it as habitual (which it may also be) may be obtained by having or imagining someone who wants to learn how to drive sitting next to you. Try to point out all the sources of danger you avoid. There are many, and as the demonstration continues, you will become aware of ones you never consciously considered.

Chapter 3 Process Models of Relationships Going Bad

1. P. G. Ossorio, *What Actually Happens*, p. 16 defines a process as "...a sequential change from one state of affairs to another." Further, "A process is a state of affairs having other, related processes as immediate constituents. (A process divides into related, sequential or parallel, smaller processes.)"

2. Throughout this section I shall use *need* and *want* interchangeably. To want is to make a more conscious, deliberate movement than to need; but adult human behavior is at least intentional, so the passivity of *need* is not completely appropriate—when it is, we are not dealing with a full-fledged adult. *Want* has connotations of activity, consciousness, and deliberation which are often not justified and in any event are not required for my arguments in this section to hold. I would have used a more descriptive term, but there isn't one in English.

Chapter 4 Conceptions of Why Relationships Stay Bad

1. Surely, couples can and do shrug their shoulders and say, "Well, I guess we both kind of messed that one up," laugh, and part good friends.

They do, but there are strong pressures against this solution, discussed later in this chapter. Briefly, if people can throw away a relationship that easily, either they didn't put much into it in the first place, or it has already come to a true end. We are concerned here with people who are still involved with each other.

Chapter 5   The Future of Sex and the Individual

1. In this discussion, I talk as if the sexual revolution were more extensive and complete than it is. It has not reached all segments of our society, even among the young; but it is clearly spreading. Not everyone is as liberated as the hypothetical people I talk about here; but many are, and many more are becoming so.

2. As in the previous section, let us assume the movement has succeeded completely. Obviously, it has not yet done so. But there is no reason to suppose it won't.

3. Not all literature is taught in these ways, but the validity of the claim that the minds of students are being desexed is not dependent on the proportion of teaching of these sorts. How much arsenic does one need?

Chapter 6   Measurement and Research

1. The presentation is directed at the lay reader; statistical and methodological considerations have been almost completely eliminated. I have also attempted to limit the ceaseless qualification to which social scientists are given. The professional reader is assured that all of these are present in the original research report (G. W. Kelling. "The Prediction of the Outcome of Personal Arguments of Heterosexual Couples: An Experimental-Field study").

2. The evidence here is only suggestive. While the difference in change among the sub-relationships was statistically significant, my interpretation of individual differences is not entirely based on individual statistical comparisons.

Bibliography

Albee, E. *Who's Afraid of Virginia Woolf?* New York: Atheneum, 1967.

Ardrey, R. *African Genesis.* New York: Dell Publishing Co., 1961.

Aronson, E., and Linder, D. "Gain and loss of esteem as determinants of interpersonal attractiveness." *Journal of Experimental Social Psychology.* 1 (1965) : 156–71.

Bach, G. R. *The Intimate Enemy.* New York: Morrow, 1969.

Bandura, A., Ross, D., and Ross, S. "Imitation of film-mediated aggressive models." *Journal of Abnormal and Social Psychology,* 66 (1963) : 3–11.

Bateson, G., Jackson, D. D., Haley, J., and Weakland, J. "Toward a theory of schizophrenia." *Behavioral Science,* 1 (1956) : 251–64.

Berger, P. *Invitation to Sociology.* Garden City, N.Y.: Doubleday & Co., 1963.

Berkowitz, L., Green, J. A., and McCaulay, J. R. "Hostility catharsis as the reduction of emotional tension." *Psychiatry,* 25 (1962): 23–31.

Bernard, J. "No news, but new ideas." In: Bohannen, P. (ed.), *Divorce and After.* Garden City, N.Y.: Doubleday & Co., 1970.

Brain, R. *Friends and Lovers.* New York: Basic Books, 1976.

Brown, N. O. *Life Against Death.* Middletown, Conn.: Wesleyan University Press, 1959.

Brown, R. W. *Social Psychology.* New York: The Free Press, 1965.

———, and Herrnstein, R. J. *Psychology.* Boston: Little, Brown and Co., 1975.

Burroughs, W. S. *Naked Lunch.* New York: Grove Press, 1959.

Byrne, D., Erwin, C. R., and Lamberth, J. "Continuity between the experimental study of attraction and real-life computer dating." *Journal of Personality and Social Psychology,* 16 (1970) : 157–65.

Cartwright, D. S. *Introduction to Personality.* Chicago: Rand McNally, 1974.

Chomsky, N. *Language and Mind.* New York: Harcourt, Brace & World, 1968.

Cuber, J. F., and Harroff, P. B. *Sex and the Significant Americans.* Baltimore: Penguin Books, 1965.

DeVries, P. *Tents of Wickedness*. Toronto: Little, Brown and Co., 1959.

Driscoll, R., Davis, K. E., and Lipetz, M. E. "Parental interference and romantic love: The Romeo and Juliet effect." *Journal of Personality and Social Psychology*, 24 (1972) : 1–10.

Flavell, J. H. *The Developmental Psychology of Jean Piaget*. New York: D. Van Nostrand Co., 1963.

Garfinkel, H. *Studies in Ethnomethodology*. Englewood Cliffs, N.J.: Prentice-Hall, Inc., 1967.

Gaylin, W. *Caring*. New York: Alfred A. Knopf, 1976.

Gergen, K. J. *The Psychology of Behavior Exchange*. Reading, Mass.: Addison-Wesley, 1969.

Goffman, E. *The Presentation of Self in Everyday Life*. Garden City, N.Y.: Doubleday & Co., 1959.

_____. *Asylums*. Garden City, N.Y.: Doubleday & Co., 1961.

_____. *Frame Analysis*. New York: Harper & Row, 1974.

Goode, W. J. *After Divorce*. Chicago: Free Press, 1956.

Haley, J. *Strategies of Psychotherapy*. New York: Grune & Stratton, 1963.

_____.*The Power Tactics of Jesus Christ*. New York: Avon Books, 1969.

Hall, E. T. *The Silent Language*. Garden City, N.Y.: Doubleday & Co., 1959.

Hamilton, D. *Death of a Citizen*. Greenwich. Conn.: Fawcett Publications. 1960.

Harré, H., and Secord, P. F. *The Explanation of Social Behaviour*. Totowa, N.J.: Littlefield, Adams & Co., 1973.

Hartman, D. T. "Influence of symbolically modeled instrumental aggression and pain cues on aggressive behavior." *Journal of Personality and Social Psychology*, 11 (1969) : 280–88.

Hellman, L. *The Children's Hour*. In: Hellman, L., *Six Plays*. New York: Modern Library, 1960.

Johnson, T. J., Feigenbaum, R., and Weiby, M. "Some determinants and consequences of the teacher's perception of causality." *Journal of Educational Psychology*, 55 (1964) : 237–46.

Jones, E. E., Davis, K. E., and Gergen, K. J. "Role playing variations and their informational value for person perception." *Journal of Abnormal and Social Psychology*, 63 (1961) : 302–10.

_____, Kanouse, D. E., Kelley, H. H., Nisbett, R. E., Valins, S., and Weiner, B. *Attribution*. Morristown, N.J.: General Learning Press, 1972.

_____, and Nisbett, R. E. *The Actor and the Observer: Divergent Perceptions of the Causes of Behavior*. Morristown, N.J.: General Learning Press, 1971.

Joyce, J. *A Portrait of the Artist as a Young Man*. New York: Viking Press, 1964.

_____. *Ulysses*. New York: Random House, 1934.

Kahn, M. "The physiology of catharsis." *Journal of Personality and Social Psychology*, 3 (1966): 278–86.

Kanouse, D. E., and Hanson, L. R. *Negativity in Evaluations*. Morristown, N.J.: General Learning Press, 1971.

Kelley, R. K. *Courtship, Marriage, and the Family*. 2nd ed. New York: Harcourt Brace Jovanovich, Inc., 1974.

Kelling, G. W. "The Prediction of the Outcome of Personal Arguments of

Heterosexual Couples: An Experimental-Field Study." Ph.D. dissertation, University of Colorado, 1972. Ann Arbor, Mich.: University Microfilms, Order #73-18, 576.

Kerouac, J. *On the Road.* New York: Viking Press, 1957.

Kierkegaard, S. *Fear and Trembling.* Garden City, N.Y.: Doubleday & Co., 1954.

_____.*Either/Or.* Garden City, N.Y.: Doubleday & Co., 1959.

Lorenz, K. *On Aggression.* New York: Harcourt, Brace & World, 1966.

Mace, D., and Mace, V. *Marriage East and West.* Garden City, N.Y.: Doubleday & Co., 1959.

Mailer, N. "The time of her time." In: Mailer, N., *Advertisements for Myself.* New York: The New American Library, 1959.

McGuire, W. J. "The nature of attitudes and attitude change." In: Lindzey, G., and Aronson, E., *Handbook of Social Psychology, Vol. III.* Reading, Mass.: Addison-Wesley, 1969.

Mischel, W. *Continuity and Change in Personality.* Andover, Mass.: Warner Modular Publications, 1973.

Morris, D. *The Naked Ape.* London: Cape, 1967.

Newman, M., and Berkowitz, B. *How to be Your Own Best Friend.* New York: Ballantine Books, 1971.

Ossorio, P. G. *Persons.* Boulder, Colorado: Linguistic Research Institute, 1966.

_____.*Notes on Behavior Description.* Boulder, Colorado: Linguistic Research Institute, 1969.

_____. *Meaning and Symbolism.* Boulder, Colorado: Linguistic Research Institute, 1971.

_____. *What Actually Happens.* Boulder Colorado: Linguistic Research Institute, 1973.

Page, J. D. *Psychopathology.* 2nd ed. Chicago: Aldine, 1975.

Piaget, J. *The Moral Judgment of the Child.* New York: The Free Press, 1965.

Proust, M. *Remembrance of Things Past.* New York: Random House, 1934.

Rubin, Z. *Liking and Loving.* New York: Holt, Rinehart and Winston, 1973.

Seidenberg, R. *Marriage Between Equals.* Garden City, N.Y.: Doubleday & Co., 1973.

Stein, D. D., Hardyck, J. A., and Smith, M. B. "Race and belief: An open and shut case." *Journal of Personality and Social Psychology,* 1 (1965): 281-89.

Szasz, T. S. *Ideology and Insanity.* Garden City, N.Y.: Doubleday & Co., 1970.

Walters, R. H., and Thomas, T. L. "Enhancement of punitiveness by visual and audiovisual displays." *Canadian Journal of Psychology,* 17 (1963): 244-55.

Zimbardo, P. "Shyness—the people phobia." *Today's Education,* 66 (1977): 47-49.

Index

Mischel, W., 17
Morris, D., 3

Newman, M., 22
Nisbett, R., 105, 189
Nixon, R., 159

O'Hara, J., 130
Ossorio, P., 39, 192

Page, J., 146
Piaget, J., 2, 9, 10, 11, 44, 45, 48, 49,
  55, 60, 61, 74, 80, 130, 165
Proust, M., 44, 52, 53, 56, 57, 59, 60,
  61, 75, 77, 80, 98, 116, 171, 195

Ross, D., 109
Ross, S., 109
Rubin, Z., 40

Seidenberg, R., 27, 79

Shakespeare, W., 59, 116, 171
Shelley, P., 187
Simon, N., 24
Smith, M., 16
Stein, D., 16
Swift, J., 99, 171
Szasz, T., vii, 24, 26

Tagore, 163
Thomas, T., 109

Updike, J., 116

Valins, S., 189

Walters, R., 109
Weakland, J., 103
Weiby, M., 188, 189
Weiner, B., 189

Zimbardo, P., 114